Images of Art Therapy

Images of Art Therapy

New developments in theory and practice

Tessa Dalley, Caroline Case,
Joy Schaverien, Felicity Weir,
Diana Halliday, Patricia Nowell Hall,
Diane Waller

Tavistock Publications
London and New York

First published in 1987 by
Tavistock Publications Ltd
11 New Fetter Lane, London EC4P 4EE

Published in the USA by
Tavistock Publications
in association with Methuen, Inc.
29 West 35th Street, New York NY 10001

Printed in Great Britain at the University Press, Cambridge

British Library Cataloguing in Publication Data
Images of art therapy: new developments in
theory and practice.
1. Art therapy
I. Dalley, Tessa
615.8'5156   RC489.A7

ISBN 0 422 60390 2
0 422 60400 3 Pbk

Library of Congress Cataloging in Publication Data
Images of art therapy.
Bibliography: p.
Includes indexes.
1. Art therapy.   I. Dalley, Tessa.
RC489.A7145   1987   616.89'1656   87–10079

ISBN 0 422 60390 2 (U.S.)
0 422 60400 3 (U.S.: pbk.)

Contents

Foreword

'Each form is the frozen temporary image of a process. Thus any work merely represents a staging point in the process of becoming, not a fixed goal.'

(El Lissitsky: *Life, Letters, Texts*)

It has been our aim to share the responsibility of this book. From the beginning we have worked together as a group, giving each other support, encouragement, and criticism. The exchanges and interchanges have occasionally been difficult, but always rewarding. We have met regularly in the two years since its inception, discussing our ideas and aims, as well as our writing. Our ideas about art therapy come from differing standpoints and are based on different experiences, but we share certain common principles which will, we hope, become evident. Although we are each responsible for our own section, we hope the book will have a cohesion derived from our profession and friendship, rather than our editing policy. It is for the reader to decide if this is successful.

The common theme of this book has developed from us all being artists, practitioners, and teachers of art therapy. We would like to acknowledge here our patients and students, who teach us, but mostly do not realize they do. As is obvious from the content, without our patients and students, there would have been no book.

Contributors

Tessa Dalley (BA Hons, Diploma in Art Therapy, Diploma in Psychotherapy, RAth). As a qualified art therapist, with a training in psychotherapy, Tessa has worked with a variety of client groups, but is now concentrating on work with children. Currently, she works part time as an art therapist in a primary school, and as a part-time lecturer on the art therapy training courses at Hertfordshire College of Art and Goldsmiths' College. She is also involved in child psychotherapy training at the Tavistock Clinic; contributes regularly to the Leeds Art Therapy Spring School; and having edited *Art as Therapy* (Tavistock 1984), made a training video to accompany the book.

Caroline Case (Cert.Ed., Diploma in Art Therapy, MA, RAth). Caroline has been in clinical practice, working particularly with children and adolescents with special needs in the education/social services fields. She has carried out research into the 'Expression of Loss in Art Therapy'. Her current interests include small group art therapy with primary school children. Presently she is senior lecturer, and course leader of the postgraduate courses in art therapy at Hertfordshire College of Art. She is a council member of BAAT and member of the Registration Board. She also works in private practice and as a supervisor for art therapists.

Joy Schaverien (DFA (Lond.), MA, RAth) is senior lecturer in art therapy at Hertfordshire College of Art, where she is MA course leader. She studied fine art at Brighton College of Art, and the Slade. Her experience in art therapy has been in a wide variety of National Health Service settings including a therapeutic community, a psychiatric hospital and an out-patient psychotherapy department. Currently she is involved in doctoral research at Birmingham Polytechnic into aesthetics and psychotherapy, focusing on the role of the picture in the transference/counter-transference relationship.

Felicity Weir (Dip AD, Diploma in Art Therapy, MA) has worked for several years as an art therapist specializing in art and psychotherapy with children and adults. Until recently Felicity was a lecturer on the postgraduate diploma in art therapy and the MA courses at Hertfordshire College of Art. She has completed an MA thesis on the relationship between art and psychoanalysis, and has recently completed her training in child psycho-therapy at the Tavistock Clinic, as well as working as a child psychotherapist.

Diana Halliday trained at the Central School of Art and in Paris, and has always both painted and taught art, realizing the therapeutic value of art very early on in her educational experience. She was one of the founder members of BAAT in the 1960s, and was employed as a child psychotherapist using art in several child guidance clinics. Having lived in Canada and the USA for sixteen years, she is a member of the American Association of Art Therapy and Fellow of the International Society of the Psychopathology of Expression. Currently, she works in private practice and runs experiential workshops and seminars at the Mary Ward Centre, London.

Patricia Nowell Hall (Cert.Ed., MA) is an art therapist with a wide experience in a variety of NHS settings. She began working with autistic children, and then specialized in art therapy within therapeutic communities. She completed her MA at Birmingham with a ten-year research project on the relationship of art therapy and psychotherapy and their long-term effects. She is currently researching into the area of 'active imagination' within art therapy. Now an associate lecturer, Patricia teaches on the postgraduate and MA courses at Hertfordshire College of Art, and on the art therapy foundation course at Goldsmiths' College. She is also a visiting lecturer in art therapy on courses for movement and drama in therapy. She is on the panel of therapists of the Champernowne Trust and also on the committee for their annual conference of Jungian Psychotherapy and the Arts, at Cumberland Lodge, Windsor Park. Her consultancy work at home and abroad involves work with individuals and groups.

Diane Waller (MA(RCA), ATC, Dip. Group Psychotherapy (ALCP)). Diane is head of the Art Therapy Unit at Goldsmiths' College, where she enjoys a combination of teaching, clinical supervision and research, and a certain amount of political activity. In 1986 she was elected Life President of

BAAT. She is consultant to a World Health Organisation sponsored research project to establish an art therapy service within the Bulgarian health service. She has found a training in group analytic psychotherapy to be invaluable in all aspects of her work as an art therapist and educator.

1 | Art as therapy: some new perspectives

Tessa Dalley

Using art in therapy is now gaining acceptance as a profession in the United Kingdom. Over the last twenty years there has been a struggle for the autonomy of art therapy to be established and for art therapists to be recognized. Recently, the establishment of independent salary scales, a professional register, and other administrative changes are formalizing its existence as a profession, while the number of different client groups working with art therapy constantly grows.

With this expanding practice of art therapy, what is its main theoretical basis? With many different approaches within the profession, is there a main area of consensus that influences current thinking? This chapter will examine aspects of art therapy theory by developing and critically examining some of the more traditional ideas on which much of our practice is based – in particular, theories of transference, creativity and aesthetics, and the psychoanalytic approach to 'art' with particular reference to Freud. Also, the work of Klein and Winnicott is discussed using their radical ideas of using play and art within a therapeutic relationship. By examining this approach with children, important links can be made for the development of the work in art therapy with adults. Two case studies are presented to emphasize these links between child and adult, what might be considered as 'normal' and 'abnormal', and the implications for this within an art therapy situation. Finally, ideas for the future are outlined, and with reference to some recent research, arguments are put forward for the development of art therapy in education.

Many of these ideas were put forward in *Art as Therapy* (Dalley 1984) which, as an introduction to the subject has proved a useful book for several reasons. It reflects some areas of consensus and disagreement within the profession, which has opened up vigorous debate, some of which will be discussed here. Secondly, it has widened the understanding of the philosophical bases of art therapy and informed other professions, with the effect of increasing knowledge and understanding and dispelling some myths.

First, however, it is important to be reminded of some concepts central to art therapy. Art therapists who use a psychoanalytic approach encourage the pictorial expression of inner experience, and in this sense art is recognized as a process of spontaneous imagery released from the unconscious. 'The process of art therapy is based on the recognition that man's most fundamental thoughts and feelings, derived from the unconscious, reach expression in images rather than words' (Naumburg 1958: 511). When used therapeutically in this way, art is a means of non-verbal communication, a way of stating mixed, poorly understood feelings in an attempt to bring them into clarity and order. 'Put more elaborately, art activity provides a concrete rather than a verbal medium through which a person can achieve both conscious and unconscious expression, and can be used as a valuable agent for therapeutic change' (Dalley 1984: xii).

This psychoanalytic approach to art therapy rests on the premiss that spontaneous art is similar to the processes of free association. It requires that 'one imagine and depict what is uppermost in one's mind and this demands both the suspension of habitual defense and a high degree of moral courage and self discipline' (Kramer 1980: 9). However, as Kramer points out, spontaneous, expressive use of art materials is not 'untramelled scribbling and messing' and the difference is comparable to that between aimless chatter and free association in psychoanalytic treatment. Although Freud's somewhat ambivalent view of art and artists does not incorporate this idea of spontaneous expression, the processes involved in dreams are in many ways similar to those of art activity, particularly in relation to the expression of the unconscious. The activity of art uses many of the symbols and mechanisms of displacement, condensation, splitting, etc. which Freud defined in the study of the dream. Having recognized the parallels that can be drawn between the art processes and dreams, we can choose to use this as central within the treatment method of art therapy as Freud outlined in his dream analysis. Similar approaches are appropriate when considering unconscious imagery and symbolism of paintings and dreams alike.

However, there is an obvious difference which lies in the fact that art activity is a conscious process which gives concrete form to feelings, which are often unconscious. The dream equivalent of this would be an attempt to make sense of a vivid dream on waking, or the understanding of it through analytic interpretation, but there is no tangible form, such as a painting, that can act as a record of the experience and thereby facilitate the process. 'It may be that the analysis of art can continue where the analysis of the dream left off' (Ehrenzweig 1967: 4).

The implication of this is that using art in this way may be more far-reaching and can be more fully developed than dream analysis, for it is the privilege of the artist to combine the ambiguity of dreaming with the tensions of being fully awake. Ehrenzweig describes this in the following way:

'The artist feels this need for expanding his point of departure and will welcome the independent life of his medium. Something like a true conversation takes place between the artist and the work. The medium, by frustrating the artist's purely conscious intentions allows him to contact more submerged parts of his own personality and draw them up for contemplation. While the artist struggles with his medium, unknown to himself, he wrestles with his unconscious personality revealed by the work of art. Taking back from the work on a conscious level what has been projected onto it on an unconscious level is perhaps the most fruitful and painful result of creativity.'

(Ehrenzweig 1967: 57)

Clearly this intensity of the relationship between artist and art is fundamental to the art therapy process. It is, however, the presence of this art form which creates the complexity, and essentially the uniqueness, of art therapy. The degree to which the art form is considered as central to the art therapy process, and the therapist's attitude towards it, is the subject of much debate. Bearing in mind that different approaches in art therapy legitimately cover the wide spectrum between psychotherapy and art education, this debate also concerns the degree to which art therapists must be primarily art trained or have some training in psychology and psycho-therapy.

Several recent articles have been concerned with this issue. Dubowski (1985) challenges those who are 'taking the art out of art therapy', maintaining that the link with psychotherapy has become too strong which leads to the practice of 'illustrative' therapy where the patient is given time to make a picture simply in order to talk about it. 'Art, a basic human behaviour, must have some selective advantage in its own right. Those of us who are artists as well as therapists understand this from our experience. We understand that the relationship that the artist has with materials, forms, images and symbols is a unique relationship and a deeply rewarding one.' He stresses that it is a very private relationship, initially at any rate, and that such a complex relationship must be given time to develop. As this develops, there is an increasing acquaintance with what develops on the picture surface, and the evolution of this symbolic language leads to a conversation between the artist and the art. 'Why is it then that all too often we deny our patients the opportunity to develop such a relationship. My feeling is that in our developing identity as "therapists" we are sometimes inclined to forget our identity as artists' (Dubowski 1985: 17).

Those who hold the opposing view question the value of the emphasis by the therapist on the art work or on any visual communication. Judd (1986) describes how this emphasis on imagery, especially when working with children, can pre-empt the session:

'This means that the art therapist may respond with more interest and enthusiasm to say, a painting, than, for example, to the child who sits quietly playing with his fingers or jumps on the couch or whatever – all equally part of what the child is "saying" or significantly not saying. This narrows down the potential awareness of communication on the part of the patient and receptivity on the part of the therapist.'

(Judd 1986: 146)

Whether the focus of the work is verbal or non-verbal, active or inactive – some art therapy sessions can be entirely one or the other – it is important that the therapist concentrate on what is most significant in terms of the therapeutic interaction. If there is resistance or reluctance on the part of the patient to enter into the art process, painting or drawing might not take place for several weeks, or conversely there may be intense, constant out-pouring of creative activity where few words are exchanged for a similar length of time. Each situation is important in terms of communication within the therapeutic relationship, and can be made more explicit through interpretation.

The appropriate use of a particular medium is also important in this communication. Art materials are enormously versatile, and yet each has particular therapeutic properties. The introduction of paint, sand, or clay at a specific point in therapy might be crucial. Many times one hears of a situation where a patient is 'stuck' in the sense of not making any significant change, and when offered another medium immediately becomes in touch with deeper feelings which were previously buried. This introduction is an intuitive and sensitive one made by the therapist through personal familiarity of working with these media and therefore knowledge of their potential effect. Here the art therapist, as artist, can facilitate through her own understanding of the art process by offering a new means of exploration.

Therefore, as art therapists we must address ourselves to the whole art process. Images emerge into consciousness, and the feelings or ideas that surface can sometimes be controlled in the encounter with art, which will result in a finished art product. But often in art therapy, as feelings are expressed and worked through using the art media, the creative process can be seen to be destructive rather than constructive in terms of the product.

'As therapists we are more accustomed to failure than to success. We are used to seeing paintings of volcanoes become a mass of red and black because explosive feelings were not depicted but acted out. We see carvings end up as pieces of wood because the act of cutting unchains aggressive drives that cannot be confined within a given shape. Before our eyes, drawings turn into angles of half-erased lines because ambivalence paralyses the capacity for making decisions.'

(Kramer 1975: 57)

The process of art therapy

This process suggests that, in a therapeutic situation, the use of art materials facilitates the breakdown of defences and the emergence of feelings, and the result is usually too disorganized to be called 'art'. The aggression, ambivalence, and explosive feelings that are experienced in this process form the essence of the therapeutic work. Those who emphasize the aesthetic importance of the finished product in art therapy tend to undermine the cathartic aspects of the process of creating it.

Art processes are a function of creativity, which is therefore central within art therapy. Ehrenzweig (1967) explains its significance in the following definition: 'In creativity, outer and inner reality will always be organised together by the same indivisible process. The artist too has to face chaos in his work before unconscious scanning brings about the integration of his work as well as his own personality' (Ehrenzweig 1967: 5). He sees the origins of creativity in the primitive 'primary processes' and, stressing the importance of the unconscious, gives a clear analysis of the ego rhythm that underlies all creative work. First there is the phase of fragmented projection, 'schizoid' in character, followed by a manic phase of unconscious scanning and integration when the art's unconscious substructure is formed. The secondary revision occurs in the ultimate 'depressive' feedback and re-introjection of the work into the surface ego. Because the introjected material was shaped on a lower, less differentiated level, it must appear to the artist more fragmented and chaotic than it actually is. 'The artist himself is cast in the role of the spectator faced with the chaos of newly created art' (Ehrenzweig 1967: 80).

This highlights the nature of the unconscious within the creative process and from this we can gain some understanding of how the concept of free association operates through spontaneous art. As creativity originates from primary processes, this is why it is important that, for therapeutic purposes, the art product is not too accomplished. In the analysis of dreams, Freud found that dreams looked particularly real, not when the dream's imagery was precise and clear, but when the dream was supported by a rich unconscious fantasy. He also noticed that the secondary revision of the dream was steered by the superego in order to polish off the unconsciously most significant symbolic details.

Ehrenzweig points out that there is little doubt that there is a similar process in art where the secondary revision tends to ignore and polish off irregularities and textural elements that seem insignificant, but which contain the unconsciously most important symbolism. Those who place emphasis on aesthetics in art therapy might be in danger of encouraging this process which may leave the patient/artist highly dissatisfied and misunderstood.

> 'If I had taken these fantasies of the unconscious as art, they would have carried no more conviction than visual perceptions, as if I were watching a movie. I would have felt no moral obligation towards them. The anima might easily have seduced me into believing that I was a misunderstood artist, and that my so-called artistic nature gave me the right to neglect reality.'
>
> (Jung 1963: 179–80)

Freud and aesthetics

Art therapists who use Freudian ideas of free association and the expression of the unconscious focus on images from patients' art work in a similar way to those brought in the patient's dreams to the consulting room. The 'Wolf Man', whose case was based on the Primal Scene, an early childhood memory, brought Freud a drawing of this which provides a poignant image of his experience (Freud 1963, XVII: 30). This was the only time that this occurred, and was not generally encouraged by Freud. For, unlike Jung, Freud's attitude to art and aesthetics was clearly ambivalent. His view of artists varied from adulation to denigration (XVI: 356, IX: 8). He maintained that aesthetic experience was not susceptible to psychoanalytic enquiry and psychoanalysis 'can do nothing towards elucidating the nature of the artistic gift, nor can it explain the means by which the artist works – artistic technique' (XX: 65). He discussed the 'formal' or 'aesthetic' as the artist's means of deceiving his audience, and expressed the awareness that the better the quality of art, the more completely have its origins been transformed and obscured.

But to remain with this early Freudian interpretation of art, that art is merely a substitute gratification for repressed desires, does not seem entirely compatible with his own aesthetic experience. For he did acknowledge that, in spite of his layman's knowledge of art, he found himself, surprisingly, affected by it.

'Nevertheless, works of art do exercise a powerful effect on me, especially those of literature and sculpture, less often of painting. This has occasioned me, when I have been contemplating such things, to spend a long time before them trying to apprehend them in my own way, i.e. to explain to myself what their effect is due to. Wherever I cannot do this, some rationalistic, or perhaps analytic, turn of mind in me rebels against being moved by a thing without knowing why I am thus affected and what it is that affects me . . . some writer on aesthetics has discovered that this state of intellectual bewilderment is a necessary condition when a work of art is to achieve its greatest effects. It would be only with the greatest reluctance that I could bring myself to believe in any such necessity.'

(XIII: 211–12)

Because of this reluctance, the emphasis in his writing has been on the artist rather than on the understanding of art. Freud's uneasiness about art bears directly on his oblique approach to the work of art itself. In fact, in his two main studies of great artists we see how Freud deals with the difficulty of his 'rebellion'. In his essay on Leonardo, the connection with art is almost eliminated in favour of the psychoanalytic enquiry. Freud reviews and interprets the successive phases of Leonardo's adult life against his childhood background. Freud used the evidence in the pictures to confirm the activity of his last phase of creativity and the infantile complex, but he established the link from the infantile memory on which Freud's analysis was based. 'We thus find a confirmation in another of Leonardo's works of our suspicion that the Mona Lisa del Grovido has awakened in him as a grown man the memory of the mother of his earliest childhood' (XI: 114).

Freud seemed to treat Leonardo's paintings as biographical evidence, but was obviously drawn towards them and affected by these and other works. He was possibly describing some personal aesthetic experience, which was incomprehensible and bewildering. Wollheim takes up this point directly. 'Part of understanding how it is that a work of art affects us is recognising the confusion or the ambiguity upon which this effect in part depends' (Wollheim 1974: 217). Some of the confusion may stem from the fact that Freud had no theoretical explanation for aesthetic experience nor artistic achievement. 'We should be most glad to give an account of the way in which artistic activity derives from the primal instincts of the mind if it were not here that our capacities fail us' (XI: 132). In his appraisal of Freud's essay on the Moses of Michelangelo, Wollheim also points out Freud's dilemma. 'It is unclear how far Freud's emphasis on understanding as prerequisite of appreciation was a purely personal avowal or whether it indicated his theoretical position' (Wollheim 1974: 217).

For art therapists working psychoanalytically, this position is ultimately frustrating. Within an art therapy relationship, the art therapist experiences the impact of the image which demands some personal aesthetic understanding that has to be brought into the theoretical framework within which he is operating. Although Freud makes a number of well-known references that equate art with recovery, reparation or the path back to reality (IX: 153, XI: 50, XII: 224, XIII: 187–88, XVI: 375–77, XX: 64), as Wollheim points out, nowhere did he indicate the mechanism by which this came about. 'By the time he found himself theoretically in a position to do so, the necessary recourses of leisure and energy were, we must believe, no longer available to him' (Wollheim 1974: 219).

How this theory might have developed remains open to speculation. As the notion of the unconscious was initially connected with repression, any positive correlation with creativity was not made. The unconscious appears in Freud's account of art only as providing techniques of concealment or possibilities of play. Latterly, he did recognize that certain unconscious operations had a constructive role to play in the binding of energy and what was later to become known as the building up of the ego. But in no sense did he regard its expression through creativity as 'therapeutic' and thereby the creative process as inherently healing. In Storr's view (1973) Freud's notion on creativity and artistic production is one of the most unsatisfactory parts of psychoanalytic theory.

'Freud never really grasped the notion that art might be a way of enhancing man's grip on reality rather than escaping from it into wish-fulfilling phantasy. For Freud the reductive approach of tracing psychological material to its infantile origin always took precedence over the possibility that the same material might contain within it the seeds of better adaptation and thus be forward looking.'

(Storr 1973: 31)

Winnicott (1971) supports this view when he points out that, when attempting to tackle the subject of creativity, psychoanalysis had to a large extent lost sight of the main theme. He points out, for example, that to take an outstanding creative artist such as Leonardo and introduce themes between his work and his early infancy and from this develop ideas of homosexuality and narcissism, bypasses the theme at the centre of the idea of creativity.

'The main theme is circumvented – that of the creative impulse itself. The creation stands between the observer and the artist's creativity. The creative impulse cannot be explained but a link can be made between creative living and living itself and reasons can be studied as to why creative living is lost and why life that is meaningful and real can disappear.'

(Winnicott 1971: 81)

Jung also departs from the Freudian position, as in his discovery of 'active imagination' he learned to value painting as a method of objectifying phantasies. Jung was aware that psychotic phantasies were similar to dreams, and was able to understand them by applying the principles of dream analysis which Freud had outlined in *The Interpretation of Dreams*. But Jung also came to realize that to take the content of the delusional system and trace its origins to infantile sexuality did not do justice to the creative complexity of the delusional material. During his self-analysis, Jung used drawings and paintings to express his phantasies, and from this we can gain closer understanding of the processes involved. What he described as taking place, in the process of 'individuation' closely paralleled the stages of the creative process.

This is important in terms of the weight Jung placed on creativity and the therapeutic significance of its inherently healing qualities. For he believed that art represented a new synthesis between the inner subjective world of the artist and external reality. The artist selects, often unconsciously, material from both external and internal reality. The work embodies a conjunction between the two, and this integration gives a sense of reconciliation and resolution. His technique of active imagination which deliberately mobilized the patient's creativity is an approach that many art therapists use today. 'What the doctor then does is less a question of treatment than of developing the creative possibilities latent in the patient himself' (Jung 1963: 16).

In this art process, the 'artist' can be seen as someone who 'lets go', allowing aspects of his personality other than the social one to take over. It is because of this collapse of ego-control that it is essential for the therapist to have empathy with the creative process. In one of the most important studies of art from a psychoanalytic viewpoint Kris (1952) expanded his influential ideas of the artist's ability to tap unconscious sources without losing control by 'regression in the service of the ego'. Kris did not depart from Freudian principles of free association in a controlled situation, but speculated that the relaxation or regression in all artistic activity, in contrast to the phantasy or dream, is purposive and controlled. He suggests that this happens as there is a continual interplay between creation and criticism, 'a shift in psychic level consisting in the fluctuation of functional regression and control'. When regression goes too far, the symbols become too private, whereas when there is too much control, the result will be 'cold, mechanical and uninspired'.

Kris noted, therefore, that creative work implies a 'controlled' regression of the surface faculties towards a primary process. But by saying that creativity does not merely control the regression but also the work of the primary process itself, he emphasized the dynamic role of the ego in creativity. This departs from Freud's more pessimistic view of the involuntary unconscious. Kris believes that the unconscious 'turns its potentially disruptive effect into a low structure and highly efficient instrument for making new links and shaping new, more comprehensive concepts and images. The conscious and unconscious are not merely linked. Surface thought is wholly immersed in the matrix of the primary process' (Kris 1952: 262). From this, he explains the 'spell of creativity', found in certain stages of the psychotic process, as attempts at restitution. When the psychosis causes the loosening of the patient's relation to the outside world, there are vehement attempts to 'recathect the objects outside'. Sometimes artistic production stops and the interest in the work is lost when the level of functioning significantly improves.

These ideas have been most influential and important for art therapy. The implications of 'controlled regression' will tie up with later discussion in connection with play and work with children, but this must be one of the special qualities of using art as a safe means for adult 'regression' and 'progression' in therapy. One essential feature of creativity is that it can express both irrational phantasies and the needs of a rational, objective task in one single image or structure. Therefore, the art process can be both ego-disintegrating, which allows the emergence of forms from the instinctual or subliminal level, or ego-building by the elaboration of those forms at a higher or 'conscious' level. These processes are clearly illustrated in the following case study.

Case study: Henry

Henry, a 21-year-old student of pure mathematics, was admitted to an acute admissions ward because of disturbed behaviour, with a content of talk about disaster and death. His work had deteriorated over the last eighteen months, and his GP had described him as an academic eccentric. His parents both worked as librarians and his younger sister had just left school. He felt hostile towards his father, but closer to his mother, and had predominantly jealous feelings towards his sister. Academically, he had always excelled.

On admission, he was doing odd grimaces and gestures, and he spoke in a mixture of religious delusions and mathematical phraseology (psychiatrist's report). He admitted to some vague hearing of voices, and feelings that he was controlled by unknown forces through the radio and telephone. He was acutely anxious and extremely restless, saying that he felt he would shake himself to death with his nervousness and tensions.

He attended art therapy sessions, one of the activities in the ward treatment programme. The groups were non-directive in the sense that patients were provided with a variety of art materials and encouraged to use these according to their own choice. Interaction between the therapist and patient was based on an individual approach to the work produced which often prompted a discussion within the group as a whole. The structure of the sessions was largely dictated by the patients themselves. They lasted one hour and took place four times a week.

Lack of space prohibits the description of each session, but shifts are clearly seen in various stages. Henry joined the sessions willingly and was at first preoccupied with aeroplanes, missiles, and complicated mathematical formulae. He would cover the page with figures as though urgently working something out. It was impossible to talk to him as he would allude to God, bombs, or other destructive powers to evade any approaching comments. In this way he would block any reference to his feelings with scientific and mathematical jargon.

The first notable change occurred after the arrival in the group of two young patients of a similar age. The young girl was over-affectionate towards him and constantly demanded his attention. He seemed to identify this girl with his sister, frequently calling her the wrong name, and when she approached he shook visibly. Becoming aware of this, he subsequently drew a picture of him and his sister and explained that their only contact was for him to help her with physics. His anxiety was equally provoked by a young 'hypomanic' boy. Threatened by his similar interest in physics and his overtly sexual behaviour they communicated in a competitive way which made Henry extremely restless and tense. After a while, Henry drew a picture of this boy. Not only did Henry acknowledge him as a person but also could talk about his feelings towards him, rather than just venting his aggression through missiles.

A succession of changes occurred after this. He drew *Figure 1* showing the words 'Cansel It' written across his complex ideas and formulae. The session following this also marked real change. Having drawn a picture of an aeroplane, he suddenly took a paint bottle and smeared red paint all over the page with his hands. He said this was blowing up his aeroplanes – it was the first time he had used paint in this way and did several pictures of aeroplanes going up in smoke.

After this he was noticeably more settled and relaxed. He continued to paint in colours and shapes in an experimental way, trying to find new ways of doing things, talking about his school days and trying to remember what other subjects he had learned. He said he was fed up with the façade behind which he was living, and talked about his maths as his 'madness' and the other aspects of his paintings as his 'sanity'. Occasionally he lapsed back to writing numbers and drawing bombs, and then covered them over with paint, speaking of the aircraft as his 'old self' and not feeling the need to draw them anymore.

Through his own symbolic imagery he attempted to clarify problems in his mind. *Figure 2* is a picture of himself – he explained that he is the white

Figure 1 'Cansel It'

part, isolated, with problems before and behind him which were all moving together along the ground. He felt like a whirlwind. Using a similar theme, he drew himself as tumbleweed blowing across the desert and commented 'My paintings tend to be several unrelated subjects which drift through my mind. I enjoy interpreting my own paintings. It gives my fantasies a concrete form.' He was becoming increasingly listless, with a bland mood and rather vacant expression. He began to question everything, particularly concerning his own identity. He drew a series of pictures of himself riding alone through a desert on horseback (*Figure 3*). These were simplistic but enabled him to articulate these important feelings. He seemed lost, as if in a vacuum, not knowing which way to turn. He said he felt 'damped' not depressed, and sometimes drew abstracts which he said were 'nothing' – how he felt. Occasionally he came to the session angry and frustrated and expressed this by painting in thick black paint as though trying to gain some sense of motivation. In all the rest of the ward activities he had become withdrawn and very lethargic. He was in a state of dependency; the reality of his situation was that he could do very little for himself. The art sessions were his only means of communication for his thoughts and feelings. As he rarely spoke, painting helped him understand his problems, but at the same time he had to use his own initiative for this.

Certain important decisions in terms of his future were now facing him,

Figure 2 Whirlwind

Figure 3 Riding across the desert

but he said he needed everything planned for him otherwise he felt panicky. With these pending decisions, his paintings became more fragmented and disintegrated – one painting was 'just a muddle – like me. My paintings have a fragmented quality, but enable me to become less tense by expressing feelings which helps problems to surface.' After a week at home, he had decided to take a bed-sitter and attend the ward on a day-patient basis. He wanted to continue attending the sessions, and having made the decision his mood was brighter and more optimistic. On discharge he drew a picture of himself at the helm of a boat commenting 'I can express my feelings through painting – it helps me feel more relaxed. It brings deep feelings to the surface.'

This study shows the duality of art which Kris (1952) was referring to. Painting provided a means through which Henry could externalize his feelings and erode rigid defences. By continuing to express himself in this way, weakened, exposed boundaries could then be strengthened and consolidated. Through this, he could identify and resolve several conflicts that contributed to his breakdown. The stages of this process can be seen. His anger and aggression, formerly misplaced in his war-like interests and obsession with destruction and disaster, were channelled more appropriately, which helped his awareness of them as emotions rather than intellectual pursuits. For a long time his hostility had been internalized and had now found release in the sessions.

His own conflict of identity was clearly expressed in his paintings. Initially feeling pressurized as a mathematician, he pursued this in a determined fashion. These barriers disappeared with his psychotic symptoms, exposing more sensitive, vulnerable parts of himself. He had to re-establish old links and rebuild a shattered 'ego'. In this sense he developed through regression. The sessions allowed him both space and time in an environment that enabled him to explore alternative paths. By 'free associating' his ideas, he became aware of unconscious, previously repressed aspects of self. The insight he gained helped his self-confidence in beginning to rebuild his identity.

At particular stages of his therapy, Henry was asked to draw some human figure drawings of a man, a woman, and himself (*Figure 4*). On admission, he drew the three aeroplanes without hesitation, saying that the person was inside each of the aircraft. At this stage it seemed that people were unimportant to him and he lived in a fantasy world of missiles. After a month, the human figures he drew were strangely primitive but at the same time like robots. The picture of himself is babylike in comparison to the crude figures of both man and woman. The third set, drawn on discharge, shows greater maturity in terms of body image and sense of self (he is clothed and perhaps feels less naked in comparison to the previous drawings). The content of the drawings gave insight into his inner world and the change

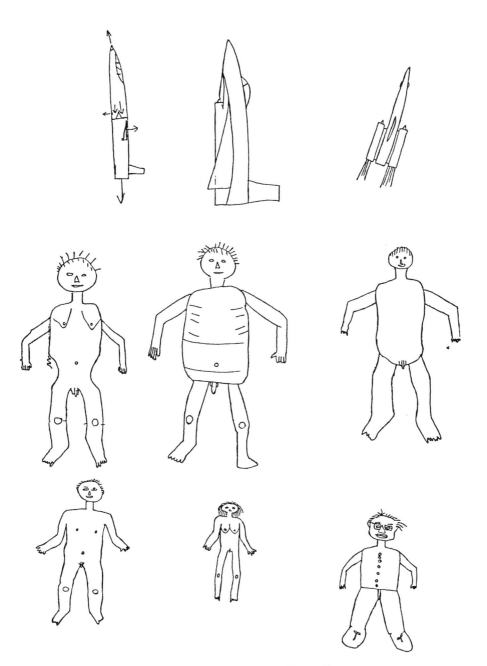

Figure 4 A man, a woman, and himself

reflected progression in the disappearance of his initial symptoms and the tentative emergence of a new 'ego' which becomes increasingly sophisticated.

Spontaneous expression through art activity can therefore be seen to have important therapeutic effects. The process of art therapy develops within a triangular relationship between therapist, patient, and the image produced in the session. Henry had to feel safe enough for his healing process to begin. When powerful emotions are being expressed, possibly for the first time, a trusting relationship between therapist and patient is vital. Containment within the therapeutic relationship enables anxiety to be held, providing a suitable environment for the safe expression through the images. 'It is essential that the high anxiety surrounding symbolic processes can be held by the therapist who also apprehends the shifts in the child's condition as he paints' (Wood 1984: 71). This has the effect of allowing the release of feelings spontaneously from the unconscious as creativity 'unblocks' and catharsis takes place. The art therapist facilitates the art process by providing this containment, but also allows transference to develop within the relationship. The art product creates the focus but is also a third factor to consider in the transference.

Transference

The importance of transference as an aspect of art therapy is insufficiently recognized and often misunderstood. This is reflected by the scarcity of literature on the subject. But some serious enquiry is needed to fully understand the effect of the imagery produced in art therapy. Transference occurs when the patient transfers strong, infantile feelings, that originate from childhood experiences or early relationships, on to the therapist. For Freud, transference referred to something that happens in the therapeutic exchange between patient and analyst; a reliving and repossessing of stages of development that had been experienced at earlier times in psychosexual development. The therapeutic use of transference is to interpret the earlier stages, to integrate them, and to understand them so that they become part of the conscious ego-controlled content of psychic life.

'The characteristic of psychoanalytic technique is this use of transference and the transference neurosis. Transference is not just a matter of rapport or of relationships. It concerns the way in which a highly subjective phenomenon repeatedly turns up in an analysis. Psychoanalysis very much consists in the arranging of conditions for the development of these phenomena at the right moment. The interpretation relates the specific phenomenon to a bit of the patient's psychic reality, and this in some cases means at the same time relating it to a bit of the patient's past living.'

(Winnicott 1958: 158)

What is of concern to us as art therapists is how this process operates within art therapy and whether the existence of a third object, the art product, made within the relationship, essentially detracts from the transference. The introduction of an art object into any situation must entail some involvement between the receiver and object. Reaction to an image or art object inevitably involves contemplation or even self-examination. Some writers have described this inner experience, or movement within the psyche of the recipient, as one which can be likened to the transference process. 'Through giving oneself up to the artist as though giving oneself up to the analyst, a transfer occurs which attaches to the present and actual experiences apparently presented in the art, emotional meanings proper to an earlier now buried experience' (Gorham-Davies 1963: 446). The degree to which this reaction takes place within an art therapy relationship and how this affects the therapeutic process is very important. For example, according to this reaction, direct interpretation of transference between therapist and client might be modified by the presence of the art product, which may provide the focus through which the transference relation then develops. Margarita Wood describes this complex triangular relationship, and makes a plea for a wider recognition of the original Freudian concept of transference, 'for only then can we respect the integrity of the therapeutic process that we observe in art therapy' (Wood 1984: 69). She argues that as some aspects of experience find uneasy containment when projected onto another person, a concrete environment can offer a more simple transference medium.

'The elements of the classical dyadic transference, the projections of the child's inner world onto the therapist are present, but their expression and resolution take place within the picture making, unless they are clearly impeding that process, or are set in direct defence against it, or yet again, if the child is unable to enter that state in which painting is possible.'

(Wood 1984: 69)

We are therefore concerned with the impact of an image within the therapy relationship – for both patient and therapist. In art therapy, both transference and counter-transference develops through the reaction to the image itself. Margarita Wood lucidly describes this process:

'as though the therapist becomes a pliable vessel with a good-enough fit around most of the yet unknown contents put into it, until the time comes for recognition through reflection. But the vessel also has to tolerate unknown contents which distort it, and the therapist realizes a burden of feelings and ideas, not personal belongings, and not necessarily evoked by the overt situation but existing concurrently with it.'

(Wood 1984: 70)

Describing how the child makes his own vessel in his painting, the art therapist is still subject to the overspill of unconscious content. 'The therapist may feel battered and useless for no apparent reason. The therapist is also in a counter-transference relationship with the painting and can feel inexplicable in response to it' (Wood 1984: 70).

Initially, the psychoanalytic term 'counter-transference' was considered to be an inappropriate response on behalf of the therapist, but recently this has been revised to incorporate ideas of therapeutic empathy and identification. Sometimes described as a 'hidden mirror', the existence of counter-transference demands that the therapist makes shifts to accommodate this process. Wood argues that one way to achieve this is to experience the hidden, inner processes that accompany image-making and thereby the mechanisms of projection, introjection, identification, and empathy which she maintains are inherent in any participation with the arts. 'As in psychoanalysis, a vicarious understanding is not enough, and personal experience of the process is needed to inform the therapist's empathy with the painting child' (Wood 1984: 74).

Here, we are approaching some theoretical way to bring closer together the psychoanalytic and the artistic processes which, as Wood suggests, do involve some similar mechanisms. In some recent literature there are moves to revise ideas and make clearer links between psychoanalytic theory and art. Kuhns (1983: 92) for example, wants to break away from the concentration of psychoanalysis on the artist to the psychoanalytic interpretation of the work of art – 'that it seems to me, is the goal of a psychoanalytic theory of art'. He puts forward some definitions of transference in terms of the art object by referring to the ways in which the artist reacts to, makes use of, reinterprets, and restructures aesthetically the tradition within which work is carried out. From this, he defines counter-transference as the relationship between the audience and the work, which involves the viewer's response to the peculiarities of the object in terms of his or her associations and interpretations. What is of particular interest to art therapists is Kuhn's concept of 'cultural' transference which he says occurs as objects become more fully integrated into the conscious awareness of individuals through psychoanalytic interpretations. This process evolves through the patient's relationship to objects which have been of crucial importance in their psychological development. A deeper understanding of those objects becomes clear through the transference relationship between therapist and patient. But this is made more complex as the objects themselves are representational in that they too present and express transference relationships to which the person regarding the object then in turn responds.

'The process is one of "mirroring", reverberating and reflecting back and forth through several layers of consciousness; the consciousness of the object; of the artist, who creates the presentation of the self through the object or in the object; and of the beholder, who responds to all the layers with an accumulation of conscious and unconscious associations which include deeply private nodal points in the unique experience to which there are correspondences, but not identities, in others.'

(Kuhns 1983: 21)

In this sense, transference, in relation to art objects, includes historical as well as psychoanalytic dimensions, in the way that person and object 'see each other'. This idea was completely lacking in Freud's analysis, but Kuhns argues that to achieve an appreciation of the object's uniqueness, these must be brought together, and this happens through response to the unconscious material. 'If the psychoanalytic interpreter is to move beyond unconscious responses to unconscious material, he must raise his response into consciousness – that is, find a language in which he can explain the meaning' (Kuhns 1983: 89).

I would argue that the practice of art therapy is working towards finding that language. Working with the transference from the images produced in art therapy demands both aesthetic and psychoanalytic interpretations. In the initial encounter with an image the response is usually directed to the aesthetic, but involves more than just the formal properties. In the further understanding of the image, the art therapist must also be aware of the expressive qualities of feeling to which counter-transference is an inevitable response. These ideas are more fully discussed in Chapter 3, by Joy Schaverien.

Play

Play is another activity in which creativity is involved, and, like image-making, takes place externally. By looking at the psychoanalytic approach to play, particularly in the areas of interpretation of symbolic activity and transference, as art therapists we can learn a great deal. In fact, it is from the ideas of Winnicott, and to a lesser extent, Melanie Klein, that art therapists have based much of their therapeutic approach and technique. Klein (1975) was the first of the psychoanalysts to use play to analyse children. She noticed that the child's natural mode of expression was play and this was the means by which the child communicated thoughts and feelings, rather than relying on the more adult use of verbal associations.

Play for the child is work – a way of exploring and mastering the external world and, through expressing and working through phantasies, a means of exploring and mastering anxiety. Klein concluded that a child's free play, with the verbal communication he might be capable of, could be used for analysis in a similar way to that of free association with adults.

'In their play, children represent symbolically, phantasies, wishes and experiences. Here they are employing the same language, the same archaic, philogenetically acquired mode of expression as we are familiar with from dreams. We can only fully understand it if we approach it by the method Freud has evolved for unravelling dreams. Symbolism is only part of it; if we want rightly to comprehend children's play in connection with their whole behaviour during the analytic hour we must take into account not only the symbolism which often appears so clearly in their games but also all the means of representation and the mechanisms employed in dreamwork, and we must bear in mind the necessity of examining the whole nexus of phenomena.'

(Klein 1: 134)

Play is of particular value to the child as it provides possibilities for anxiety-provoking situations to be faced in a symbolic way, so that the anxiety itself is reduced to a tolerable and manageable extent. But the child will break off playing if the anxiety is too great, and it was Klein who drew attention to the inhibition of play as an important symptom. Free play can be arrested by a complete stoppage or by rigid unimaginative repetitiveness indicating an inhibition of phantasy life and of development generally. Underlying anxiety can be lessened by interpretation as this brings unconscious conflicts into consciousness, which goes towards resolution. This process is similar to the resistance to free association with adults or the incapacity to paint in an art therapy session. Klein's technique, therefore, consisted of analysing play in much the same way as the analyst of the adult interprets dreams and free associations.

'The play which was interrupted, owing to the setting up of resistances, is resumed; it alters, expands and expresses deeper strata of the mind; the contact between the child and analyst is re-established. The pleasure in play, which visibly ensues after an interpretation has been given, is also due to the fact that the expenditure necessitated by a repression is no longer required after an interpretation.'

(Klein 1: 134)

Art and play

As Klein noticed that the child's drawings and the associations to them were particularly instructive, it is important to consider aspects of Kleinian theory that might be useful in art therapy. Art and play have a number of features in common and it is worth examining these similarities further. For what is essential about play is that it has to be spontaneous, and therefore if we are to consider art in the same way, particularly in therapy when analysis of the material is taking place, then there must be the equivalent element of spontaneity. Once spontaneous painting is taking place, an image formed and the understanding of it ensues within the therapeutic relationship, then analysis of the transference can also follow. Klein stressed the similarities between child and adult analysis, the difference being purely one of technique not of principle. Of particular importance is the similarity in the nature of the transference relationship, and the therapist's understanding of the anxieties and phantasies shown by child or adult, directly or non-directly, in the relationship with her. Playing and painting, if they are spontaneous, can thus be used for interpretation of symbolic activity and transference in the same way.

Connected with this, if child's free play can be closely allied to the spontaneous painting of an adult, then both are used to express preoccupations, conflicts, and phantasies. At the same time, both play and art can be used to master anxiety and thereby set up some capacity for controlling the situation. The child's conscious phantasy is not contained in his mind like an adult but experienced in his play activity, and to a large extent the child is compelled to play in order to think things out. 'Play is a form of behaviour, an active externalisation of mental experience which makes use of symbolical objects and of dynamic, dramatic interaction relating to those objects' (Hoxter 1977: 19). Hoxter goes on to talk about adults:

> 'The adult uses his verbal capacity, his system of word symbolism, to express and communicate to others his thoughts and feelings. But he also uses words, to a great extent, for inner thought, for the actual process of thinking. The mature adult has considerable capacity to contain his thought processes in his mind. But from time to time the adult will find it useful, perhaps essential, to clarify his thought by externalising his mental imagery in the form of talking, writing, doodling and so on. It appears that children have a similar but much stronger need to externalise their mental experience. The young child tends to do so by creating a three-dimensional play situation into which he can put himself, or a toy representing himself.'
>
> (Hoxter 1977: 19)

The need for spontaneity is essential within an art therapy situation for the same reasons that play can be altered by compulsion and rules. 'Play to order is no longer play; it could at best be a forcible imitation of it. By this quality of freedom alone play marks itself off from the course of the natural process' (Huizinga 1970: 47). If spontaneous art work made in a therapy relationship is tailored by ideas of technique, a pressure to conform or to produce a satisfactory aesthetic result as a major consideration in its creation, then the essence of its communication is lost by the rules of making a picture.

In a recent session, with a group of four children, two boys, aged 8 and

10, decided to play draughts – the black child adamantly wanting to be 'blacks'. Their racial battle was played with fierce competition, but as it was bound by the rules of the game, they were inevitably frustrated. They then abandoned the game and began to fight verbally. Later in the same session, the same two children came together and decided to build a battleship, and with negotiation and some disagreement, they constructed one, spontaneously painting it part black and part white. They then played out their battle, which although at some stages was bitter, was more satisfactorily resolved through their play. Games that involve boundaries do not provide the flexibility for personal expression. To have therapeutic significance, image-making must be similarly free from rules as ultimately personal control rests in the process itself.

Adults need games with defined rules to be able to play. Spontaneous play is associated with fooling around or being childish, and so for adults when introduced to art therapy, there is often the need to conform to stereotyped ideas of picture-making. Initial anxiety is often linked with the actual art activity, with associations of school experiences and inhibitions, but once engaged in the painting, themes tend to emerge concerning childhood, memories and the 'child' part of themselves. Frequently in art therapy with both individuals and groups, the process of painting allows the emergence and expression of very early childhood experiences. So the very activity of painting can have this strong effect of facilitating a regressive process, which involves initial associations of being free, spontaneous and possibly losing control – all aspects of the adult self that tend to be buried or certainly lost sight of, but quickly re-emerge in art therapy. Like playing, spontaneous painting forms the focus for therapeutic work, and like free association, unconscious material can be made conscious through this process. Art enables adults to be able to play.

It was Winnicott (1971) who pioneered the idea of playing in the relationship between patient and therapist and the 'potential' space between them – 'the creativity-bearing intermediate region which joins and separates the mother and the playing child' (Deri 1978: 43).

> 'Psychotherapy takes place in the overlap of two areas of playing, that of the patient and that of the therapist. Psychotherapy has to do with two people playing together. The corollary of this is that where playing is not possible then the work done by the therapist is directed towards bringing the patient from a state of not being able to play into a state of being able to play.'
>
> (Winnicott 1971: 44)

He stresses that only in playing is the child or adult free to be creative. 'The reason why playing is essential is that it is in playing that the patient is being creative' (Winnicott 1971: 63).

The therapeutic implication of playing is the search for the self. But by recognizing the connection between creativity and play, he also emphasizes that the playing has to be spontaneous, not compliant, nor acquiescent, if psychotherapy is to be done. He speaks of this particularly in terms of art:

'In a search for the self the person concerned may have produced something valuable in terms of art, but a successful artist may be universally acclaimed and yet have failed to find the self that he or she is looking for. The self is not really to be found in what is made out of products of body or mind. . . . The finished creation never heals the underlying lack of sense of self.'

(Winnicott 1971: 64)

By emphasizing the importance of the process of creativity, through which the self can be found, he expresses the dissatisfaction for the simplistic psychoanalytic view of sublimation and the idea that creativity is a straightforward substitute for instinctual expression.

For our purposes, we can understand the process of creativity, play and the activity of playing as similar to our approach to the process and activity of art. 'The thing about playing is always the precariousness of the interplay of personal psychic reality and the experience of control of actual objects' (Winnicott 1971: 55). The potential space or playground between mother and baby is equivalent to the therapeutic arena between therapist and client. The unpredictable nature of painting evokes feelings and anxieties which may be less easily mastered and in this sense, might be more 'precarious' than play. However, in either case, the therapist plays a role similar to that of the adult in the background whose accessibility is essential for the 'game' to take place and to whom children and adults turn when the symbolic nature of the play breaks down and they are overwhelmed by the force of their own feelings. The use of the adult/therapist as the container for painful states of being is the prerequisite for the ability of the self to establish this capacity.

If we look at the relationship between mother and baby, we can learn a great deal about communication and containment of feelings. The earliest forms of communication take place without verbal or non-verbal symbols. The baby conveys its feelings to mother with directness and rawness. As Hoxter (1977) explains:

'If the baby is alarmed or distressed, what he does about this is to arouse alarm or distress in the mother, he makes the mother experience in her own feelings what he cannot yet bear to keep inside himself. And the mother has to cope with these feelings of alarm and distress in herself before she is able to respond appropriately and give relief to the baby.'

(Hoxter 1977: 13)

The baby's experience might have been that the distress was not accepted, understood, or coped with, but that it was met by the repercussion of mother's own not-understood, not-coped-with anxieties.

These are familiar situations that are commonly faced within a therapeutic relationship. To help in the understanding, as Harris (1970) describes in her article, the observation of mother–infant interaction and development has been an important contribution to analytic training. The essential intimacy and nakedness of the analyst–patient relationship (which Winnicott describes as the 'white-hot' experience of a consulting room) is, Harris points out, probably more analogous to the mother–baby relationship than to any other.

Infant observation involves weekly observation of an infant with his mother for the first year of life, detailed recording, and discussion of this experience. Discussion of the process enables the observer to participate in a more unconscious way and learn from her own counter-transference. The observer must allow herself to feel, but needs to think about these feelings in order to restrain herself from acting them. By learning this receptivity, the analytic student will be able to receive increasingly the projection of the more primitive infantile parts of the patient's personality.

'The central truth one can learn through one's own experience as an observer and through observing the development of a mother who is learning to be a mother is directly applicable to the analytic couple. It is more painful to wait, to remain receptive, and not cut off, to bear the pain that is being projected, including the pain of one's own uncertainty than it is to have recourse to precipitative action designed to evacuate that pain and to gain the relief of feeling that one is doing something.'

(Harris 1970: 10)

This reminds us of a similar approach put forward by Winnicott when he refers to the essential dangers of the need of the inexperienced therapist to make interpretations (Winnicott 1971: 102). Perhaps it might be argued that the experience of infant observation is not central to the art therapy relationship, but it is important that the art therapist can also experience and learn this receptivity, and thereby understand the underlying dynamics of the relationship and origins of transference. As art therapy is essentially activity-based, it is perhaps tempting for an art therapist to cut across difficult feelings or painful processes when the therapist is unable to contain them, by the initiation of further art activity or the introduction of a theme, rather than waiting, experiencing, and thereby working with the conflict. McNeilly (1983) describes this as a 'safety mechanism' and sees the whole process of suggestion by the therapist as one of control and a need for structure, which is really the therapist's need to avoid transference and counter-transference.

Observing the development of symbol formation as the infant grows is perhaps more specifically relevant for art therapists. This is discussed more fully in Chapter 4 by Felicity Weir, but if art therapists are relying on their training as artists for a special knowledge of the intimacy of creative processes, some other experience of non-verbal communication patterns, such as that between mother and baby, is invaluable. This rigorous and exacting experience helps in understanding the nature of the unspoken word, the symbolic gesture.

Winnicott's therapeutic approach was based on his observation of children, where, like Klein, he recognized the importance of play for both communication and 'the continuous evidence of creativity which means aliveness' (Winnicott 1964: 144). He linked the importance of creative play with self-revelation which is equally important for art therapy.

> 'Play can be being honest about oneself just as dressing can be for adults. This can become changed at an early age into its opposite, for play, like speech, can be said to be given us to hide our thoughts, if it is the deeper thoughts that we mean. The repressed unconscious must be kept hidden, but the rest of the unconscious is something that each individual wants to get to know, and play, like dreams, serves the function of self revelation.'
>
> (Winnicott 1964: 146)

Children in art therapy

For self-revelation through play and art to take place, Winnicott stresses the need for a 'facilitating environment' which encourages patients to play and explore various art materials. Children in therapy have often experienced 'good enough' mothering at an early point in maturational development, but may have been traumatized by a premature separation from mother, or had the experience of an unobtainable emotional response. It is important therefore to provide an environment where the child may safely regress and re-experience this early trauma, but this time in a controlled setting and with a more empathetic, understanding, and containing 'environmental mother'. This may be the first opportunity for many children to experience themselves in such an environment, where they are given the freedom to explore within this personal space which has structures and boundaries. This can be viewed as the recreation of the 'potential space' between mother and baby.

The therapist as 'environmental mother' accepts, sets limits, and even frustrates according to the ability of the child to tolerate such frustration. The introduction of art materials enables the child to feel free in using his creative art experience as a means of tolerating the frustrations that inevitably arise. These have their roots in early relationship with mother and can now be re-created in a less traumatic form. The ultimate re-experiencing of these instinctual feelings, along with a growing capacity for symbolization and sublimation, permit the child to 'work through' and integrate them. The following case study illustrates the importance of this process.

Case study: Chris

Chris attends an inner London primary school, which serves a largely immigrant community. Given the general climate of racial tension and social deprivation, priority is given to special needs. The art therapist works with the most difficult or disruptive children from each class, and maintains a close liaison with the teachers.

Chris is an 11-year-old boy, third son of West Indian parents. He has a pale skin, is overweight and physically clumsy. Mother is over-protective and rather controlling, father is ambitious for his sons and though apparently rather remote, puts them under great pressure to achieve. Chris is probably of high intelligence, but has achieved badly at school. As an infant, he was an extremely bright child and so with parental pressure, was moved up a year. When he came into the juniors his progress tailed off, and in the last couple of years his application in the classroom has been very poor. He has appeared vague and apathetic, with low achievement which has constantly frustrated the expectations of teachers and his parents. He seemed to evoke exasperation in anyone trying to teach him anything as in his lessons he 'escaped into day-dreaming'. He was moved down from the top form, where he was the youngest, and so is presently the eldest of the juniors. This also had the effect of postponing his move to secondary school. At first this caused him some distress, but the class into which he was moved was more controlled and less violent and so he was seen to be making progress. However, after an initial improvement, he returned to his old ways.

It was at this stage that he was referred to art therapy, which for the first two terms was on an individual basis for one hour. The art therapy room is large, well equipped with art materials, clay, sand, and 'junk' – boxes, stones, shells, etc. The child is free to choose his own activity within the boundaries of the session, which is in contrast to the more structured and controlled lessons. At first Chris appeared vacant and listless, but showed a lively imagination. Each session he started immediately to work on a model, a drawing or an idea he had thought up or seen. He worked inventively, but in a secretive manner, usually in silence, not disclosing what he was doing until it was completed. His work was concerned with weapons – guns, aeroplanes, bombs, parachutes – which he constructed in great detail.

As the sessions developed, he began to talk more, to trust the therapist and by being more open about his work, not hiding it or working with his back turned, he began to disclose more about himself. He was beginning to show some commitment to the sessions, illustrated by a large chalk drawing of a monster on the blackboard which he turned to the wall so that it would stay there, and not be rubbed off. He referred to this creature as 'Fred', and regularly checked that he was still there and 'all right'. It remained there throughout his therapy (see *Plate 1*). He was sometimes quite playful and childlike – drawing silly pictures of the therapist, telling jokes and trying to engage her in other ways. One of these ways was to constantly pick faults in the therapist, or the materials she was using, showing that his anxiety about not achieving was very near the surface. As he was such a complex child, it was often difficult to know how he felt. His bland façade prevented the vulnerable and sensitive parts of himself from showing. When these were allowed to surface, one realized the real difficulties that he experienced. For example, once when working with polystyrene, the small balls started sticking to his clothes which caused him acute anxiety and he jumped around the room in great distress trying to get them off.

The next term he worked in a group of three. This was to some extent to 'accommodate' the other children in the school. But in discussion, it was felt that some 'sharing' of the session with his peers might help in his relationship with them and in the difficult transition to secondary school. At that time he remained isolated, was not well liked, and was often teased and bullied, and he tended to escape this by reading comics. He was in the habit of resorting to comics when faced with any kind of pressure.

The other two in the group were both girls, an 11-year-old West Indian and a 9-year-old Cypriot. It was felt that this trio would be a 'safe enough' group in which Chris would be able to achieve, assert himself and become confident enough to develop, while working alongside the others who would provide a peer 'sounding board'. One immediate consequence of their interaction was that Chris became more sexually suggestive and openly aggressive which was expressed particularly in his drawings. The guns and missiles changed to monsters fighting and eating each other, with gaping jaws and sharp teeth – though these were often obliterated afterwards by splashing paint and folding or destroying the painting (see *Figure 5*).

Up until now, several overriding factors seemed to account for his behaviour. He felt threatened by his peers, and therefore avoided competing with them, and as he greatly feared criticism, doing nothing prevented this possibility. Most destructive of all was his own self-criticism, and so he sabotaged things before anyone had the chance to get close enough to comment. Chris had to be in control – only then could he function, but this ultimately prevented him from doing anything, particularly under pressure. Because of this he was happiest on his own and potentially extremely isolated. In the sessions he was learning to relax these controls and

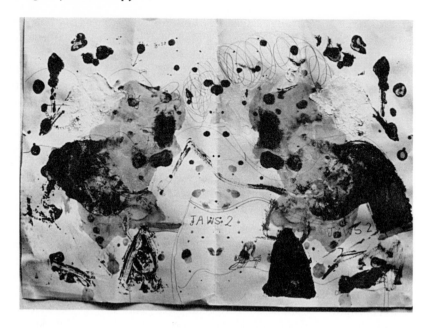

Figure 5 'Monsters'

experience feeling open and vulnerable. These aspects of himself were extremely sensitive and were only allowed to surface occasionally. Only by losing the controls could he learn to function without them.

Over his last year, the inclusion of a fourth member, an 8-year-old West Indian boy, made quite an impact on Chris. The new boy in the group provided a younger male influence which was not too threatening. He felt able to be 'big' brother to him rather than 'baby' which it seemed he was always made to feel at home. This had the effect of enabling him to relate in a relaxed, spontaneous way without feeling the need to be so much in control of himself or others. As he was exploratory and inventive in his art work and model-making, he gave the others enthusiasm to be likewise in an ingenious way. He was learning to be included and integrated in the group without letting them get too close to impinge on him to a point which he found intolerable. He was getting in touch with his own ability to be powerful, something that he had always felt lacking with his over-protective mother and older brothers. His new-found role as leader was a new experience which made him feel reassured and self-confident.

Throughout this time of growth his art work continued to develop and become more expansive and spontaneous. The enclosed nature of his work was beginning to change, but, at the beginning of his last term, he experienced a severe bout of new difficulties when he became totally preoccupied by his health and eating problems. During this time his academic work suffered as well. It was recognized that he was getting in touch with some acute separation anxiety, as this was his last term at the school and art therapy sessions would be terminating. Working through the transference, he had been able to be experimental and test out new boundaries and ways of being. He made many references to how much he would miss the sessions but by the end of the term he came to accept the separation. This seemed bound up with the intensely close relationship with mother who refused to let him go. He was able to talk about some of these issues and work through many of his own, and felt sufficiently strong to insist on going on the school journey in spite of parental opposition.

For the last few weeks before he left the school he made an enormous aeroplane out of cardboard, which he hung up in the hall with pride. During its construction he became covered with paint, spreading it on with a sponge and enjoying the sensation of squeezing it through his hands, a new departure for a boy normally so conscious of cleanliness. The others joined in this with equal delight. The sheer scale of this object, in sharp contrast to the tight, controlled style of his first aeroplane, indicates some real changes in his self-image. One hopes that he will now be able to make the problematic transition to secondary school with more ease. His art therapy experience has enabled him to break down many of the defences that he put up and emerge more assertively, which will put him in a better state of mind to cope with his adolescence. Without this experience, Chris might have become totally 'lost' behind the wall he built around himself, as he found it too difficult to let his 'real' self emerge.

Art therapy in education

What is striking about Chris's situation is the parallel that can be drawn with the case of Henry, whose breakdown might have been prevented with earlier intervention. More and more it is being realized that if young children are given the opportunity to experience some therapeutic intervention it may prevent future problems during early teens and adolescence. Encouraging specialist workers such as therapists and special-needs teachers to work within the normal school environment, and have regular contact with social workers and family clinics, can prevent the need for care and treatment orders, and the subsequent stigmatization that inevitably ensues by the removal from the 'normal' institution. Removal sets up a course of treatment for 'maladjustment' and it becomes increasingly difficult to re-adjust or return to the mainstream of 'normal' life. With a view to this problem, Winnicott (1964) advocates the interesting idea of 'educational diagnosis' which would follow the same lines as medical diagnosis in identifying the widely different needs of children in school. He points out that what troubles teachers is not so much the varying intellectual capacity of their children, as their varying emotional needs, and he encourages teachers to approach these difficulties, once specified, in an appropriate way within the existing institution.

In the United Kingdom, this is only just beginning, but in the United States of America there are reports of art therapy being introduced into school systems in the 1970s. Cohen (1975), for example, outlines the problems encountered in her school when attempting to introduce art therapy into the curriculum. Most of the problems centred around 'educating' the staff and other personnel at the school in order to dispel suspicion and ignorance about the aim and objectives of such a programme. She suggests intensive in-service training for the staff, and points out that video (see References) is often a good medium through which to do this – 'perhaps the most informative and dynamic way for educating such large groups'. She also comments that there was pressure to delete or change the word 'therapy' but it was soon realized that the children were very keen to participate in the programme and 'recognised and wanted to have an avenue of expression as well as a professional with whom they could share their feelings'. She concludes

'Every child is a special child and has a right to be happy and yet so many are so miserable. Situations arise that they are unable to cope with. Often they cannot function with or relate to members of their families or with their peers at home or at school; they have worries and fears as well as undesirable habits. It is difficult, if not impossible, for such a disturbed child to achieve in school and to relate to his family and peers. And yet these factors are essential if the child is to sustain himself and if he is to become a desirable and useful member of his community and his society. This, then, would be a prime objective of an on-going art therapy program in . . . schools.'

(Cohen 1975: 135)

This is exactly what I have found working as an art therapist within a primary school. The children recognize the freedom of expression that is gained through art – only very rarely do they ever ask for direction. Many enlightened, therapeutically orientated teachers would agree with this. 'As educators, we want the child to move forward intellectually through opportunities to master the outside world. We want this growth not to be restricted to cognition but to include emotional growth. Therapy can be viewed as a special kind of learning that deals with a person's inner world and the immediate social world' (Pine 1975: 91).

An art therapist in this situation works with individual children or small groups and has a relationship essentially different from that between teacher and pupil. In therapy the child might learn how to use the art materials to his own advantage, but he is not taught. The relationship between art therapist and child flourishes in an atmosphere that is free from competition and judgement. As we have discussed, an accepting therapist attitude frees the children to be themselves, and begin to discover themselves. Acceptance does not mean that the therapist gives the children permission to act out, but it does mean that there is encouragement to be themselves and feel expansive. This attitude or 'containment' fosters the child's trust in the relationship and this relationship forms the basis for corrective experiences. In art therapy, the child may shift from play to art, or he may choose to do nothing at all. 'Through the process of doing in art, in the course of psychotherapy as in art education or in art therapy, one communicates with oneself. Viewing each work as an expression of the child who produced it, we can see in it to what extent the child was able to communicate with himself' (Pine 1975: 93).

If this is the case, why is it so rare for teachers and therapists to work alongside each other within the same institution? Perhaps this is a subject which requires special consideration. In a recent interesting study, Katrin FitzHerbert (1985) argues for a different approach to 'maladjustment' in primary schools by giving positive prevention a chance. She makes the claim that most of the education money spent on children with behavioural problems in the normal schools goes on adolescents, special units for disruptives and persistent absentees, or on home tuition. She suggests that if a proportion of what goes largely on containment, on satisfying the letter of the law, could be spent on positive prevention in primary schools, then many children who now fail the system (or whom the system fails) could survive successfully in the secondary school mainstream.

The essence of the preventive approach tested out experimentally was child-centred in that it provided a 'safety net', geared to identifying children 'at risk' and to dealing with their individual needs before these could produce unmanageable behaviours, troublesome to the school as well as the child. In her study, 200 children aged 8 and 9 were subjected to some 'systematic' welfare procedures in the last seven terms in junior school. Three years later the group was followed up and the majority was found to be surviving happily and doing well academically or socially, or, where their achievements were limited by low ability, they were at least working. A few were still socially isolated, teased, and even shunned by their peers, as they had been in junior school, but they were displaying resilience in the face of this treatment.

When matched by the control group, the scale of the difference between the groups lent support to two hypotheses – first that primary teachers can predict fairly accurately which of their pupils will get into trouble in secondary school and secondly, that a conscious attempt at prevention successfully averts these sad outcomes, at least for some children. Having formalized these findings she outlines the difficulties of introducing such a preventive programme, as they are inter-disciplinary and would require co-operation from social services, education and possibly other agencies. However, she concludes 'The Warnock Policy on making provisions for children with special needs in the ordinary school, now creates a wonderful opportunity for launching preventive projects as an integral part of the education service'. She makes the point that if these opportunities could be used, teachers would be spared much of the pain our society cynically asks them to bear. 'We know how accurately teachers can predict which of their pupils will have troubles – and will be troublesome – in the secondary school. We should put their powers of prediction to constructive use by developing prevention in the junior school, not creating more and more sin bins' (FitzHerbert 1985: 237).

The practice of art therapy in schools would go some way in providing this effective preventive measure, as it is seen to be doing in the school which Chris attends. Since the programme of art therapy was introduced there, many children have been prevented from being expelled or placed into special schools. In times of economic stringency, to integrate a programme of art therapy into the school system might prove to be financially beneficial. Where school is the main source of stability and continuity for some children, to be removed from this environment and placed in another for treatment is extra punitive. Where home is unstable and unloving, an art therapist working within a school can be seen as essentially integrating, and by containing the child's emotional needs, can be seen to facilitate learning. An 8-year-old boy, recently put into care, has been attending individual art therapy sessions throughout this traumatic time. He has used the sessions to talk about this experience and express his feelings, centring on his ambivalence about his mother. He felt loyal and protective to her, in the absence of any father, and yet he also felt entirely let down by her. He had been through an almost psychotic stage of confusion, with outbursts of aggression and bizarre acting out, but managed to use the consistency of the sessions to help focus his thoughts and feelings through his paintings, models, and games. He is a very creative child and, becoming more secure and self-confident, he is now gaining friends among his peers, who were largely antagonistic to him. In his art and play he has worked through and expressed many of his difficulties and experiences. He waits regularly outside the door at the appropriate time and is rapidly changing into a good-humoured and likeable child.

Another boy, aged 8, who has four younger siblings, is forced into the role of carer since the arrival of the new baby. Taking the place of the largely absent father, he tends to extend this role at school, but in art therapy sessions he is permitted to regress and become the 'baby'. He puts his thumb in his mouth, asks to go home and be with his mother, and he is able to work through many of the difficulties he experiences with his domestic responsibilities at home. He finds containment in the sessions which prevents regressive behaviour spilling out in his general contact with his class mates, as some of his emotional needs can be met. His class teacher, another stable mother figure will also be changed next year by a class move and so the sessions provide continuity and stability in an otherwise fragmented and chaotic life.

Children must develop emotionally and intellectually, and when this gets out of phase and emotional needs are not met, the resultant blockage tends to arrest learning and general functioning. Many children with whom I work are not sufficiently stable emotionally to function intellectually and therefore they find learning very hard. An immature 9-year-old struggling with a repressive Cypriot home is learning through basic tactile and sensory experiences, by squeezing and squashing clay through her hands and getting as messy as possible – a stage to which she needs to return in order to progress. She needs the structure of the sessions to experiment and find her own boundaries, which are ruthlessly imposed upon her at home but which she is unable to provide for herself. I have worked with a 9-year-old experiencing the anguish and conflict of divorcing parents for whom she is carrying much of their bitterness; an 11-year-old involved in the constant custody battle of her estranged parents; a 7-year-old for whom this bitter process is about to begin. For children to be able to express these feelings, often unconsciously, through their paintings, drawings, models, and play provides a fundamental 'space' for their personal stability, which undoubtedly helps their learning process.

It is this spontaneous need that is taken up by the presence of an art therapist. Art provides a most appropriate medium through which to work, as children in distress and with special needs often find it more difficult than most to articulate their feelings. Art provides release, enjoyment, play, catharsis, splashing and messing with the materials – often essential for children whose emotional development has been severely arrested. This is clearly the case when working in groups, when one large painting indicates how children interact together and highlights issues such as competition/co-operation, authority/leadership, and other dynamics that emerge in the group. Conflicts that arise can be resolved and worked on through the activity of the group task. This might include 'projects' such as scenery painting, murals for special events such as Guy Fawkes and so on. The art therapist's skills can be of great assistance in facilitating a group towards such an aim by looking at the group dynamics, but also by helping to build an aesthetic appreciation of the overall product which might involve the whole school. The social learning process of art activity can also produce aesthetic results, and the talented can enjoy the satisfaction of this achievement.

Some acknowledgement and containment of emotional difficulties in schools is essential if we are to prevent enormous social upheavals in the future. I would argue that art therapy is of great value and importance for children, for expression of their feelings, thoughts, and difficulties. I think it is important that we take steps to recognize this now, and I hope that this chapter has provided some convincing argument and sound theoretical basis to help establish a system of provision by art therapists in education of the quality that now exists within our National Health Service. The power of this process is well described by Edith Kramer, the pioneer of art therapy with children, and it seems a fitting ending:

'There is no way to bypass the crucial moment when the making of a picture becomes an independent act, when the young painter confronts a blank surface with the will and desire to make a statement and the inner strength to overcome the fear of committing himself. This desire and this fear are at the core of all creative work. We can give support, encouragement and help, but we cannot deny the difficulty and should not try to circumvent it.'

(Kramer 1975: 40)

Art therapists must meet the challenge of making this process available to all those who might benefit from this experience.

© 1987 Tessa Dalley

References

Cohen, F. (1975) Introducing Art Therapy into a School System: Some Problems. *Art Psychotherapy* 2: 121–35.
Dalley, T. (ed.) (1984) *Art as Therapy.* London: Tavistock.
Deri, S. (1978) *Transitional Phenomena: Vicissitudes of Symbolization and Creativity, Between Reality and Fantasy.* New York: Aronson.
Dubowski, J. (1985) Who Took the Art out of Art Therapy? Unpublished paper, presented at the International Review of the Arts in Therapy, Goldsmiths' College, London.
Ehrenzweig, A. (1967) *The Hidden Order of Art.* London: Paladin.
FitzHerbert, K. (1985) Giving Positive Prevention a Chance. *Education* 15 March: 236–37.
Freud, S. (1963) *The Standard Edition of the Complete Psychological Works.* London: The Hogarth Press and the Institute of Psychoanalysis.
Gorham-Davies, R. (1963) Art and Anxiety. In Philips, S. W. (ed.) *Art and Psychoanalysis.* New York: Meridian.
Harris, M. (1979) *The Contribution of Observation of Mother–Infant Interaction and Development to the Equipment of a Psychoanalyst or Psychoanalytic Psychotherapist.* London: The Tavistock Clinic.
Hoxter, S. (1977) Play and Communication in Child Psychotherapy. In M. Boston

and D. Daws (eds) *The Child Psychotherapist and Problems of Young People.* London: Wildwood House.

Huizinga, J. (1970) *Homo Ludens.* London: Temple Smith.

Judd, D. (1986) Book Reviews. *British Journal of Psychotherapy* 2(4): 145–51.

Jung, C. (1963) *Memories, Dreams, Reflections.* London: Routledge & Kegan Paul.

Klein, M. (1975) *The Writings of Melanie Klein.* London: The Hogarth Press and Institute of Psychoanalysis.

Kramer, E. (1975) Art and Emptiness: New Problems in Art Education and Therapy; The Problems of Quality in Art. Both in E. Ulman and P. Dachinger (eds) *Art Therapy in Theory and Practice.* New York: Schocken Books.

Kramer, E. (1980) Symposium: Integration of Divergent Points of View in Art Therapy. In E. Ulman and C. Levy (eds) *Art Therapy Viewpoints.* New York: Schocken Books.

Kris, E. (1952) *Psychoanalytic Explorations in Art.* New York: International Universities Press.

Kuhns, F. (1983) *Psychoanalytic Theory of Art: A Philosophy of Art on Developmental Principles.* New York: Colombia University Press.

McNeilly, G. (1983) Directive and Non-Directive Approaches in Art Therapy. *The Arts in Psychotherapy* 10: 211–19.

Naumburg, M. (1958) Art Therapy: Its Scope and Function. In E. F. Hammer (ed.) *Clinical Application of Projective Drawings.* Springfield, Ill.: C. C. Thomas.

Pine, S. (1975) Fostering Growth Through Art Education, Art Therapy and Art in Psychotherapy. In E. Ulman and P. Dachinger (eds) *Art Therapy in Theory and Practice.* New York: Schocken Books.

Storr, A. (1973) *Jung.* London: Fontana.

Winnicott, D. W. (1958) *The Maturational Process and the Facilitating Environment.* New York: IUP.

Winnicott, D. W. (1964) *The Child, The Family and the Outside World.* Harmondsworth: Penguin Books.

Winnicott, D. W. (1971) *Playing and Reality.* London: Tavistock.

Wollheim, R. (1974) *On Art and the Mind.* Cambridge, Mass.: Harvard University Press.

Wood, M. (1984) The Child and Art Therapy. In T. Dalley (ed.) *Art as Therapy.* London: Tavistock.

Video (1985) Art Therapy: A Training Video. Made at Goldsmiths' College, London by J. Beacham, T. Dalley, and D. Waller. Available from Tavistock.

2 | A search for meaning: loss and transition in art therapy with children

Caroline Case

Introduction: the context of practice

At the time of writing, there is no statutory provision for art therapists in the education or social services systems. Official opportunities for working with children are quite limited and in some ways analogous to the situation in the National Health Service some years ago (see Chapter 7). There are, in fact, art therapists working in the areas of child guidance, intermediate treatment, family therapy, and special schools. In this chapter I am going to discuss some aspects of working in two further areas – the areas of assessment and observation, and of normal primary schools.

In an educational setting what kind of room is relevant or indeed essential to practice? The setting gives many significant indicators to clients and staff of other disciplines about the sort of work that goes on in there. An art therapy room is unlike the traditional consulting room of the psychotherapist where a neutral setting, limited furniture, and the clients' 'own box' or 'drawer' of pencils, toys, paper, etc. focus the interaction on the relationship between the two people, the engaging of a working alliance between child and therapist. It is also unlike an art room where a group of children is taught; for an art therapy group will focus on the group processes of the group, reflected in and thus part of the paintings, as well as focusing on the individual significance to the maker.

As a practising artist, an art therapist has an aura from a different tradition to a psychotherapist, which conveys the message that they have a working relationship with their own creativity which often has visible products. Adolescents frequently ask questions such as 'Can you draw a horse, Miss?' Whereas a psychotherapist's skill might be patently demonstrated by interpretation (and indeed might be tempted to a display of virtuosity) a parallel pitfall for an art therapist might be to draw that horse!

What seems important is that the art therapist in a studio brings a personal history of apprenticeship at making, and for this reason has, for instance, a range of interventions available different from other therapies. As well as verbal interactions there are possibilities in painting and modelling, working together, drawing the client, modelling feelings, and ways of recognizing and feeding back.

The externalizing of inner images will have an effect on the maker whether or not there is also a verbal relationship with the therapist. This does not exclude or discourage other forms of communication, particularly when working with children.

In a relatively new profession, the lack of tradition leaves the context of practice quite flexible. My own history of working initially in the assessment setting has influenced the type of space and facilities I feel to be appropriate. Beginning with an almost empty room and the most basic materials, areas of a different character emerged in the room according to children's needs. A pattern gradually developed of seeing children in small groups of three or four, often of mixed ages, with the possibility of further sessions too for those most deprived or disturbed and likely to benefit from individual therapy. Unlike the more usual pattern of eight clients in group therapy with adults, I find the smaller number more appropriate for younger children. It reflects family patterns or sibling relationships, it feels a more productive size, and children respond well to each other. Seeing children individually and in a small group makes for a much fuller assessment of potential and problem areas.

The assessment centre where I worked received children aged 4 to 16 years, who had been taken into council care. The children were likely to have at least one or more of the following problems (as well as being under immediate stress because of being taken into care): emotionally disturbed; ascertained maladjusted; young offenders; drug abusers; school truanters; refusals or phobics; battered children; or children with problems expressed sexually, e.g. prostitution. The art therapy room was part of a system of assessment involving different professionals. Residential social workers worked with the children in the house, field social workers with the child's family. Children were interviewed by a child psychiatrist and tested by the educational psychologist. The particular function of the art therapist and room was partly a counterpoint to the teacher and classroom, the child encountering two different structures. A certain amount of self-control and application to school work was expected in the classroom, which was necessary to keep children to standards of learning they had attained and to remediate any learning problems that became apparent. A different set of rules could apply in the art and play sessions where in a small group one could choose one's own activities. This enabled assessment of children's ability to respond to the different structures, to peers, to younger and older children. At the same time different working relationships would develop with the teachers and the therapist, with possibilities of short- or long-term therapy.

In the art therapy room the following areas emerged to be the most useful for children in these circumstances, which are, of course, residential, though in transition. A group table area in the centre of one part of the room proved to be a natural meeting ground, both for more structured adolescent groups and as a place to sit while working or talking for those who wanted to interact socially. A large walk-in alcove gradually developed into the 'messy area' where the children could paint on the floor, walls, or ceiling, and throw and pound things. This area had its own light which was most useful, and it could also be partitioned off from the rest of the room by a curtain or a wall built up of cardboard or wood. For children in transition the possibility of building a den or home or private room is very necessary. It is a place to be private, to sit in the dark. Space to reflect, to think things out is often hard to find in an institution. It is so valuable, however, to these children facing enormous decisions or preferences to be conveyed at a court hearing.

A quiet drawing area with books also doubled as a dressing-up/play area for younger children. Three categories of books collected on the shelves: art books, often at times pictures would be used as a model – as if in making pictures, artists had looked at 'what they could become' in terms of a new identity; reference books, on natural objects (animals, birds, etc.) but also man-made objects; and lastly, fairy story books, used by children of all ages, again for unconscious guidance to find a way forward, very like the art images. This area was also used for dressing-up, enactment, and story-telling when it needed to be contained (otherwise the whole room might be utilized).

About a third of the room comprised an ostensibly infant play area, partly carpeted. This contained all the non-fixed image-making materials. It was an area for experimentation, trial, and play, and for those too insecure and tentative to risk a more traditional medium. There was also sand and water and ready-made objects, a blackboard with a full range of coloured chalks and the doll's house and accoutrements; here things could be arranged, disarranged, and leave no trace. This part of the room was almost divided off from the rest by two large cupboards, leaving a narrow passageway as its entrance. On the carpet by the doll's house were two easy chairs.

I decided to have a desk, as I like a point of reference by which children can orientate themselves in a group in relation to me as well as to each other. How children respond to it and me becomes part of their exploration of authority and a component of transference. It is often used as a non-messy base for dens, beds, or nests, i.e. under the desk as well as in the chair for play or security.

Mainly for the sake of the short-stay children who could not start any real treatment programme, a variety of crafts seemed productive. This meant that from their stay something visible could result, and be taken away. Therefore, pottery, candle-making, lino-printing, woodwork, etc. were all available around a large tiled sink area.

The above description of the art therapy context might encourage a fallacy that all children love painting and play! In fact, children might have lost the ability to play, they might come to talk, or an enormous range of things might happen, even, apparently nothing at all. Art therapists might spend weeks of treatment just waiting. Like any other therapy, timing is all important. The relationship of art, play, image-making, enactment, and story-telling suggested by the different areas enumerated will be taken up in the following section and examined in more detail.

The grief process

One of the cardinal issues lurking behind all assessment work is that of loss. Children generally enter the centre in a state of stress because a situation has broken down and they have been taken into council care. Whatever the precipitating reasons for coming into care and however they are labelled, all children share the state of being in transition. The spectrum of feelings about arrival at the centre may vary from seeing it as a haven of safety to a place of imprisonment. Whatever their emotion they need to be helped to look at the changes they are having to undergo, to come to terms with what they are leaving behind and to be able to face the future.

Behind these immediate issues of loss and change may lie previous losses, e.g. of a parent or a significant other, by separation, divorce, imprisonment, or mental or physical illness, as well as from a natural or early death. Research by Colin Parkes (1971) has documented the reactions to other forms of loss in adults, e.g. retirement, unemployment, change of occupation, amputation, disablement. In these terms, grief is seen as one of several psycho-social transitions which involves the same sort of 'realization' and the giving up of old models of the self and world. This I feel could be extended to include in children the reaction to a change of environment, change of school, teacher, children's home, foster home, loss of residential or field social worker, as well as the various forms of loss of a natural parent or relation.

Most art therapists are likely to be working with special-needs children, and experience of multiple loss may be quite common. There may be several losses inextricably mixed in tandem so that it is difficult to be quite sure what one is working with. It is not unusual for images to do with bereavement to surface spontaneously in a child who has been referred for another problem. For example, intense, aggressive acting-out can hide a depression caused by loss. Sometimes images seem to reflect or monitor progress, to be portents of a disclosure or climax to come. Sometimes they would focus a re-enactment of events, an emotional discharge, or more simply share the multitude of nuances of feeling surrounding a loss. At other times, pictures or play manage to forge a satisfying new configuration which expresses a struggle for meaning accompanying a loss which may only be expressible non-verbally.

Early grief studies (Lindemann 1944: 141) were aware that 'the essential task . . . is the sharing of the grief work'. It is necessary to reassure the grief-stricken that the peculiar physical, and psychological accompaniments of grief are, in fact, quite normal to that situation. Curiously, bereavement, following which one mourns one's loss, has particularly concrete manifestations. The intensity of attachment to the person is replaced by a correspondingly intense sensation of emptiness which feels physical. It is understandable why early studies of the meaning of death (Nagy: 1948) found death personalized in the figure of the Grim Reaper taking someone away, as the sensation is of being robbed and one needs a robber to blame. Bowlby's research (1981) has shown that grief not worked through in childhood inevitably has repercussions in adult life, from the difficulty of trusting relationships to later psychiatric illness at another death, or underlying depression and anxiety. Despite it being such an important factor little is done to help the grieving child, although it has long been observed: 'He who remains passive when overwhelmed with grief loses his best chance of recovering elasticity of mind' (Darwin 1872: 129). There is a necessity to explore grief thoroughly. In other research Marris has concluded that: 'Until grief is worked out, the conflict itself becomes the only meaningful reference for behaviour' (Marris 1974: 56).

Before going on to look at two case studies in some detail, it might be useful to give a skeleton outline both of the main stages of the grief process (which in some form accompanies all losses and transitions whatever one's age or understanding) and also of the different theories of the nature of grief work. This literature is now more readily available than it was twelve or fifteen years ago when I was first encountering grief, and the references will indicate further reading suggestions to explore for those interested.

Early studies of grief postulated bereavement as a six-week crisis, but after modern sociological studies it is now recognized that a major death might take from eighteen months to two years or longer, for recovery. A sense of time necessary can be felt through this comparison: 'As in the case of a physical injury, "the wound" gradually heals' (Parkes 1975: 19). There are three main stages, though the length that each individual might remain within each stage would vary.

Stage one: The initial response is one of shock and disbelief. The person can feel cold, numb, dazed, empty, and confused. There is often a complete denial of the fact that has been communicated. This gives way to crying and all-encompassing sorrow. The person has to deal with run-away anxiety and fear of breakdown, as well as many other psycho-physiological symptoms.

Stage two: The second stage of grieving is one of pining, despair, and disorganization. There is restlessness and pre-occupation with thoughts of the deceased. There might be obsessional review of the precipitating events. There is anger, and a tendency to feel guilty about the death or to blame others. There is crying and an urge to search for the lost person. People tend to develop a perceptual 'set' for the person and to see them in the environment. Anger is often mixed with a depressive withdrawal associated with apathy and a loss of aggressiveness. There is a loss of interest in the self, concentration, and personal appearance. With the more pervasive sadness of depression, there is a search for the meaning of death, its purpose or significance in the larger moral order.

Stage three: This last stage is one of reorganization and recovery. There are attempts at social participation, awareness of strength to deal with emotional crisis and the development of new skills. 'If there is anything positive about surviving the death of someone close to us, it is the possibility of increased growth and self-confidence, although this self-improvement comes at a very high price' (Schultz 1978: 51).

What exactly is happening in the stages of the grief process? There is much internal opposition in mourning. Freud explained: 'Reality testing has shown that the loved object no longer exists, and it proceeds to demand that all libido shall be withdrawn from its attachments to that object' (Freud 1917: 243). The opposition arises because people will not willingly abandon a relationship in which so much is invested. Time and energy is needed while the 'emancipation from the bondage to the deceased' takes place. 'Each single one of the memories and expectations in which the libido is bound to the object is brought up and hypercathected, and detachment of the libido is accomplished in respect of it' (Freud 1917: 244). It is only when this work of mourning is completed that the ego is free to make a new attachment.

Melanie Klein developed Freud's theory of mourning by relating it to a revival of an earlier experience of mourning in infanthood at weaning (see Chapter 4). 'The poignancy of the actual loss of a loved person is, in my view, greatly increased by the mourner's unconscious phantasies of having lost his internal "good" objects as well' (Klein 1940: 398). The mourner then feels that his internal 'bad' objects predominate and that his inner world is in danger of disruption. Both Freud and Klein believed that the mourner reinstates the lost loved object in the ego, but Klein also believed that the mourner had to recover what he had already attained in childhood. 'His inner world, the one which he has built up from his earliest days onwards, in his phantasy was destroyed when the actual loss occurred. The re-building of this inner world characterises the successful work of mourning' (Klein 1940: 398).

Parkes's term, 'psycho-social transition' is extremely helpful as it emphasizes the inner-world and external-world changes that have to be made. It is a 'time when we reassess our picture of the world and our means of being a part of it'. He suggests that a crucial factor may be the way in which the individual copes with the process of change. Marris discusses why change is so problematical: 'The anxieties of change centred upon the struggle to defend or recover a meaningful pattern of relationships' (Marris 1974: 39). He suggests that there is an ambivalence towards change because of the 'impulse to defend the predictability of life'. The social studies take into account the emotional tie, the disruption of family relations, change of status, finance, housing, etc., all of which may occur in social reorganization resulting from a death in the family. These adjustments have to be seen as part of the grief work.

A case study from the Observation and Assessment Centre: Hyacinth

Hyacinth's story illustrates how energy is bound up with the preoccupations of mourning (Case 1980: 47). It is only when these have been worked through that the person can reapply themselves to everyday life. Hyacinth's mother voluntarily asked for her to be assessed when she was 9 years old. Hyacinth had been born in England of immigrant parents and at less than a year old was sent to live abroad with her grandmother. When she was nearly 9 she returned, to rejoin her mother and sister. Hyacinth's mother referred her to social services after a few months, because she was withdrawn, not eating, and unresponsively playing alone in her bedroom.

In the Centre School she lacked concentration and would listlessly slump over her desk, lost in thought, usually sitting with her shoes off because she found them uncomfortable. Previously she had worn them infrequently. From the immediate description of the circumstances, it can be seen that Hyacinth had lost the whole world as she had known it – her country, the most significant adults in her life, and her school. Not surprisingly she was rejecting her unknown mother and had withdrawn apathetically. Fantasies or expectations on joining her mother may have been disappointed. She had little application of energy to her schoolwork. It was easier for her to respond to staff and other children in the house as there were less expectations and demands put on her and she had no specific role to play or functions to perform.

In the first art therapy session she began to paint a self-portrait, which became 'a man crying'. It's a strange smeary figure, balancing something black on his head, either a hat or carrying a load. Her only comment was 'It's a man crying'. She then began a second picture, starting with a more controlled felt tip drawing of me on the left (*Figure 6*). She had, in earlier exploring the room, found a box of old templates and went to get a dinosaur, a tyrannosaurus rex, a monster. This she outlined lightly in pencil, putting in more detail on the face, teeth, eye, nose. She then began to draw more firmly in felt tip a picture of herself overlapping the monster, which 'went wrong'. She started to paint the monster's tail red, then left the picture to begin a third, of a block of flats, painted yellow, in the rain. This picture she took away with her, but it was very similar to the block of flats painted in the next session, though this time she painted herself superimposed on the building, which was in snow. The windows, the eyes of the building, were dark. The chimneys were red as the dinosaur's tail had been. In general there was a blanketed feeling from the dark windows and falling snow.

The session seemed to begin and end in tears, first the man crying and then the flats mournfully in the rain. Sandwiched in between seemed to be

Figure 6 Hyacinth: Dinosaur, therapist, and Hyacinth

the expression of some conflict. I felt as if I had been given health and vitality, complete and coloured. Hyacinth had depicted herself as a composite of monstrous feelings, barely recognizable, just the beginnings of a painted red tail, and of great emptiness and confusion, a sense of her stomach in her mouth in the intestine shape, a brimming over of feeling not expressed consciously. The lack of emotion accompanying the pictures made them feel like portents, pre-disclosure pictures of depression, with a sense of something looming behind.

At the end of this first week in the Centre, Hyacinth began to be physically unwell, complaining of stomach aches and not feeling like eating. Her stomach seemed distended, but from no clear cause. The next session she drew a picture of herself and her friend, Genevieve. Genevieve had blonde hair and a roughly painted red dress. These were the same colour as the block of flats and also the red of the dinosaur's tail. For the first and only time, Hyacinth drew herself with dark hair and dark skin on her arms. This was very similar in pink and yellow to the picture of me in the first session. In some ways it's a healthier, more complete picture of herself though the mouth is conspicuously absent. In fact, Genevieve's teeth are most conspicuous, more like the dinosaur's mouth. The mark of the water pot and dripping yellow paint testify to the difficulty of concentration, the apathy of mood, and the lack of energy accompanying the picture. Yet Hyacinth's eyes in the picture are wide open and watchful. Her lack of mouth echoed her withdrawnness emotionally and her not eating, not taking anything in. Hyacinth's quietness and sadness became more marked at this time. She began just to sit in a quiet area of the room looking at some art books and got particularly taken with a book on the French Impressionists. Her favourite picture was Claude Monet's 'Femmes au Jardin' 1867. In the picture there is a woman on the left in a striped dress with a bonnet with ribbons, holding a huge bunch of flowers. The following session Hyacinth quietly copied this lady, quite small in the middle of the page (*Figure 7*). She wrote 'Eat' above it and my name, and gave it to me as a present. In this rainbow-stripey dress, I felt as if I'd been asked to hold onto all the good things – the hope of the all-coloured dress and the life of the flowers. It's as if I'm the picture of health and able to 'eat'. I have brown-skinned arms, so I feel I am standing for the healthy side of Hyacinth, which must feel far away. As the stomach aches persisted, Hyacinth went to hospital for two days to be tested. She returned looking better, though nothing had been found. This seems a typical symptom of bereavement – the acquiring of strange physical symptoms, sometimes mirroring symptoms of the deceased, which cause great anxiety.

Over the next few sessions Hyacinth returned to the French Impressionists, sitting quietly looking at the ladies in their fine dresses, occasionally beginning a drawing from the book, but not finishing any. I felt through this

Figure 7 Hyacinth: Striped lady (1)

time that she must be missing her grandmother badly or reacting to the changes in her life.

The arrival of some older children at the Centre from her home country precipitated a new phase. Hyacinth began to talk about her life there. She painted flags, which often symbolize a uniting of factions or a statement of origins. These were taken to be hung in her room. Then one session she talked of a donkey she had known, called Vinigan, and drew a picture of Vinigan, with a man bringing a bucket of milk or food, saying 'Vinigan up'. The picture suggests the positive transference existing, her feeling of being fed, her positive relationship and her encouragement to her own instincts to survive – to take in from those around her. The striped, all-colour clothing persists in a slightly different form on the man. Hyacinth's father is an absent presence, living fairly near her mother but married with a new family. It is difficult for her to form a positive relationship to this part of herself.

The turning point in this depression came when she went to the sand trays one session and began to move sand from one tray to another, saying, 'I'm clearing up in here, I'm making it clean'. I asked if she was about to make a picture in the sand and she replied, 'No, just cleaning'. She then called me over shortly afterwards and I saw that she had made a mound in the middle of a tray, saying 'It's a grave'. She then needed a coffin and put a doll's-house boy in a black box and buried it under the mound. She began to make another mound. 'Lots of them, like they are.' She grouped a set of people around the first grave with a doll's-house granny prostrated across the grave. 'The granny is crying and crying.' She 'acted out' the granny's sobs. I asked who was in the grave and the story emerged of her younger cousin who had died. She had not been to the funeral, but had been 'to the place with graves to look'. She was very sad and gradually began to cry as she told me of her cousin falling into a river, it was too deep, and drowning. Another cousin got him out, he was lying curled up at the bottom. She began to mark out a river on the sand and put a boy figure in there. The older cousin carried him home. She had been at the shops, she didn't believe her cousin. She shouted, 'You're lying, you're lying' at him and he had hit her. Her granny screamed and screamed and cried and so did Hyacinth. Her granny had had bad head-aches for a long time after and had taken to her bed. She rarely got up now. Hyacinth was now crying fully and saying angrily 'I dream about him and I see him and say you mustn't go down to the river again, you mustn't do it'. She had dreamt about him last night and it made her feel very sad. She ended, 'I don't like to talk about it'.

All this time, Hyacinth was talking very clearly, much more than usual. Other children in the group were demanding attention. As usual, I drew the sand picture in a special book. Hyacinth was pleased to see it put in there, still crying gently. She went to sit in an armchair at my desk and began to draw in a wobbly way while I attended to other children. She drew a picture of herself, blonde hair, long 'Impressionist' dress and a strange shadowy figure of her cousin. She wrote 'sad' beside it.

Several characteristics of mourning were apparent in Hyacinth's distressing story. She had not actually been to the funeral, but had been to the graveyard to look. Children often seem to have part knowledge of or part access to the necessary rituals surrounding death. She had witnessed and been frightened by the power of her granny's cries and sobs and had cried and screamed like her. Children usually model their reactions, and need a model to follow through the grief process. She could not believe the truth of her older cousin telling her her younger one was dead. For the first time some anger – most characteristic of mourning – breaks through the depression. She is almost telling him off in the dream. The feeling is, if he hadn't gone near the river, he wouldn't be dead, he wouldn't have left her. Also she feels some guilt, because she was at the shops. There is the unspoken thought – could she have prevented it?

The importance of sharing grief, of reliving the traumatic experience and the feelings of sadness, anger and guilt are apparent in Hyacinth's opening description at the sandbox of 'I'm clearing up in here, I'm making it clean.' It's really like a spring-cleaning of the head, a necessary clearing out.

After this session, Hyacinth rejected painting, drawing, and sand play for two weeks, announcing that she was going to make dolls' clothes because 'it was more sensible'. Despite this reaction to her outburst of emotion and communication, a remarkable change seemed to be happening. Her posture and her schoolwork dramatically improved. She was sitting up, alert and paying attention, both taking in and giving out. The giving of new clothes to her dolls seemed a symbolic taking on of a new identity. At the end of the fortnight she began to play in a huge cardboard box, which had held a large washing machine. This became her home and she would sit in it with her toy bendy monkey, with the lid shut up. The first session she sat in there for some twenty minutes, so that her presence in the group was almost forgotten. Then an eerie wailing began to emanate from the box, a crying and the words 'My son, my son'. As I gingerly lifted the lid, I saw Hyacinth wailing over her monkey, cradled in her arms, apparently how her grandmother had wailed over the body of the dead child. This wailing continued off and on through the next fortnight, woven into the 'house' play. Eventually becoming a ritual, it gradually extinguished in intensity, until the last morning she came into the session, leapt into the box, announced briefly 'My son, my son!' and leapt out to begin another activity, the box not being used again.

Her sense of change and growth was reflected outside the session saying 'I'm a big girl now' at the swimming pool, and that she didn't need any help changing in the cubicle.

The next session she sorted through her entire folder of paintings – which often accompanies the end of a phase. She discarded all the 'poor' unfinished pictures from her depressed phase and finished colouring in the second striped lady which she had begun many weeks earlier (*Figure 8*). She

Figure 8 Hyacinth: Striped lady (2)

then put her name on this lady and experimentally pinned it up next to the one that was me, which had been on the wall, alternating names and positions until satisfied. She held on to me, saying she was like a big baby. She then admired the pictures, very pleased with the arrangement, and began to talk about 'being grown-up' and about living in England. It feels as if in the completion of this picture she has been able to take back the 'good things' which I had been holding for her. The identification with her school-friend, Genevieve, is very important, and both in this and the drawing after the sand session she has given herself Genevieve's blonde hair. So Genevieve too was representing her vitality or English self. In the talk of 'growing-up', it feels as if she is launching herself into a new life in England. The loss of her cousin and the loss of her previous life, and her granny, etc. seem very entangled. I felt in the picture after the sand session as if the shadowy figure of the dead cousin also represented herself or an identity left behind. In her identification with Genevieve, and myself as a model of a grown-up English woman, there is a conspicuous absence of her origins. Instead an idealized English notion seems represented by the Monet ladies.

It is not uncommon for immigrant children to draw blonde selves. It appears to be a stage one goes through, and it seemed likely that Hyacinth would get a stronger sense of her own identity at adolescence. The cross-hatching under the second striped lady suggests some insecurity in this image already. Throughout this session with the two striped ladies, she was singing and humming, emanating a sense of happiness. She was about to go back to her mother's street, not to her mother's house, but to be privately fostered by another immigrant family, which her mother had arranged.

At the end of the final session, after saying goodbye quite formally, we had tidied the room, to leave it at the end of a Friday afternoon. Hyacinth began to travel around the room off the floor – across tables, cupboards, high railings, sand pits, desks, pottery wheels, etc. At some distance from the door, she asked me to open it. She then did a death-defying long jump from the sink cupboards out of the room into the lobby. She had thus devised her own leaving ritual by not touching the floor, as if some part might be left behind intact.

A case study from a primary school: Richard

Moving on from the complicated multiple losses that one might work with in assessment centres, it is slightly easier to monitor the implications of bereavement in a primary school setting, where a child's total situation is more stable. Even though a child's home may stay the same and their school the same, there is still a profound alteration in living circumstances following the loss of a parent. The whole pattern of relationships in a family alters, as well as material changes that might follow a loss of income, etc.

My first experience of working as an art therapist in a primary school was as a researcher, working with children who were under-functioning in their schoolwork and who had suffered a significant loss. I believe teachers are very aware of the temporary special-needs children for whom there is so little provision in our educational system. These are the children who suffer a temporary stress or are recovering from a traumatic happening in the family. They just miss the need for child guidance as they are normally well-adjusted and functioning well at schoolwork, but are often severely affected by some special situation at home. It is in these circumstances that the educational therapist is needed. She has the art and play therapy skills to take the burden off the general classroom teacher, who cannot deal with such issues while working with a large number of children. The sort of issues I have in mind are the effect of sudden unemployment in the family, divorce, separation, hospitalization of a member of the family, the birth of a new baby, beareavement, etc. (see Chapter 1). In all these situations a child may need temporary support by group work or individual sessions. I worked with a group of six children over a period of two terms in a mixture of group and individual sessions. The children's teachers were enthusiastic and gave me much useful information and feedback on how the children were after a session.

Richard's experiences in the sessions encompass both social readjustment and the struggle for meaning that accompanies mourning (Case 1980: 55). Richard was 10. His mother had died from cancer two years before and had been a dinner-lady at the school before her illness. He had an older brother and sister in their late teens, and a father who had a building firm. His father had reacted to his wife's death by frequently attending spiritualist meetings and seances, and returned home recounting to the children the conversations he had had with the mother. He believed he was being guided by spirits and that they had even told him the name of the woman he would next marry. Richard had been a problem at the school since his mother's death, so the deputy head had seen his father frequently about him. His father found it difficult to accept that Richard was a problem at school or that the underlying causes might be as a result of his mother's death, but gave his permission for him to attend the art therapy sessions, thinking that there would be no harm in them. Richard seemed to be constantly in trouble for fighting and 'general naughtiness' and refusing to comply with female staff. Richard was sturdily built, intelligent, and when I met him I thought there was something likeable about him, as if his surface aggressive behaviour hid a rather pleasant, even shy, nature.

One of the discoveries made after an introductory series of art therapy groups for staff was the experience of not wanting to finish a picture and also not always wanting a 'perfect finish'. Such groups led to discussion of the place that art often has in a school of being used to illustrate other work or to make a suitable display for adults visiting a school. I decided to ease the children into working from their own inner direction, by having a few sessions centred around fairy tales. Half-way through the term all the children were coming in, choosing their activity from their own volition.

To the first group I read 'Puss in Boots' (Lang 1965) and then suggested that the children paint either 'something from the story' or 'an animal that they would like to help them'. Richard knew the story and liked it, and said that he would paint 'a helpful animal'. He began the 'windmill' picture which was to occupy him for several weeks (*Figure 9*). He drew all his figures and objects from the bottom left-hand side, right-handedly, working up and over and down the right side. He bent over the work nearly obscuring it, using a great deal of pressure and much heavy breathing. During this session he worked on the windmill only and left the blades plain black and a plain brown mound at the bottom. The blades were drawn at right angles rather than diagonal to the building, making the construction look like a clear cross above a mound.

Figure 9 Richard: Windmill and three sons

The following conversation took place in the group of three – Richard (10), Sally (11), and Laura (9):

Sally:	'I'm going to do white eyes on my cat.'
Laura:	'That's like a ghost.'
Richard:	'I've seen a ghost of my mum.'
Sally:	'She used to be a cook here, didn't she, but she died of cancer?'

Richard: 'Two years ago, she had an operation, but they put something back wrong, that's what my mum said, and she's a nurse.'

A general discussion followed on death, ghosts, hospitals, and heaven. Later on:

Sally: '. . . but she's alive in heaven, isn't she?'
Richard [to me]: 'What are pearly gates?'

I replied that they were a description of the entrance to heaven, to show what a special place it was. The topic of conversation changed.

Several things occurred to me from the conversation. First, that Richard's mother had been known to the whole school as a dinner-lady, therefore, what a public happening it must have been and difficult for Richard to bear. Secondly, how ready he was to talk of his problem when given the opportunity in a small, fairly non-threatening group. His teacher had said he 'never mentioned' his mother or family to her. Although it was clear that they had a good relationship, the classroom was not the right place. Thirdly, how his natural interest rose up despite the emotional subject to ask what were the 'pearly gates', which I took to be a good sign that his natural curiosity and wish to learn were not too affected. His teacher said how pleased he seemed to be with the session. He came back 'smiling and relaxed'.

Every session for six weeks Richard continued to add something to this picture, all painted very carefully. In this way the windmill was several times re-painted, the eldest brother by the windmill, the wall, and the youngest brother sad, because he only has a cat. The sixth session was a group of Richard (10), Sally (11), Laura (9), Famil (11), Nina (9), and Ben (9). Richard had arrived in a belligerent loud mood, and Famil and Sally were very argumentative with each other. Unpleasant, provocative remarks were scattered throughout the afternoon.

Richard began to paint the donkey and the middle brother. Famil began a painting of a witch. As they bickered, Famil suddenly countered to Richard:

Famil: 'Your mum's a witch, like this.'
Sally: 'Yes, you'll go to the devil, where your mum is.'
Nina [mostly to herself]: 'In hell the fires will burn you up, you'll roast for ever and ever.'

Richard stopped his careful painting and began to paint the yellow very thickly and vigorously across the painting. His taking of the comments very stoically made me suspect he had taken a lot before. He pretended he would go and hit them, standing up and posturing with fists raised defensively, but he didn't.

Famil: 'I've seen her in her grave.'

Richard for the first time looked really angry and then said calmly, and surely:

'You don't know where her graveyard is.'

He painted a black face on the sun and left the picture. He then took a new piece of paper and painted the 'Shark'. He said of it when finished,

> 'It's a shark, it's fri[ghtened], alone, it doesn't eat men, eats anything else he sees, apart from dangerous fish, which could eat him, like piranhas.'

Richard rose in my estimation that afternoon. He showed remarkable control and safety in his unique knowledge of where his mother was buried, which no else knew. Painting the yellow seemed to free him from a certain control, letting out some aggressiveness/depression in the shark and the black face of the sun. Seeing himself as a shark seemed appropriate to his behaviour at school. It is aggressive to other fish – other boys? But not to men – adults? It has a healthy respect for more dangerous fish.

Anger in mourning seems to provide a certain drive to get one through a period of time. It can also defensively avoid depression which will mean the working through of unwelcome facts. When a calm control bottles up both anger and depressive thoughts, a burst through like this is most necessary and effective at releasing behind it a trail of material that can be worked with.

Now that the windmill picture was completed, I noted the absence of any 'helpful animal' which was the central part to the story. The older brothers have the windmill and the donkey and are facing away from the youngest, who is sitting unhappily. Aware of the background of spiritualism, seances and messages, I suggested to Richard that he might do a kinetic family drawing[1] in order to help him focus on who remained and how the family was now composed. This was completed in a long, drawn-out session, with some agonizing. His father was drawn first and coloured in, in a fast car, encapsulated from the rest of the family. Next, after much deliberation, he drew and coloured in just his mother's head at the top of the picture. He then attempted his older brother, who he said 'lay about in front of the TV all the time'. He made a joke and drew a large bum on the TV screen, then rubbed it out and drew a man. Then he tried his sister, bottom right, dancing to a record. He tried to add more to his mum, scribbled around it and finally drew himself, bird-watching.

Several things were striking about the picture. First the fragmentation and isolation of each family member. No attempt is made to show them together in one environment. Richard is facing away from them (like the youngest child in the windmill picture). He is nearest to his mother. He seems to be interacting with the bird in the tree more than anything else. He had talked to me about birds quite often. His mother is included in the family, yet is of the world and not of the world, high in the picture, half drawn and coloured in. I puzzled about the slant of Richard's figure and 'whirly' head. Could this be a sense of reeling from environmental or mental pressures? A picture of a tree done at the end of another session has a similar feeling of being buffeted by pressure or of reaching out for warmth to a non-existent sun. It contained a nest of eggs in a crook of branches, but no mother bird. Both trees have scarred holes in the trunk. The family picture seemed to show a lack of a central figure – a focus to hold them together.

I had seen Richard for eight weeks now and he was developing a very playful attitude towards me. We would have to race from the classroom to the art hut when I collected him. He would not want to leave, would try to hang out the sessions and try to stop me leaving by holding the door, all in great fun. His teacher was amazed at this and said she thought he really needed 'a warm female to play with' which she felt unable to be in the classroom. He was beginning to ask me if I was coming back after Easter, which I felt was a crucial question because it was saying 'Is it worth opening up anymore?'

One difference between working at the Assessment Centre and at the primary school is that children entered in a state of stress at the Centre, received by a body of professionals who would be involved in trying to sort it out. Education for children is in some way equivalent to an adult's work and may be experienced by them as a place of safety from family problems. In a school where children are outwardly, at least, dealing with a situation, should they be encouraged to open up and explore or to utilize defences to forget and get on with schoolwork? I felt that the children I worked with both in this setting and in a subsequent pilot art therapy scheme in a primary school, consciously chose whether to use the opportunity or not. For instance, one child in Richard's group of six asked to stop coming after a few weeks because he didn't like any of the materials I had to use – he wanted to do metalwork. I thought he didn't want to work with me or with my method of working. He didn't want to delve into any difficult areas. He wanted to construct some 'manly' defences. This seemed an honest appraisal on his part, and we stopped working together. The other children all chose to work to different levels of disclosure and indeed awareness.

I felt that Richard wanted to share both his confusion and depression in the weeks to come. In the next session he decided to paint a pattern in a circle, copying the idea from another child in the group. He began the pattern, a circle of red and then blue around the outside, while recounting his father's war stories from service days. He then began to talk about 'spirits', which were obviously on his mind. At the same time the pattern 'went wrong' and he began to fill in the circle in black. This is how the conversation went:

Richard: 'It's family workshop tomorrow.'
Me: 'What happens there?'
Richard: 'They have a meeting and a seance. I'm the only child allowed to go.'
Me: 'Oh, are you? What's a seance? I haven't been to one.'
Richard: 'They talk to spirits, ghosts, through a medium. People die, and if they've learnt enough they stay a spirit, but if they haven't they come back – that's reincarnation. You have four bodies and you go travelling while asleep, that's why you think you've been to places before. My dad's been born three times, once in Peru . . . '

His voice trailed off, and then he said:

'They don't really allow children in.'

All this while he painted round and round.

I wondered what to make of this fantasy, that they had seances at 'family workshops' and that he attended. I felt after this conversation that Richard was probably being inhibited from resolving and coming to terms with the loss of his mother by his father's need for consolation from spiritualism. It was tantalizing for Richard to hear messages from someone with whom he was unable to communicate directly himself. I thought that this was impeding his own struggle for meaning. I wondered what the solution was to this.

The deputy head was having regular meetings with Richard's father, but it is difficult for parents to be aware of children's needs when they are wrapped up in their own grief.

The next session Richard added marks of blue, yellow, red, green, and white to his black circle. It seemed as if the components of a pattern or design were all there, but they were disintegrated, or unable to organize themselves into an arrangement – a rather bleak symbol of the self. Then he decided to paint Corfe Castle which he had visited on a school holiday the year before. Whilst mixing and stirring some yellow paint, he hoped that Nina wouldn't arrive for the next session – 'I want all the attention for myself'. This was typical of his honesty and quite good humour about his needs. He carried on stirring and we talked:

Richard: 'Just like my dad's porridge.'
Me: 'Does he do all the cooking now?'
Richard: 'He's the only one who can.'
Me: 'Can your brother or sister cook?'
Richard: 'She's worse. My dad makes bricks on toast.'

Me: 'Bricks on toast?'
Richard [laughing]: 'Beans on toast.'

There followed a graphic description of an awful stew they had had to eat.

Me: 'I expect you miss your mum's cooking?'
Richard: 'I do.'
Me: 'I expect your dad does too. He's doing his best, isn't he?'
Richard: 'He is, but it's awful.'

Much stirring of yellow paint followed. Then he painted a black wall around the castle, saying 'I've finished'. This last conversation reminded me of Parkes saying: 'Loss and deprivation are so inseparably bound together, that it is not possible to study one without the other' (Parkes 1975: 25). There is a sense of Richard losing love and affection from his mother, but also the whole quality of life altering.

It seemed to me that the importance of the sessions to Richard in the first term was partly the contact individually and in small groups and the opportunity to talk to a sympathetic adult. This was only possible when the first lengthy windmill picture had been painted out and a certain degree of trust had been established between us. The windmill picture is both a statement of the situation, with three children left, and a time of gathering forces which became conscious through the activity of painting. At times it felt as if the painting provided a 'cover' for talking or it allowed a fluidity of stuck thoughts. The image of the father is of one cut off from the children emotionally. He was in the fast car or, in the case of the castle, he was defending or making his own resolution through spiritualism. The regularity of Richard's conversations around his mother's death were a way of his trying to understand what had happened to him. During this term he kept up a constant dialogue and never got 'lost' in a painting.

In the second term, Richard used the sessions differently. He seemed to be slightly oppressed by school pressures – worrying about reading tests, etc. This was his final term at junior school and also our last series of sessions. He became more involved with his paintings, which were done very silently around the theme of the tree. The symbol of the tree seems to appear when there is a pressing need for a supporting image of growth and integration. I want to discuss three of Richard's pictures from this second term, when there were less verbal clues to his preoccupations.

In the first session, Richard pastelled a tree, grass, two smaller trees or bushes, a sun and some clouds, and then in black charcoal added a bird, a black hole and some marks across the tree. The marks on the tree suggest emotional scarring, and the leafless one-dimensional branches suggest a feeling of impotence, a lack of growth. Richard drew this in a group session and obviously wanted my individual attention. He wandered around afterwards, unable to concentrate. Sylvia Antony in her study of the development of a concept of death did 'story completion' tests with the children, and she remarks on the persistently recurrent theme of bird nesting (Antony 1971). The bird in the nest with eggs seemed to symbolize the mother with her young, or fertility. She felt in her study that it was the expression of the Oedipus conflict at the latency period. Richard had the not uncommon boys' interest in birds and bird nesting at this age. The bird often also represents the human soul, and I felt from his pictures that the interest was in reaching out to the parent mother bird rather than the eggs, particularly in the family drawing. The drawings all show part of a combination of bird, nest, or eggs, but never the whole together.

Two weeks later Richard asked to be left alone and quietly painted while I cleared up in another part of the room, instead of sitting by him. He called me over when he had finished and showed a painting of three trees (*Plate 2*).

Me:	'What kind of trees are they?'
Richard:	'A daddy, a mummy, and a baby' [laughing and pointing to them in turn].
Me:	'What time of year is it?'
Richard:	'It's winter' [and pointing to the 'baby' in the middle] 'Its evergreen.'

He was very pleased with this painting, as he had been proud of the previous tree picture. This seemed to be an encouraging painting of himself as growing and surviving, despite the bleak emotional winter he was in, of his fading mother on the left and his leafless father on the right.

Two weeks later Richard charcoaled and pastelled another drawing. This session he was more confiding and talkative. He talked about taking his cycling-proficiency badge and this, with the pride in mastery of a new medium, suggested his moving into a new phase. The drawing was heavily sprayed with fixative at regular intervals, with cries of 'into the attack!' as Richard pretended to be an aircraft. There was no danger of losing any part of the picture. He talked of RAF war stories and his father while drawing the large tree. He mentioned a favourite TV programme, 'The Saint' and put him in. Then he talked of his brother and sister while drawing the two smaller trees or bushes (*Plate 3*). The drawing seemed to reflect the first tree/black bird picture and to be a progression. He is very concerned about his brother taking A levels and his brother and sister being 'bone idle' in the house. He was very pleased with his picture. That week there was an open day at the school and the school hall was full of children's work. He suddenly asked:

Richard:	'Why do they put my crappy pictures in the hall, and not my real pictures?'

| Me: | 'Why are they crappy pictures?' |
| Richard: | 'Because they ask me to draw things I can't draw.' |

The work in the hall included illustrations of the last school journey, with pictures of birds that the children had seen. I think that what was important was that although Richard could actually draw them they came from no inner necessity, but were of external things, seemingly irrelevant in view of his preoccupation with his mother's death. This is why the pictures drawn in the art therapy sessions seemed like his 'real' pictures. I felt that this third picture was a sort of family portrait of the surviving members and also a further stage of progression in his struggle for meaning. It in some ways tries to resolve the obvious splintered feeling in the earlier family picture. The picture defies an exact reading yet clearly satisfyingly contained all the family elements for Richard. I thought that the large tree was somehow both his father and him, scarred heavily and reaching out for warmth to the sun. The scarring has been a regular feature of the trees. It first appeared on the kinetic family drawing and the earlier tree drawing. The black circle can be seen as a close-up of the 'wound'. It appears again on the pastelled tree and here growing up and presumably out of the tree eventually. There is the first tiny spot of green on this larger tree. The two smaller trees, brother and sister, are firmer and more established than in the earlier pastelled picture. Richard seemed to be taking strength from his hero, 'The Saint', but the 'saint' and 'other worldliness watching out for you' inevitably bring his mother to mind. In his comments on his brother and sister, Richard was worrying that 'home' was not as it should be and trying to come to accept the new standards of behaviour, cleanliness, and the order of relationships. This appears symbolized in the paintings, only half conscious and verbalized. This was the end of my sessions with Richard, who was moving to the senior school.

In the study at the school it was difficult to isolate from the sessions factors that might have affected or improved schoolwork. Richard's teacher was tremendously enthusiastic about the effect of the sessions on him. She had been particularly aware that his self-image and self-esteem had become very low and she felt that it had vastly improved by his attendance at a small group. She knew that he needed an adult with whom to talk over the experience but there were too many demands on her attention in the classroom, besides which she had a different role. She also felt that Richard's father had been helped to think about him a bit more.

Grief in childhood

Both Hyacinth's and Richard's case studies verify the view that any remaining adults' attitudes to grief are overwhelmingly important to a child, as they are likely to model their reactions upon them. In her study, 'Reactions to the death of a mother', Marion Barnes (1964) describes how a 4-year-old's grief was a straightforward identification and working through with the father's grief, and how a 2-year-old's was delayed for nine months because of denial, like the grandmother's, but then resolved. Here, Hyacinth's 'illness' paralleled her grannie's 'taking to her bed'; and Richard had fantasies of attending seances like his father.

One of the disadvantages for many children is that they are likely to be 'protected' from the truth, given part information, told nothing for a long time, or told euphemisms or nothing at all, so that someone might disappear and never be mentioned again. Children may not be allowed access to rituals surrounding death which provide both a socially accepted expression for grief, and a framework to hold the very basic fears which arise. In Marion Barnes's study the two questions which most concerned other children hearing of the death of a mother were 'Will I die?' and 'Will my mother die too?' Rosemary Gordon writing of rituals feels that ritual helps mourners to reintegrate into the community: 'Their own death wishes are stemmed and counterbalanced' (Gordon 1978: 40). These fears need discussing with children. Gorer, however, found in his research that: 'Traditionally British parents find it embarrassing to talk to their children on subjects of deep emotional importance' (Gorer 1965: 41).

Because many adults cannot provide a verbal description or definition of death or the way in which people remain, it is all the more valuable for a child to be able to explore issues and feelings in some concrete medium. How does a concept of death develop? The studies of Nagy (1948) with Hungarian children and Antony (1971) with English children, are most useful. In brief, death to children under 5 is seen as a departure, a sleep, as with any separation. This is also accompanied by an interest and confusion in such terms as cutting, killing, dying. Death may be seen as reversible. In the stages which follow death is personified, and people may be seen as 'dead' but imagined in another life, living just the same, e.g. Sally's comment in Richard's case study, 'But she's alive in heaven, isn't she?' Death is then later seen as not reversible and as the cessation of corporeal activities, 'a body that has no life in it'.

Children are often romanticized as having youth on their side in terms of their adaptability to new situations. In the context of bereavement they have particular difficulties, because of their very youth, and they are more likely to form pathological mourning symptoms. There is a remarkable lack of consensus in the available literature as to what age children are able to mourn. I found the most useful approach to be that of Furman (1964) who suggests that a lack of developmental approach accounts for the discrepancies in the literature, e.g. some infant children will mourn successfully, whereas some latency children will not. There will be many contributing factors, e.g.

how a child is being looked after, the need for a new person to become attached to, the importance of previous life experiences, and the circumstances of the loss – in fact, all the same problems which face an adult and which may cause pathological mourning. Furman suggests that there are two tasks for the child: acceptance of a fact in the outside world and corresponding changes in the inner world. Clearly, a lack of intellectual development and an immature ego will work against a successful mourning, so that chidren are more likely to develop pathological symptoms than adults, e.g. denial or delayed grief. However, at the Assessment Centre, it seemed as if children of all ages could work successfully through grief issues, given support and time of their own, unless they had been too severely damaged earlier in life to reach a resolution.

All children will have experienced some form of loss in their normal development. As they progress to a new stage they leave an earlier one behind them. Watching children regressing under severe stress at the Assessment Centre one can see what they have to gain – an escape from facing difficulties which are often overwhelming, and a familiarity with an old 'baby' stage. But they lose their competence and their pride in their development and acquisition of new skills. In mourning they need help so as not to deny death, retreat into fantasy or to be stuck in a stage of anger or depression. It cannot be so clear to them what they will gain by taking on the struggle of the grief-work, which is often a struggle against despair, a struggle for comprehension. They need support, an adult model and opportunities to share their unique feelings, whether verbally or through art and play.

The playscape

In this part of the chapter, play in the art therapy room will become the main focus of interest, in particular the counterpoint of art and play in treatment with children. My starting points are the three types of play that appeared whilst working with Hyacinth, i.e. sandplay, play in the box, and leaving play.

Sandplay

In her therapy the sequence of events that led up to her sandplay was as follows. An initial build-up of images, which combined with an early engagement in transference, culminated in the first 'striped lady' picture. During this period the unexpressed feelings emerged in a psychosomatic illness which gave her leave from normal school and social pressures. A further sequence of images called forth reminiscences from her home country, which restated her identity. Then came the session of sandplay, precipitated by anxious dream images of guilt and warnings.

Sandplay was, therefore, used at a moment when an exact representation of a real event was needed. This could have been shown in a picture, so why was play preferred? The events in the past needed to be relived by Hyacinth. It was an empathic type of play – she was becoming the people, partly imitative, partly to understand their actions and feelings. The repetition of an experience which had strongly moved Hyacinth meant that it was externalized, meditated upon, and assimilated, and led in this case to a dramatic change in her behaviour. She became more animated, her posture straightened, and her schoolwork improved. Her energy, which had been keeping these overwhelming feelings repressed, was released.

The key seems to be the transformation from passivity to activity. The need is to assimilate overpowering adult emotion and the whole effect of the events. Sandplay often seems in this way to express a need to have control or mastery of the forces acting upon one, whether external (school or family pressures) or internal, unconscious forces. Freud comments on 'play' in *Inhibitions, Symptoms and Anxiety*:

> 'The ego which experienced the trauma passively, now repeats it actively in a weakened version, in the hope of being able itself to direct its course. It is certain that children behave in this fashion towards every distressing impression they receive, by reproducing it in their play. In thus changing from passivity to activity they attempt to master their experiences psychically.'
>
> (Freud 1925)

Hyacinth's words, 'I'm cleaning, clearing up in here' suggest the spring-cleaning feeling which accompanies such re-enactment, leaving ugly events and emotions behind in the sand. This use of the sand – out of context of the seashore – is peculiar when one thinks about it. The use of the sand-tray by disturbed children is very like the sea sweeping a stretch of sand clean with the change of the tide. The blackboard, which can similarly be swept clean, is often the preferred method of expression at times of great anxiety. Both can also be used to express the fragility of connections, so that it is not unusual for a child before a holiday break to make a sand or blackboard picture to be left in the room over the gap. Their wonder and delight at finding it intact on return, parallels their often precarious experience of relationships. Their picture, and the therapist, have survived the angry and anxious feelings which accompanied the separation.

What of sand, water, and ready-made objects as a medium of artistic expression? Sand and water can be formed into objects and can be used for play materials like clay. They cannot be transformed by fire, but they can return to their original state, which can be a reassuring quality. Sand has a flexible nature, i.e. it can be punched, cut, sifted, wetted, sculpted, hollowed, and shaped. It can be thrown and reconstituted in the sand-tray ready for use. It can be swamped under water and return overnight, dry, ready to be used. It survives attack, which is a useful quality for a medium to have in therapy. It can also have a silky, delicate, sensuous feel, running, smooth, moveable. It can encourage and give room for a state of reflection or waking dream, or for the business of building and construction. Like any other art medium, sand and water and objects can be a non-verbal way of thinking.

People working in the sand-tray experience a balance between structuring and experiencing, passing through stages similar to any other creative activity. There is often an initial playing, messing with the sand, experiencing some of its qualities, preparing a suitable texture. Then ideas take shape and objects are selected – a period of intense involvement. Often, afterwards, the 'story' of the picture is spontaneously told to the therapist. The picture is then recorded, and may be returned to later in therapy to be reconsidered in the light of later pictures.

There is a universal appeal to all ages in this way of working. Faced with hundreds of miniature ready-mades, some are regularly used to 'stand for' an aspect of the psyche. It is important to have damaged figures, animals, vehicles, dilapidated buildings, etc., as well as ones in prime condition. Professor Pickford (Bowyer 1970) in 'Lowenfeld World Technique' mentions the 'importance of mutilated objects in fantasy', although Virginia Axline (1969) in 'Play Therapy' suggests the immediate removal of any broken pieces. I find that children may identify with a marked or damaged object, and may eventually wish to repair it, while recognizing also that it might be very necessary for a child to be aggressive, to break and destroy an object as well.

When holding a play workshop/seminar with a group of mature social work students, I suggested a period of free play with the sand-tray toys. People naturally grouped or decided to work alone. During the first phase of initial exploring and searching, two men began to pick out all the damaged toys, e.g. a man with no head, animals with legs missing, etc. There were some jokey references to horror films, video nasties, and accidents. One man began balancing a large grey plastic hollow rock on a pole, and under this nuclear mushroom cloud the Chernobyl disaster began to take shape. The broken toys lay face down around the cloud in the centre. A fortress wall was built, towers representing a traditional Russian 'Kremlin' look. Tiny soldiers surrounded the area. The mushroom cloud loomed with terrible significance, not a plaything anymore, not a rock, but something invested with many meanings. It had become a visual symbol. Another person could use the rock differently. The whole context of use determines its meanings to the individual on each occasion.

Play in the sand can also be an interior conversation on a symbolic level. An example of this was provided by Rashida, aged 12, who was referred to us when her father left suddenly on a trip, leaving her locked out for the weekend. She had been under a lot of stress and anxiety, crying and worrying about where he was and unable to paint or do anything in the art therapy sessions, except cling to the radiator. Then on the third session, she came in and depicted the snow forest (see *Figure 10*). The 'world' is full of animals and people all going about their business, some going home, some just standing, some fallen in the snow, hurt or lost. No one seems to see each other, all are isolated with their own problems and the staff are busy, rushing on and off duty. It seemed to show, and help her understand, her situation, and it communicated to me how she was feeling. When it was finished she was able to talk about her experiences of being left by her father, her fears of being taken into care and her fear of the Centre, staff, and children. This sand picture contains so much pain, of wishes to go home, of isolation, and alienation. It expressed both subtle and deep emotion. Its power left words of explanation almost superfluous. It signified the end of this first state of crisis and the re-emergence of her independence or own volition, the end of a feeling of things happening to her, of her passivity. The making of it changed her status in events.

Dora Kalff expresses this clearly:

'An unconscious problem is played out in the sand box, just like a drama; the conflict is transposed from the inner world to the outer world and made visible. This game of fantasy influences the dynamics of the unconscious in the child and thus affects his psyche.'

(Kalff 1980: 32)

Play boundaries

Hyacinth's 'house play' in the large cardboard box is just one aspect of another category of much needed play for children facing transitions. Here, play was being used in a repetitive way to 'exhaust' a feeling or emotion experienced, with Hyacinth in control and the bendy monkey used as her object/companion. Although the art and play therapy room in a large institution can often feel like a place of sanctuary, where normal rules may not apply, the boundaries of the room and therapist may not feel enough to very vulnerable children, who may need further containment. A useful quality of a large cardboard box is that one has four walls around and control of the lid and therefore the light source. People in a state of transition, of waiting, are intensely vulnerable to the projections and fears of others. This need to shut out other people is often symbolized by a need to sit in the dark and quiet. 'To be in the dark' is to acknowledge a state of 'not knowing'. In this state one needs not to make a conscious decision, but to allow a solution to surface.

In therapy children are involved in meeting unconscious forces. Being in a

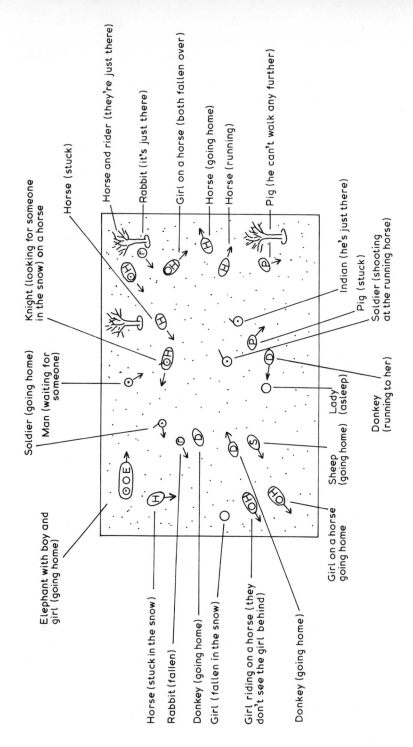

Figure 10 Rashida: Snow forest

cardboard box or another construction is rather like a package tour on a coach. One can control the amount and quality of the 'foreignness' that one can bear to meet, and rush back to the safe, known coach or box when necessary. The messy area could sometimes serve this purpose. Carole, aged 16, for instance, took over the messy area for a fortnight, at a time when she was waiting for a court decision on her future. She stripped it of all paint and mess and redecorated it as her sitting room. She painted pictures for the wall, picked flowers from the field for her table and spent several therapy sessions sitting in there, reading with a candle. This acted as an outlet for her intense anxiety about where her future home would be and gave her some much needed privacy and quiet for her to sort out her thoughts on her future.

Hyacinth and Carole were both putting themselves into sanctuary or a special place, their vulnerability needing a taboo on contact. The doll's house can sometimes be used as an attempt to prepare for later life, but in a different way. Here the doll's-house families act out possibilities for us in a contained space within our control. They are puppets to our desires. One 15-year-old girl, Sharon, 'took over' the doll's house for several weeks and redecorated it in stunning 'Hollywood-style' silver wallpaper and fur rugs. Every time she added to the house, she made up fantasies of her life-to-be when she was grown up. Using this piece of creative play as a base, we had many discussions surrounding her hopes and fears for the future, and it led into painting various trial selves. This projection into the future alternated with some fairly abstract paintings called 'my mind at the moment'. Here we are moving back and forth between fantasy and reality, playing and projecting. Out of this process gradually a realistic balance develops.

The uses of the doll's house, messy area, space beneath my desk, or cardboard boxes or other constructions, all show a need for 'personal ground' within an institution. Sometimes the whole art room might serve this purpose or, more often, the carpeted area and the easy chairs.

At one time I did not know how to be of use to a 16-year-old boy, David, whom I had first seen at the Centre when he was 12. He had been back and forth between the Centre, children's homes, and home, all repeatedly breaking down, but he kept up an unrealistic hope that he could return home. This was unlikely, as his relationship with his step-father was non-existent in any positive way and was doing him great harm. He had been physically, and psychologically, battered. He seemed unapproachable in his despair and would not talk, paint, or do anything, but would nervously bite his nails curled up in a chair. After several sessions like this he brought in *Treasure Island* by Robert Louis Stevenson and I began to read it to him by request. This was a success in that he was calmed and contained by the reading and went away relaxed, but I was worried that I couldn't get any nearer the problem or help him in a more positive way. Then one afternoon our near-silent session was broken by his suddenly saying 'I love my mother, miss'. How should I reply? Phrases suggested themselves to me quickly, but none seemed quite right, but as I began he said forcefully, '*Don't* say anything miss. You are not a social worker.' Chastened, I carried on reading, and felt my role had been redefined explicitly. My presence was what was important. To discuss his situation would be to admit the unbearable truth that there was no way he could go home, but he needed silent support and time to work it out undisturbed, which was often hard to get surrounded by professional helpers. The quest in *Treasure Island*, the search for buried treasure, represents the hidden heart – the difficulty of saying 'I love you'. I am equating here hidden treasure with hidden feelings. Treasure is usually found underground or in caves, a mother image. The hero is usually battling through trials to reach the treasure which is also paradoxically a journey away from a mother, from childhood to manhood. David, too, was going to have to painfully grow up by separating from his mother, eventually leaving home to live in a hostel.

Leaving rituals

Hyacinth's third piece of significant play, her leaving ritual, suggested the need to visibly mark or to enact a ritual of ending. This might take place verbally, with a formal goodbye and exchange of kisses and good wishes. It might be marked by the making of cards or the exchange of presents attempting to fill the coming space between us. There was a ritual of selection of objects made to take away, to keep or distribute to particular staff, marking the relationship. In the house there was usually a stage of preparation for leaving – a day off school to buy new clothes to depart in, and a goodbye party. So at times of transition one looks forward, making advance preparation, and backward, reflecting on the meaning of the relationships left behind. Hyacinth's piece of play somehow ducked the issue of leaving in that she could not physically walk from the room. There was, I think, some denial of the ending – an attempt to leave the experiences in the art therapy room intact, though somehow sealed off from her new life. This could be contrasted with another leaving session.

A week before leaving, Mark, aged 11, came into the art room and refused to let any of the children near him, although he was usually sociable. He generated feelings of 'aloneness'. He was very excited about leaving, although confused, and he acted out these feelings. He cut up a polystyrene block, painted a face on it, and marched round the room. He then cut himself 'shackles' for his head, arms, and legs. He walked around the room, saying 'They chain you up here.' This referred to the common idea among the children that the Centre was really a prison and that you were sent there to be punished. He then pretended to be knifed, and a long dying scene followed me round the room until I buried his 'dead body' under a pile of cardboard in the messy area. He then emerged as a 'ghost' and went to sit high up on the wooden rails watching the other activity in the art room, but refusing to be part of it. This play expressed his complicated feelings about leaving. He put on a mask to hide his real feelings which were sad, exaggerated the worst feature about the Centre for the children – the regulations about going out – by saying 'They chain you up here.' He 'dies', symbolic of his leaving, but then participated as a 'ghost'. His ghostly presence seemed a correct analogy for that 'limbo' feeling when one is awaiting an event. As one's thoughts withdraw, investment in the situation withdraws as one begins to anticipate the move, the new life. One is literally still part of the old, there and not there, but projected into the new. The long dying scene needed an intervention. It suggested burial, and the messy area seemed right. He chose his own moment to emerge, making ghostly 'whoo, whoo' noises. So he was able to call attention to his special state, and find his own means of expression.

Malleable mediums

In the therapy session, whatever the named focus, i.e. art, play, drama, or verbal therapy, all activity becomes representative communication of the relationships between child and therapist and between child and group. The communications reflect the stage of engagement with the therapist and group in the work in process. All actions and activities may be invested symbolically with personal material and, through projections and identifications, with the relationships in the room. The clear significance of certain pieces of meaningful play helps one to value every moment of a session. Even apparently aimless scribble or chatter is valuable, as it is usually a necessary stage on the way, a lack of focus that allows a redirection to emerge. It seems that play can flow into art, and art into play. For children, does play have the same function as art, or are they different? Does play have the same function for children that art does for adults?

Play has been written about exhaustively, but continues to defy exact definition, partly because of the vast number of contexts in which play takes place. It is more productive to limit one's comments to the specific context of the art and play therapy room.

Some of the play took place at a time when a child was in no condition to benefit from an art experience. Rashida, for example, was in a state of shock, of severe separation anxiety. She progressed from clinging to the radiator, satisfying a primitive need for warmth and comfort, to the sand-tray. She would not have been able to form objects at this time, but could manipulate and arrange ready-mades. Here one can see sand, water, and objects as another medium. This had an ordering effect on her, bringing the elements of her experience under her control and enabling her to express an interior state. Similarly, Mark's leaving play expressed anxiety at a stage of transition which included separation anxiety. This type of imaginative play shows the need to act out feelings, to take parts, to represent the feelings by action rather than a symbolic configuration. It is, in the leaving play, and in Sharon's doll's house play, a trial run for a real event. To some extent it is the use of theatre rather than the visual arts. The very action uses the pent-up energy of the tension around a situation. Once this has been released the making of art objects often follows. This leads to reflection, the object being the focus for thoughts and feelings which are also contained and often need to be unpacked from it. Some play, therefore, results in renewed powers of concentration for art.

Play often enters a twilight world of fantasy and day-dream. Here, there is a leave-taking from reality, sometimes to enter a 'space' set apart, whether messy area, box, or den. Here one can 'lose oneself', just as David lost himself in *Treasure Island*. Frequently intense experiences happen in this 'set apart' space. One emerges with a solution, just as answers may be found in dreams. What play is doing is to be a medium both culturally and psychologically for the child. 'It makes the bridge between the child's consciousness and his emotional experience, and so fulfils the roles that conversation, introspection, philosophy and religion fill for the adult' (Lowenfeld 1935).

Some writers on art and play have been anxious to distinguish the separating characteristics of art, usually in a hierarchical vein. Kramer, for example, is clear: 'Sand and water are useful in play therapy, but cannot be used to make art works' (Kramer 1977: 10). These distinguishing characteristics are not always so clear to the children themselves. There is often real distress at the realization that sand worlds cannot be kept permanently, though they can be recorded diagrammatically, or photographed. One child would stand back proudly after making her sand worlds and say, with great confidence, 'It looks good enough to go in an exhibition, I wish it could!' She knew that this was a good piece of work aesthetically.

When Lowenfeld refers to play performing the same function for children as art, conversation, introspection, philosophy, and religion do for the adult, she is referring to the same area of human experience that Winnicott (1971) would define as the creative impulse. Winnicott sees the role of the creative impulse being a prerequisite for human development. This starts in a small way, through the use of objects between mother and child. As we develop into adults, the ability to use objects to communicate with the world, to make space and belongings personal, becomes the basic mechanism by which we attempt to maintain degrees of health over ill-health on personal, environmental, and cultural levels. A transitional object is a first object that

Plate 1 'Fred'

Plate 2 Richard: Mum, dad, and baby tree

Plate 3 Richard: Trees and Saint

Plate 4 Tina: Brick wall

Plate 5 Con: Fire dream

Plate 6 Con: Effigy bowls

a baby attaches importance to. Winnicott suggests that the mother's breast is first perceived to be part of the infant. The object seems to come into the space between the mother and baby. This potential space is an illusionary area between the the inner world of the baby and his actual external reality. It fills the gap of the first transitory experience of separateness for the baby. It is the first 'not me' possession, and is treated with affection. At the same time it is a comforter to the baby and so is seen as a first manifestation of 'symbol formation' in that it stands in for the mother. It illustrates the infant's capacity to create, think up, devise, originate, or produce an object. The infant's experience gradually expands as he becomes aware of an immediate environment beyond the potential space. When maternal support is withdrawn on occasions, he is able to use objects for temporary emotional support. He may, for example, fix on a light source and be able to maintain an illusion of maternal holding of anxiety. The child develops thought-out, constructive responses to filling the potential space, thus channelling emotions into rationalized creative responses when possible. The ability to play comes into being. He is able to manipulate transitional objects to meet his needs. A range of creative responses develops, including drawing and painting. It is within the potential space that the location of cultural experience can be found. It becomes an area of experience that is not inner or outer, but an overlap of both, enabling one to accept and work with inner and outer reality. The original play with an object develops into the arts, religion, philosophy, and creative scientific work, as well as all forms of imaginative living.

One can feel the perfection of the illusion, the times of loss of anxiety, the comfort of containment, when one is 'lost' in a painting or piece of play. All creative activity involves movement between conscious and unconscious states of mind. At one point one is interchangeable with the medium. People experience 'the painting taking me over, directing me what to do next'. Often, as one physically steps back from a painting, one seems to fall out of a special space, an area of containment. One has fallen[2] from unconscious involvement to a conscious awareness which spaces the maker from the object. One has left an inner world for an outer reality. Sometimes the illusion that we have created, been joined to, is recognized at this moment of conscious return after painting. It is sometimes expressed by clients when a painting dries – how it 'doesn't look the same anymore'. They are really saying that the illusion has broken, returning them to a perhaps unwelcome reality. But it is a reality which has been pieced together again, and a move forward has been made. Even though it didn't last it has 'worked' for a time, and it has acted on the maker who will begin creating at another time from a different point. As one becomes more experienced, more well-oiled in the process of making, one can recognize the illusionary element, the fact of playing and imagining, and use it. Until clients become more confident 'players', the role of the therapist is vital to bridge the anxiety of separateness and to assist the creation of satisfying objects.

What is happening when one 'loses oneself' in a painting, in a book, in an imaginary world in a box, or in a piece of clay? Marion Milner's experience of painting and work as an analyst clarifies this area in 'The role of illusion in symbol formation' (Milner 1977). The temporary 'loss of self' is a return to a state of early fusion with the mother in order to experience a oneness of realities. One mingles a subjective vision with an external world. From this experience, often an illusion so satisfying as to feel ecstatic, one sees the personal in the external, and moves forward in the adaptation that must be made in living. In her words there is 'a temporary giving up of the discriminating ego which stands apart and tries to see things objectively and rationally and without emotional colouring'. This experience is shared in a analytic hour, in playing, in painting and in all making of art, but also has the same 'aesthetic moment' experienced by a spectator. In each, one enters a moment when 'time and space are abolished and the spectator is possessed by one awareness'. Through this process one changes one's perception of the world. From a different perspective Huizinga (1971) discusses the 'illusion' in play. He contrasts the 'cheat' and the 'spoilsport'. The cheat is far less hated than the spoilsport. One can see that whereas the cheat stays within the playspace or frame that allows the loss of self, the spoilsport destroys the framework and subverts the validity of the game, robbing it of illusion.

Play and art

Play and art are both manifestations of symbol formation in their use of objects to represent concepts and emotions to bridge inner and outer worlds. Symbol formation seems to be part of play in the designation of matter as a toy, and part of art in the forming of shapeless matter into an object. Many artists bridge the gap between art and play, e.g. Kurt Schwitters, who equally finds, makes, combines, and creates. His ability to use found objects and ready-mades in new combinations in his visual art and literary works closes the apparent gap between these activities.

Play, although given a particular value by art therapists like Edith Kramer, is somehow kept in its place, as 'lower' than art. For her, the making of an art object has a 'higher' value. This is likely to reflect western society's use of art objects as merchandise, or as investments. Does the value given to art objects by the élitist art system of galleries even affect consideration of children's art and play?

In her writings on art therapy and play, Kramer's focus is clear. She says of the art therapist: 'They must encourage playfulness to stimulate imagination, yet intercede when art threatens to dissipate into play; must tolerate regression from art to play or assist in the transition from play to art' (Kramer 1979: 44). In making the art object the prime focus of a session, all other activity becomes secondary. Sessions are product-orientated. Yet it is the child that is the prime focus of a session. As therapists, we are helping a child to work on material, to disclose emotionally areas that they would not be able to explore on their own. If we are helping them from a situation of ill-health to health, all stages on that journey must be valued and experienced as fully as possible.

Something does not have to be recognizable to be art. Kramer says that small children can make shapeless lumps out of clay which are 'symbolic' representations that can outlast the moment. One child at the Assessment Centre attended weekly for part of a mainly home assessment. The first week she made two breast-shaped lumps which she painted whilst wet. These 'lived' in a special corner of the room, and every week her first activity would be to take them down and repaint them with several layers. She called them her 'cakes'. They lasted for several weeks, till she stopped coming to the Centre. What did we have here? Mother's breasts, cakes, clay art objects, a named toy, something of herself left in the room for me to look after, a symbolic part of me and her, a transitional object? It seems the boundaries are very weak. Edith Kramer contrasts the 'magic of play' where anything can be designated as anything, with the 'miracle' of art which depends on 'the arduous creation of new objects whose sole function resides in their symbolic meaning'. This seems to be too smooth a classification of activity.

One element of play that is distinguishable from art is the possibility of its being a 'safer' area in which to experiment. It is non-judgemental. Its very impermanence might draw children to it, for, like adults, children find the expectations accompanying a blank sheet of paper daunting.

Although I find Kramer's writings very valuable and thought-provoking, I would disagree that 'playing is easier than creating' and feel that both take place in the same inner/outer world of the child, and both allow symbolic representation of inner forces leading to growth in the child. It would seem retrogressive to attempt to make a hierarchy out of children's art and play activity in therapy.

Art and play sessions for children are rare moments, particularly within the education system when they are not being evaluated. The pressure to change, to know oneself, has to come from within to be of any value. Children are rarely trusted to set their own goals or choose their own activities without negative comment. Many children have great difficulties with choice, with self-direction. To help them through this painful time of facing a challenge, to choose activities or none, to sit and talk, or whatever, is to aid them towards some independence and internal security.

Notes

1 A kinetic family drawing shows everyone in the family doing something. It is usually more informative than a family line up. See Burns and Kaufman (1971).
2 When one thinks of 'falling out of a painting', it brings to mind the phrase 'falling from Grace' and the myth of Adam and Eve. One can see this as a symbolic tale of the original perfect containment in the Garden of Eden, the fusion of children and maker; and the snake as the original spoilsport, breaking the boundaries of the sanctuary.

References

Antony, S. (1971) *The Discovery of Death in Childhood and After*. London: Penguin.

Axline, V. (1969) *Play Therapy*. New York: Balantine.

Barnes, M. (1964) Reactions to the Death of a Mother. *The Psychoanalytic Study of the Child* 19: 334–57.

Bowlby, J. (1981) *Attachment and Loss*. Harmondsworth: Penguin.

Bowyer, R. (1970) *The Lowenfeld World Technique*. Oxford: Pergamon Press.

Burns, R. C. and Kaufman, S. (1971) An Introduction to Understanding Children through Kinetic Family Drawings. *Kinetic Family Drawings*. London: Constable.

Case, C. (1980) The Expression of Loss in Art Therapy. Unpublished MA thesis, Birmingham Polytechnic.

Darwin, C. (1872) *The Expression of the Emotions in Man and Animals*. London: John Murray.

Freud, S. (1917) Mourning and Melancholia. Standard Edition (1963) Vol. 14: 243–58. London: Hogarth Press and the Institute of Psychoanalysis.

Freud, S. (1925) Inhibitions, Symptoms and Anxiety. Standard Edition (1963) Vol. 20: 77–175. London: Hogarth Press and the Institute of Psychoanalysis.

Furman, R. (1964) Death and the Young Child. *The Psychoanalytic Study of the Child* 19: 321–33.

Gordon, R. (1978) *Dying and Creating, a Search for Meaning* Vol. 4. London: Library of Analytical Psychology.

Gorer, G. (1965) *Death, Grief and Mourning in Contemporary Britain*. London: Cresset.

Huizinga, J. (1971) *Homo Ludens*. London: Paladin.

Kalff, D. (1980) *Sandplay*. Santa Monica: Sigo Press.

Klein, M. (1940) Mourning and its Relation to Manic-depressive States. *International Journal of Psychoanalysis* 21, I: 317–40.

Kramer, E. (1977) Art Therapy and Play. *American Journal of Art Therapy* 17: 3–11.

Kramer, E. (1979) *Childhood and Art Therapy*. New York: Schocken.

Lang, A. (ed.) (1965) *The Blue Fairy Book*. New York: Dover.

Lindemann, E. (1944) The Symptomatology and Management of Acute Grief. *American Journal of Psychiatry* 101 (September): 141–48.

Lowenfeld, M. (1935) *Play in Childhood*. London: Gollancz.

Marris, P. (1974) *Loss and Change*. London: Routledge & Kegan Paul.

Milner, M. (1977) The Role of Illusion in Symbol Formation. In M. Klein (ed.) *New Directions in Psycho-analysis*. London: Maresfield Reprints.

Nagy, I. (1948) The Child's Theories Concerning Death. *Journal of Genetic Psychology* 73: 3–27.

Parkes, C. (1971) *Psycho-social Transitions* Vol. 5: 101–15. London: Pergamon Press.

Parkes, C. (1975) *Bereavement*. London: Pelican.

Schultz, R. (1978) *The Psychology of Death, Dying and Bereavement*. London: Addison-Wesley.

Winnicott, D. (1971) *Playing and Reality*. Harmondsworth: Penguin.

Acknowledgements

First, thanks to Iris O'Brien and Elizabeth Oliver, both innovative teachers who were instrumental in creating situations in which art therapy could be made available to special-needs children in the Assessment Centre and in the primary school. Secondly, to Nick Cocks who has shared my life through much of the work described.

3 | The scapegoat and the talisman: transference in art therapy

Joy Schaverien

The scapegoat transference

In this chapter I plan to consider an idea central to the concept of transference, the main pivot of psychoanalytic theory, that is, the idea of the magical transferability of attributes and states. This idea was evoked by reading Cassirer's (1955 and 1957) *Philosophy of Symbolic Forms*, particularly Volume II, *Mythical Thought*. I have used, and I hope not abused, Cassirer's work for my own purposes rather than doing justice to his ideas. In this chapter I consider the idea that the picture is the object of a transference in art therapy, and subject to this transference, it subsequently may become a scapegoat. This may be considered, as was the original scapegoat, a positive enactment, as opposed to a negative acting out.

The scapegoat

In its original sense, in the Bible (Leviticus XVI: 21), the scapegoat was a white goat, on to which the sins of the community were laid, in a religious ceremony. The goat was then cast out into the desert to die, taking the sins with it. In this way the sins of the community were atoned.

The process of scapegoating entails two related actions which take place in two separate stages. The first stage is the separation of the sins or the guilt from an individual or the community. This is accomplished through a ritualized transference, an unburdening, off-loading the sins. The ritualized act, the religious ceremony is in itself an acknowledgement of the sins. The priest is empowered by the community, and the shared belief and investment in his authority, to take the burden and to lay it upon the goat. (At this stage we could consider the goat to have become a talisman, in that it is magically invested with the power of the sins.)

The second stage of the scapegoating process is the sacrifice of the goat. It is rejected, cast out into the desert to die, taking with it the sins which are thereby absolved. This we might see as the stage of disposal.

Frazer (1922) and Cassirer (1955) show that scapegoating, the ritualized disposal of unwanted or evil aspects via magical transference to objects or people, is a universal process which can be found in practice in slightly different manifestations in many diverse cultures:

'It is reported that the Hupa Indians look on pain as a substance. And even purely "spiritual", purely "moral" attributes are in this sense regarded as transferable substances, as is shown by a number of ritual rites regulating this transference. Thus a taint, a miasma that a community has brought on itself, can be transferred to an individual, a slave for example, and destroyed by the sacrifice of the slave. The Greek Thargelia and certain Ionian festivals included a similar ritual of atonement, going back to the most ancient mythical origins. Originally these rites of purification and atonement were based not on a symbolic substitution but on a real, physical transference. A Batak suffering under a curse can "make it fly away" by transferring it to a swallow. And the transfer may be to a mere object as well as an animate subject, as is shown, for example, by a Shinto usage. Here a man desiring to be relieved of guilt receives from the priest a sheet of white paper cut in the form of a human garment called katashiro, "representative of human form". On it he writes the year and month of his birth and his family name; then he rubs it over his body and breathes on it, whereupon his sins are transferred to the katashiro. At the end of the purification ceremony these "scapegoats" are thrown into a river or sea, in order that the four gods of purification may guide them into the underworld, where they will disappear without trace.'

(Cassirer 1955: II, 55–6)

A ritual transference such as those illustrated here assumes a faith, a belief that an object can become empowered. A belief of this nature involves magical investment in the thing, which effects a transformation of the mere thing into a talisman. This has considerable implications for the practice of art therapy. When art therapy is fully affective there is a transference of attributes and states to an object which, subsequently empowered, becomes a talisman. Once an object is experienced as a talisman any act of resolution in relation to it becomes significant and might be seen as an act of disposal.

The talisman

> 'Talisman: Charm, amulet, thing capable of working wonders. Magical figure cut or engraved and capable of benefiting its possessor.'
>
> (*Oxford English Dictionary*)

The qualities of a talisman are qualities which are also invested in works of art. Sometimes this investment is made by the artist, sometimes by the culture. It is most clearly evident in religious works, which were created for worship. Examples of this would be icons or pictures by Giotto, depictions of sacred scenes, in which both the making and viewing of the pictures was a religious act. There is a comparable magical investment by the viewer in works which were not intentionally created for religious purposes. Great art transcends time and generations, embodying universal elements which still, after hundreds of years, engage the spectator and evoke profound responses – a message from an artist, long dead, to a new generation of viewers. Such immortality is evident in the pictures which are viewed in museums and galleries across the world and across the centuries. This quality is additional to the actual power of the visual image; it is something which we, as viewers do; it is an investment we make. This is one reason why reproductions of great art, no matter how good they may be, can never be acceptable as replacements for the original. In the work we can see, even touch, history. The work has transcended time, death; we can touch the surface, the material that was once touched by Leonardo, by Goya. The object which has long outlived its mortal creator embodies a vision, an emotional charge, which leaves more than mere traces of the human being who so long ago painted it. As viewers we invest the object (in addition to its visible properties) with this power, and are awed by it. In this way all great art may be empowered, and is then potentially a talisman.

Certain analysts are similarly empowered with the qualities of a talisman. In analytic circles there is great importance invested in being 'in touch' with the originator. Ideas change, are discussed, and modified over the years, but it is still the case that, for example, a Freudian analyst who was in analysis, with an analyst, whose analyst was Freud, is in a sense passing the 'magic baton' through the relay race of generations. This magical idea of 'touching the cloth', in part, accounts for the closed nature of the various analytic schools. Critics of psychoanalysis (Malcolm 1980, Gellner 1985) draw attention to this with objective scepticism and some humour. But there is a serious aspect to this which concerns a human need, often neglected in this rational, western culture, to invest power, to have faith; a need for magic, for links with the ancestors. In the cases of both great art and analysis there is a magical investment, disguised beneath layers of sophistication, in the object or in the person as healer.

One way of describing this type of experience would be in terms of investment of primary infantile material in the object. In psychoanalytic terms the empowering of objects, or of people, may be classified as an infantile phase of identification and idealization (Klein 1980, Segal 1981). In Chapter 4 Weir explores this approach in depth. My position tends more in the direction of Jung (1972), Hillman (1979), or Neumann (1970) who accept magical thinking as an innate aspect of human existence – as an irrational layer of the psyche which harbours the seeds of self healing. This is clearly evidenced in the images made by our clients, and indeed in our own.

The power of the image

Art therapists are sometimes concerned that in some forms of therapy the picture is used merely to facilitate the verbal exchange. I consider that there are two distinct types of picture made by people in art therapy, and for my purpose here I need to clarify this distinction.

The diagrammatic picture

The majority of clients are initially not used to the medium of art, and are inhibited by it. The first pictures they make are often diagrammatic, and are used by the patient to tell the therapist something. Although at times it can be a useful pointer or guide in talking, this pictorial diagram does not, in itself, effect very much in terms of moving the inner world of the client. Here the image follows the word. This type of image could be equated with a sign. Certain types of therapeutic intervention seem to produce this kind of picture. For example, asking a patient to make a picture of her family often results in a drawing that is a diagram with stick figures. This may be revealing in many ways: accidental juxtapositions and relationships within the diagram may surprise the client, who may realize previously unconscious aspects of her role in the family. But the actual pictorial image is not significant in itself. These pictures are like maps of the client's world, which have definite reference points outside the paper.

Let us look at an example of how this might be. A client makes a picture of a crying face.

This type of diagram obviously indicates sadness. It portrays the idea of sadness in a representational way; it is a conscious description of a state, similar to saying 'I feel sad'; it describes a sensation. This is a pictorial description of an emotion, and as such can be detached from that emotion.

Although the client may have felt sad when she made it, the picture itself does not convey sadness to the viewer in any convincing way. A diagram such as this rarely evokes a corresponding feeling in the viewer. From it we can discern only that the artist consciously wished to let us know that she feels sad. There is minimal investment in the image itself. This image is an *illustration* of a feeling, rather than an *embodiment* of feeling. It is, then, unlikely to be empowered, and unlikely consequently to become a talisman.

The embodied image

A client may be unaware at the start of therapy that she has any feelings about the therapist – indeed she may not have at first – but gradually feelings become involved. It is similar with the pictures. The merely diagrammatic picture refers to a situation or tells a story to the therapist. It points to feeling, but does not embody it. As the client starts to feel about the therapist, therapy starts to become alive. The pictures become alive and meaningful in the context of the relationship. When the client feels safe enough with the therapist, when she has sufficient trust in the holding environment, she will dare to allow the image to lead. When she opens herself to the power of the image-making process, the images start to become affective. When this is recognized by the client the subsequent images are invested with more affect; and so they become a powerful way of contacting unconscious forces and engaging with them. It is as if the picture-making process 'takes over'. No matter what the original intention, an image may be suggested by a line drawn a certain way, and an accidental splash or mark may become incorporated. Provided that the original intention is not too rigidly adhered to or fixed, the whole has a life, an evolution of its own. Deriving from a combination of inattention and conscious attention, there is a tension, an energetic process. Even when, as on many occasions in therapy, the artist fails to bring the whole to a successful conclusion, the energy which has been part of the process is embodied in the picture. Such a picture, though inexpertly executed, may be imbued with life; a product of total absorption of its maker, and also a product of a 'live' relationship with the therapist. Thus, in the therapeutic context, it is 'living form' (Langer 1953).

I hope it can now be seen that there is a considerable difference in the emotional investment in the descriptive picture and the embodied image. The embodied image is rarely comfortable, containing, as it does, the tension between opposing forces which are temporarily reconciled 'out there' on the paper. This image has reverberations in the emotional response, the unconscious of both artist and viewer.

It is the task of the art therapist to form a relationship with the client in which trust can develop, and feelings become engaged. It is then that pictures change, that life emerges in the images. Images which were fused, locked in, appear outside on the paper, evidence to the client that she has these feelings, which then become inescapable but separate. It is at this point, at the point of recognition of the feeling, that the aesthetic quality of the images frequently changes, and develops. The pictures start to exhibit opposing elements, conflicts. Emotions which were repressed, which felt too difficult, too painful to face, become accessible, contained as they are 'out there' in the image, within the frame of the picture. It is this type of image which can take the lead for a while, and it is this type of embodied image which, carrying power for its maker, is experienced as a talisman, can be a container of *a* transference, and is experienced as a scapegoat.

Transference

Theories of therapy that work with transference have in common an understanding that attention must be paid to the transference feelings. Any notion of change, of individuation, or reconciliation comes about through this emotional engagement between the two people involved. When the client becomes aware of feelings about the therapist, when such feelings become activated, that which has previously been fixed and rigid becomes potentially alive, fluid, and mobile, thus change and growth is possible. The transference/counter-transference relationship is an encounter in which both people are changed, in which both feel many things, and in which the therapist is often incorporated, in a powerful way, in the imaginal world of the client. The therapist may be seen as many-faceted, a person both loved and hated, envied, feared, respected, and despised. She may be experienced as an embodiment of the client's fears or idealizations. She may be seen as only part human (a monster or demon), or as only a human part (a breast or a phallus); a body for comfort or a disembodied emotion. In other words, in analysis or dynamic psychotherapy, the client, in part, creates the therapist.

When we say we are working *in* the transference, we are indicating that we are working in the inner world of the client. This is another way of saying we are working in the 'imagination'. If we accept that we are working in the imagination, the source of the imaginal, then the embodied images, the paintings made in this context, may be seen as a focused container for this, and, in consequence, at times, they will incorporate the transference.

Initially Freud regarded the transference as an obstacle to treatment. Subsequently he realized that it could be the main pivot of treatment (Freud 1912, 1915, Jones 1953, 1955). Since Freud the concept has expanded and now it may potentially include the whole therapeutic relationship, and all verbal and non-verbal communications which take place within this setting (Segal 1981, Langs 1980, Kernberg 1975). In art therapy this extends to include, in addition to the above, the pictures with which we work within the therapeutic relationship. The pictures which embody feeling, consciously and unconsciously, can be objects of a transference and as such the central focus for intra-psychic movement to begin. There are times when the pictures merely exhibit the transference; these pictures enhance and widen the scope of psychotherapy but are distinct from the pictures which embody feeling. When the picture embodies feeling, and movement starts to occur in relation to the image created, it is then that change is possible through the medium of the picture itself. This is similar to the transference relationship to the therapist but here the focus is the picture. It is when a picture embodies unconscious forces that it can, in a very real sense, become a scapegoat.

The scapegoating process: acknowledgement

In psychotherapy groups, and in other social situations too, we commonly refer to scapegoating. What is usually meant by this is that a person is being punished or ostracized for something which is not entirely their own fault. It is often the case that the person is rejected or blamed for exhibiting or expressing behaviours which those doing the rejecting may fear, or need to display themselves. The group fantasy may be that once this individual is removed, everyone else will relate harmoniously. The bad is all invested in this one person. The situation may be resolved when underlying fears in the group are made explicit, and when the projections, recognized as such, are offered back to the group or individual members as aspects of their own psyche, not solely belonging to the scapegoated member. The attempt to make a scapegoat is thwarted when unconscious motivations become conscious. Unless the scapegoated member does leave the group, there is ultimately no scapegoat. There is no disposal.

In the description of the original scapegoat, I said that the act of separation 'takes place through a ritualized transference, an unburdening, off-loading the sins. This act is, in itself, an acknowledgement of the sins.' Before continuing, I need to clarify what I mean here by 'acknowledgement'. Among its definitions of acknowledgement the *Oxford English Dictionary* gives: 'Admit the truth of; own to knowing; take notice of; recognise the authority of.' In the scapegoat process the sin, the guilt, is transferred by a religious ritual. This ritual is an acknowledgement, in the sense of owning to knowing the guilt. It is also the first stage in separation from it. If a feeling, such as guilt, is undifferentiated, or fused, it is not known as separate; we might call it unconscious. The ritual transfer to the goat might be seen as a first stage in differentiation, or of becoming conscious. To acknowledge, then, is to stop, to turn and face the unacceptable. The guilt does not belong to the goat, the goat is merely called in as an offering, it is sacrificed, not for *its* sins, but in lieu of those of the community. It would be pointless to dispose of the goat without first subjecting it to a ritual transference. The ritual empowers the goat, which then becomes an embodiment of the sins. In the act of empowering the goat there must be a recognition of the guilt and a ritual separation from it. Without the ritual the undifferentiated state remains, and the casting out might then be seen as unconscious 'acting out' as opposed to an enactment, by which different levels of consciousness are achieved. (I will return to this later with regard to the scapegoat picture.)

In psychotherapy groups, where there is an attempt to scapegoat one member, it is as if the first part of the scapegoating process, the separation, is attempted, but it is a false separation. It is as if the goat is being disposed of without the ritual transfer. It is a false separation because there is an unconscious refusal to own the bad feeling. There is no ritual which admits the 'bad'. Instead, a premature separation is attempted, casting out without owning what is being ejected. In this way the second stage, the disposal or casting out, is attempted unconsciously, without awareness of what is being thrown out or why. This, then, is clearly acting out, as opposed to enactment. In a group, conscious understanding is essential, because that understanding prevents the blame falling entirely on one individual. It enables mediation and negotiation to take place, and projections to be recognized. In psychotherapy groups it is clearly undesirable to have a scapegoat, because that scapegoat is a person who may be irreparably damaged by the experience. In social situations there is no disposal, because there can be no disposal of a person. It is obviously unacceptable that there should be a scapegoat in a social group because we cannot project our unwanted aspects on to other people and then dispose of them. The consequences of such actions are ultimately disastrous. For example, Hitler's projection of all the bad in Germany in the 1930s on to the Jews led to the attempt to dispose of the whole race.

In individual psychotherapy we can observe a similar process in the transference, if we return to the idea that the client creates the therapist by seeing her as an embodiment of her own fears or as an idealization. The client here is projecting aspects of herself, those that she cannot easily accept, on to the therapist: she experiences them as belonging to the therapist (Klein 1961, 1980; Searles 1965, 1979; Kohut 1971). This may be understood as an unconscious attempt to off-load, to separate from, or fuse with, the therapist. This may take the form of a consciously or unconsciously expressed attempt to blame, punish, or reward the therapist for the emotions experienced. In this sense we may see the client as unconsciously attempting to scapegoat the therapist. Such attempts may evoke feelings of responsibility in the counter-transference. The therapist may be inclined to feel guilty or responsible for the client's feelings, and this she has to deal with. She has neither the power to cause the pain or guilt, nor the power to take it away. Through the therapeutic relationship, through a constant process of interpretation and feeding back, the projections are eventually reintegrated within the client. Eventually the therapist is seen as a separate person, rather than a projection of the client's inner world. The point of this schematic version of a complex and lengthy process, is that the psychotherapist does not take on the role of scapegoat, in the sense of accepting and carrying away off-loaded projections. This would be wholly undesirable and would not help the client. No therapist can do this because in doing so she takes responsibility from her client. Whatever is projected on to her, she remains and waits until it is recognized and owned by the client. The separation here occurs through the client's eventual realization and owning of her projections. There is then no disposal of the therapist.

It is here that art therapy can claim its distinct nature, and it is here also that a difference between art therapy and psychotherapy emerges. All that has been said above about the psychotherapist applies equally to the art therapist. The person of the art therapist may be subject to fantasies and projections and attempts at scapegoating. She may respond similarly to the psychotherapist as a person. The difference lies in the transference to the image. The embodied image may be the central focus of projected feelings. There is no moral reason why either bad or good aspects should not be projected on to a piece of paper or a lump of clay. The crucial difference here is that this object of transference *can* become a scapegoat. The second stage of the scapegoating process, the disposal, *can* take place. There is a real possibility of magical investment and enactment with the image, without necessitating harm to anyone.

The image which is invested with power, the talisman image, may function in many different ways. As a scapegoat, the talisman may be disposed of by an act of destruction, but it may also be guarded and kept. Both these processes are integral aspects of art therapy.

Baring the phenomenon

The image feeding back

Earlier I used the term 'acknowledgement' to describe a process whereby differentiation and separation from a state of fusion occurs as a result of an act. This act is empowered through ritual, and so becomes an 'enactment', as opposed to 'acting out'.

Before discussing examples of scapegoat pictures in art therapy practice, I need to clarify what I mean by acknowledgement in relation to pictorial imagery. What I am exploring here is levels of knowing – those which occur via action and those which occur through regarding the object which results from that action. There are layers of familiarization, or acknowledgement, which occur without necessarily subjecting the work to conceptual interpretation. These are contained in a phrase commonly used by art therapists when they talk of 'the image feeding back'. This is a form of the image interpreting itself. My understanding of this has developed from art therapy practice, but also from reading Cassirer (1955), and so it is to his work that I refer in an attempt to clarify what I mean. It is Cassirer's phrase 'baring the phenomenon' which I use to name this part of the process.

What Cassirer terms the 'I "coming to grips" with the world' may be seen as similar to Jungian 'individuation'. These ideas both seem to be based on philosophies which have a phenomenological root and are also subject to a hierarchy of consciousness. Cassirer discusses the development of consciousness from an undifferentiated state of literal and concrete thought, through mythical consciousness, to a religious one. We could compare the undifferentiated state to Jung's 'collective unconscious' (Jung 1959a) and the journey towards individuation as the process of separation–differentiation. For Cassirer this process leads eventually, via gods of action and tool making, to naming, the word, a sense of self, and ultimately to free will. This is explored in depth in *Volume II: Mythical Thought* (1955) and can be understood as a process of both individual and of cultural development. This is not a simple formula for a limited understanding. Rather, it generates an awareness that these different possibilities of evolutionary consciousness are simultaneously present in each individual. Thus the scapegoating process, which has its roots within mythical and religious consciousness of earlier generations, also manifests itself in our 'sophisticated', scientific society. In both interaction and in art therapy pictures, if we regard the state prior to the scapegoat process as the state of fusion, we may see the next stage, the empowering of the talisman via a ritual transference, as an early attempt at differentiation. It is the start of separation and recognition. The disposal of the scapegoat would be seen as a further stage, an additional action with additional consequences. We might see this process as being recreated anew with each embodied image – not always an exact copy of this whole process but always manifesting aspects of it.

'All true action is formative in a twofold sense: the I does not simply impress its own form, a form given to it from the very outset, upon objects; on the contrary, it acquires this form only in the totality of the actions which it exerts upon objects and which it receives back from them. Accordingly, the limits of the inner world can only be determined, its ideal formation can only become visible, if the sphere of being is circumscribed in action. The larger the circle becomes which the self fills with its activity, the more clearly the character of the objective reality and also the significance and function of the I are manifested.'

Cassirer (1955: II, 200)

This idea, that an object upon which we act gives something back to us, is a familiar one for the art therapist. *'The "I" . . . acquires this form only in the totality of the actions which it exerts upon objects and which it receives back from them.'* In art therapy the client makes an image, and in so doing performs an act, which very act affirms a sense of self; the 'I' exists. In seeing the result of the action, in the marks made on the paper, or the forms elaborated in the clay, there is immediate 'feedback' from the object. An action has taken place, something has been created which cannot be denied, it is out there, outside of self – '. . . *the limits of the inner world can only be determined, its ideal formation can only become visible, if the sphere of being is circumscribed in action'*. Hence, picture-making could be seen as a meditative and a reflective activity, which renders the inner world visible – 'formulates it for our cognition' (Langer 1957). It is a way of knowing oneself through that which one makes. This corresponds to ideas of 'active imagination' (Jung 1956, 1959b) – the idea that if we can allow our conscious, adult selves to relinquish control, and permit the image to lead, unconscious forces will become manifest. We then see, in our images, a reflection of our inner world, a very effective mirror which reveals aspects we may wish to deny, as well as those we are prepared to own. However we may wish to reject the image, once seen it can never again be entirely unconscious.

'The use of fire, the ability to fashion certain tools, farming and hunting, the knowledge of certain medicaments, the invention of writing: all of these appear as gifts of mythical powers. Here again man understands his activity only by removing it from himself and projecting it outward. . . . Here the world of mythical images, like that of language or art, serves as one of the basic instruments by which the I "comes to grips" with the world.'

Cassirer (1955: II, 204)

The image interpreting itself

The idea that an image can 'interpret itself' again indicates a distinction between art therapy and other forms of therapy. Here again, I refer not to all images, but to the embodied image – that which is effectively empowered. Once an image exists 'out there', in the world, it interacts with and affects the artist. It also interacts with and affects other people, the consequences of which have repercussions for the artist. For the client in therapy, who is unable to relate easily to other people, who is also perhaps unable to relate to herself, the image-making process may play a fundamental part in enabling her to begin to do so. To make something that can be seen can authenticate her experience and even her existence.

'What previously was concrete unity despite all its inner antithesis now begins to separate and in this analytical differentiation to interpret itself. The pure phenomenon of expression has as yet no such form of dichotomy. In it a mode of understanding is given which is not attached to the condition of conceptual interpretation; the simple baring of the phenomenon is at the same time its interpretation, and the only one of which it is susceptible and needful.'

Cassirer (1957: III, 93–4)

Here I understand Cassirer to be arguing that there is, at root, no split between different modes of expression. Just as experience is initially undifferentiated, so images and words are also fused. The split, or differentiation between these modes of expression, arises through a gradual process of separation, a development of consciousness. In its initial stages the 'pure phenomenon of expression has as yet no such form of dichotomy'. There is no division, and no opposition. When an artist, or a client in art therapy, has just made a picture, it may be the case that she is in a state of fusion with the object. If so, to ask her to give words for the content of the imagery at too early a stage, may be to demand premature separation. With confidence in the process we find that separation will occur in its own time. We find that words will come, based on the artist's own motivation, from her own need. A form of interpretation is then taking place in relation to the image being seen, the phenomenon bared, and this is a private process between the artist and her image.

Words have their place in all therapies, and art therapy is no exception. It is not my intention to suggest that in art therapy we don't talk or that we don't talk about imagery. I merely wish to clarify times when words can be invasive, and can interfere with the process of recognition and reconciliation which is taking place between the artist and the image. Words potentially fix meaning and conceptualize experience. When the phenomenon is bared, when an image is newly exposed it needs space. The artist needs to get to know it before she can talk about it. She needs to find the words that fit. For the therapist to demand explanations too early can be to rob the client of her own process. We must have confidence in the process, and wait.

We are all subject to imagery and, as we have seen, this imagery may exist on different levels of consciousness or awareness. It may not always have a clearly pictorial form, but it emerges in our dreams, fears, fantasies, and imaginings. At times of stress there may be an overflowing of such imagery, which may become impossible to contain; it needs an outlet and will inevitably find one. This may take the form of behaviour which is considered socially unacceptable, or 'mad'. The fear of experiencing oneself as 'mad' or 'bad' may be so great that an attempt may be made to stifle the imagery connected with these feelings – to keep them in the dark. The fear may be that, if allowed into the light of day, these images and the actions associated with them would overwhelm and threaten us and those in close relation to us. If such images are kept within, unexpressed, they remain fused with the person. Unacknowledged, they can cause unpleasant symptoms like depression or angry outbursts, or they may be projected, transferred, or attributed to other people. If a picture is made which reveals such imagery, the feeling is owned on some level of consciousness. The picture may be denied or destroyed, but even when this happens something has changed because the image has been glimpsed in the light of day.

This image has been projected, transferred outward, but unlike in the accepted sense of transference the image is transferred, not to a person, but on to an inanimate object – paper or clay. It cannot be escaped, or attributed to anyone else. It has undeniably been made by the client. The image is thus owned, if only briefly. Instead of 'you are bad', for example, it reflects back 'I am bad'. Painful as that may be, it is a first stage in admitting the projected image and its associated feelings. The first stage in the scapegoating process, the laying down of the burden, thus takes place. The burden, however, is not off-loaded on to another person, nor on to a goat. Instead, the picture is empowered with the image, and the first stage in separation from it takes place. The picture becomes a talisman. The artist knows that this is her pain or guilt, and from the moment the picture is made she starts to take responsibility for it. There is no way of denying it. It may be a long time before the emotion is assimilated, or can be discussed. It may never be more clearly accepted than in this brief glimpse, but even so, in its manifestation, there is a form of acknowledgement, of taking responsibility and of accepting ownership.

To summarize, we have seen that the picture in art therapy at times interprets itself for its maker. There are levels of knowing or acknowledgement within a process of familiarization: to see one's own picture is to know it on one level. Living with it we get to know it better, and start to understand it conceptually. To talk about it is to get to know it differently, to both fix and negotiate meaning. When we keep it safe we respect and nurture its power, and when we destroy it we take action in relation to it.

Disposal

The second stage in the scapegoating process I have called disposal. Once the transfer to the goat is achieved it is, so to speak, disposed of – cast out into the desert to die. The community is left clear of its sins. It is the same in the examples cited by Cassirer, in the passage quoted in the opening of this chapter. The slave is killed, sacrificed, and the taint is thus removed from the community. The Batak's curse is transferred to a live swallow, which flies away, carrying with it the curse. The katashiros are thrown into the water 'in order that the four gods of purification may guide them into the underworld where they will disappear without trace'.

To dispose of a thing is not necessarily to destroy it. To dispose of a thing is to settle or deal with it in some way (*Oxford English Dictionary*). The sense which I mean when I refer to disposal includes other ways of dealing with the empowered image. Most often in art therapy the images are kept, usually by the therapist, on behalf of the client. This too may be seen as a type of disposal where the artist assumes power over the image by making the decision to keep it. This is discussed later in the chapter. Here I wish to emphasize that disposal offers a very real distinction between art therapy and other psychotherapies. If the image is a talisman, its destruction is a meaningful act and offers a genuine opportunity to enact the scapegoat process in full. Keeping it is also a meaningful act which offers the solution of a different type of disposal. The client has dominion over the picture or art object, in a way that would never be possible with a person.

To examine in more detail the role of the scapegoat picture in art therapy practise I will describe two different incidents, both of which took place in a therapeutic community. People in this community were not given diagnostic labels, but I consider it relevant to indicate that neither of the people discussed was considered schizophrenic.

Scapegoat transference 1: enactment

Sally, an intelligent 18-year-old, was emotionally very much younger. She had an air of child-like, but detached, innocence. One day I was in the art room with other community members. I was vaguely aware of Sally in the adjacent room where she was engaged in some activity. Eventually she invited me to come with her and see what she had made. She showed me, with some pride, a piece of paper smeared with faeces. Though confronted with initial distaste and an instinct to reject the object, I was also aware of many possible interpretations or ways of understanding such an act. The pride with which it was shown reminded me of the small child, proudly presenting her mother with the precious gift, her faeces, something she has made, 'all her own work'. It could also be seen as a way of testing the therapist, in the transference. It posed the question of how far I would go with her, what was an acceptable part of her and what was not. It was certainly a challenge to the therapist's tolerance, and might be seen as infantile aggression. It raised the question of whether I, or we (the other members of the community), could allow Sally to be the shitty, messy little girl she felt herself to be, as well as the intelligent, well-behaved young woman she usually presented to the world. Acceptance of the picture was, then, a symbolic acceptance of this previously rejected aspect of Sally. Verbal interpretation of the meaning of this act would have been one way of accepting it, and a way of attempting to bring to consciousness the underlying unconscious meanings of it. Acceptance of the image was another kind of interpretation, a non-verbal interpretation, an act based on an understanding of her image and acceptance of her. It left something unspoken and yet understood. It left the image, such as it was, open to its manifold meanings.

To interpret is to limit. To make a verbal interpretation is to fix meaning, even if only for now. It indicates the therapist's position and puts the client's behaviour and image within the therapist's control. If we merely accept the image, with a nod in its direction, we remain open to the multiple potential meanings, those which we don't perceive in the first glance. If we wait, we allow these potential meanings to gradually permeate consciousness not only for the therapist, but more importantly, for the client. Images do not evaporate as words do, so we can afford to wait – to allow understanding to creep up on us, rather than fixing the meaning, here and now. There are, of course, times when the right word, the right interpretation, accelerates the process and brings relief by bringing the unconscious material to consciousness. On these occasions the word fixes the unformed idea, and is just what is needed to help the client differentiate her experience. In the case of Sally, no verbal interpretation was made.

For a week Sally carried this 'picture' with her wherever she went. It was a topic of discussion in the community. She was fearful of losing it and would lock it in her car when she couldn't carry it with her – but then she was fearful lest the car be stolen with the picture in it. Eventually, after discussing it in community meetings, she decided that she could not keep it for ever, and a week later she burned it, in a ritual which other members of the community were invited to witness. Subsequently, she made many images from thickly smeared brown and green paint on paper.

I would suggest that the original smeared paper had been experienced by Sally as very literally a part of her. In Cassirer's words, it was not 'a symbolic substitution, but a real physical transference' (1955: II, 55). It was in this sense fused with her – hence her attachment to it. She was reluctant to leave it anywhere or to be separated from it, and she really feared that her car would be stolen with the picture in it. The fear was not just that she would lose something she owned, with the implication that to own something it must be separate. It was more, in a literal sense, that she would lose part of herself. This is evidence of what Cassirer calls 'mythical identity thinking in the form of substance' (1955: II, 66). The object was empowered, experienced by Sally as magical and significant.

Carrying the smeared paper around and discussing it was the beginning of resolution, of acceptance of the 'image' and of the aspect of herself it represented. It was the beginning of separation from the fused state, the beginning of a process of symbolization. The ritual burning served the disposal function of the scapegoat. Its disposal by fire did two things. It disposed of the problem of what to do with her shit. She had to let it go, she couldn't hold on to it for ever. Letting it go in this way also released something else. It allowed her to experience the idealized product as separate from her, no longer fused. This was the start of a very necessary separation from fusion with her environment and from people in close relation to her. It helped her to acknowledge her own power – her power over the image but separate from it. Destruction by fire is a powerful act. It is one which can be a positive 'enactment' containing the spark of future life. Fire is frequently seen as a symbol of regeneration and rebirth. The enactment, the burning of the paper smeared with faeces, could be understood in terms of Sally assuming responsibility for something which she now felt *belonged* to her, as opposed to something that was fused and part of her.

A word of caution needs to be stated here. This happening was in no way directed by the therapist. It was Sally's idea, and she did not first tell me that she was going to do it. If she had I might have intervened with an interpretation, which would perhaps have halted the process. Destruction, particularly by fire, is potentially a very dangerous act, in more ways than the obvious. Fire has the potential of total destruction. In this case I assume this was a positive enactment. It was Sally's own solution to her own problem, and she took responsibility for the object and the enactment, only telling me after the event. The point here is that the lead came from the client. For a therapist to suggest destruction, of any kind, would be a very dubious intervention.

The later works which Sally made in thickly smeared paint could be seen as an abstraction or symbolization of the literal material of the original. They were *like* shit, but not made of it. I suspect the act of destruction enabled her to move on to the symbolic level. These later works had an 'as if' quality, which may be seen as a developmental stage further on from the magical identification with the image. A similar process to Sally's is described by Segal (1981: 56). She says that when a 'symbolic relation to faeces and other body products has been established, a projection can occur on to substances in the external world, such as paint, clay, etc.'. She says that a symbolic relation to faeces precedes the symbolic relation to paint and clay, the art object. By actually making use of her body products, which then became part of the symbolization process, Sally pre-empted this. For Sally I suspect that the faeces smeared on the paper were experienced in Segal's words as a 'good product of the ego's own creativity' (1981: 56). It was fused, undifferentiated, so at this stage it was not sublimation, nor symbolization. It contained all the elements of fusion, but it was outside of her. It was an 'out there' extension of an inner state – it was visible. It was perhaps an 'art symbol' (Langer 1957) at a crude level. It was a metaphor for her inner life, as well as the actual substance.

In Cassirer's description of the scapegoat (quoted at the start of this chapter) he describes how the katashiro was first marked with the name of the protagonist, who then rubbed it on his body and breathed on it, making his own very personal mark on it. The katashiro was then banished to the water, where the gods of purification took it away and with it the guilt. In a similar way Sally's paper was marked, touched by her, and then destroyed in a ritual burning, with the affirmation of an audience of sympathetic people. It is as if, intuitively, she performed this ritual. Her picture became a scapegoat in the way no therapist could ever have been. No human relationship, no interpretation could in any way have been substituted for this experience. Conversely, this experience could not have taken place without the therapeutic relationship, which in this case included, in addition to the therapist, the peer group of the community members. Here the image was given space to lead. Intuitively Sally decided how to deal with it. She consulted others and discussed the problem, but no deep-level interpretation was made. The interactions with others helped make sense of it, and held her. The art therapist was not her only, nor her prime, therapist, so transference interpretations would have been inappropriate.

In retrospect I see real dangers in not interpreting such actions at some stage in the process. Verbal interpretation, appropriately timed, does act as a positive limiting frame. To allow such an enactment without sufficient containment is dangerous. Here the community and the therapist were all aware of the process and involved enough to provide effective containment. Without this, if the patient is in too fragmented a state to conceptualize the experience, there is a very real danger of additional, and this time, destructive, acting out. It is possible that the primitive or latent material can be projected on to the world, not merely on to the paper, so that the power which may be seen as positive in relation to destroying a piece of paper, may be dangerous, if for example, it is extended to relationships with people. A ritual enactment, such as Sally's, is a way of bringing unformed contents to cognition, but it is also a potentially hazardous enterprise. A person who cannot distinguish between things, internal objects, part objects, and people needs the clear and safe boundaries of a therapeutic relationship as an outer container. The picture and the paper may be seen as the inner container. The burning of the inner container needs a carefully constructed outer boundary which is inviolable. The scapegoat transference in art therapy is a transference within a transference.

This event was the beginning of a long process of separation for Sally – of recognizing her own power. It was both a literal and a symbolic gesture of separation and purification. It was an experience different from that which analysis or psychotherapy without the picture-making process would have provided.

Scapegoat transference 2: baring the phenomenon

The second example of a scapegoat picture concerns Louise, a young woman in her mid-twenties. Louise had a dream which was so real that she awoke with a clear and vivid image of a corpse in the room with her. The next day she was haunted by this image and, in an attempt to come to terms with it, to put it outside of herself, she made a picture of it. She told me about the dream and about the picture, but she did not initially show me the picture. Her fear of the image was so great that she was convinced that it would affect me similarly. She thought that I too would be frightened by it, and that as a consequence I would know how 'bad' she was, and would reject her. She had made the image and was convinced it was visual evidence of her innate 'badness'. This image was no mere description of her dream. The image itself was experienced as powerful and fearsome.

As we saw, Sally's smeared paper was experienced as fused. Louise's image too was, I suspect, experienced as fused but in a different way. Her image was made in response to a powerful need to look at what she had glimpsed – a need to face that which she feared. Louise invested the picture with power, so that it became powerful in the process of its making. There was a 'real physical transference', in that the paper carrying the terrifying image was experienced, at this stage, as part of her.

> 'The dancer who appears in the mask of the god or demon does not merely imitate the god or demon, but assumes his nature; he is transformed into him and fuses with him. Here there is never a mere image, an empty representation; nothing is thought, represented, 'supposed' that is not at the same time real and effective.'
>
> (Cassirer 1955: II, 238)

Looking in more detail at this process, we could say that prior to its pictorial manifestation this image was 'homeless'. The dream had so frightened Louise that she wanted to reject the residual image; but it was relentless. She couldn't ignore it, and it wouldn't go away. She was obliged to take action, to do something with the feelings evoked by her dream. In the act of making the picture she unburdened herself. She put the image down, and faced it. As in the scapegoating process, previously described, she transferred the image to the paper. In making the picture she came to identify with the image she created. This, I suggest, was a 'transference of attributes' to the paper, in which the 'phenomenon was bared'. The picture had become an embodiment of her present emotional reality. In this way it also became empowered, a talisman. The picture acted as a container within which this unmanageable aspect was framed, 'out there' on the paper. The image itself, within the frame was, I suspect, experienced as fused, as part of her. The image of feeling was not projected out on to a person, though as therapist I may well have featured in her fantasies around the image. The transference was to the picture, which thus became, potentially at least, a scapegoat. In the act of making the picture Louise assumed some power, some authority over the image. She turned to face it and in so doing she started to accept responsibility for it. It was no longer denied or abandoned. It was contained but, at this stage, only in part owned.

We spent some time talking about her dream before Louise decided to show me the picture. Then we regarded the picture for a while, agreeing that it was indeed frightening. We talked around it, and around the feelings associated with it. With the image still present and visible to us both, we talked of other less directly related issues. What we did not do was approach its meaning directly, in an attempt to fully apprehend it. We worked with it, and we allowed it space in the light of day. In the context of a relationship, it was acknowledged. Gradually it became a little less frightening for Louise. It was starting to become familiar, and as an image becomes familiar it may begin to lose some of its power. When such an image is newly exposed it may be felt to be too threatening to look at or to discuss. The identification with the image at this stage means that it is experienced as too close, undifferentiated. Very often the necessary first stage of separation, or of symbolization of distancing from the image, is a private, self-reflective relationship between the artist and her picture. I am aware that it could be said that the reason that we didn't talk, at this stage, about Louise's picture was because we were both afraid of it, and what it might have implied. There may have been an element of this, but it was not the main reason. If I had made interpretations at this stage, or demanded explanations, I would have invaded the reflective process between Louise and her picture. An interpretation, even a very astute one, would have pre-empted the process and prematurely drawn her out of the necessary familiarization with, and assimilation of, the image. I suggest that by staying with Louise, and staying with her picture, I was giving her a message, the message of acceptance. By respecting the image and staying silent about it, its potential meanings and future directions were left open. It was allowed to grow for her in the direction it/she needed. This was evidenced in subsequent pictures.

Louise's image might be seen in the context of Jung's description:

'During the process of treatment the dialectical discussion leads logically to a meeting between the patient and his shadow, that dark half of the psyche which we invariably get rid of by means of projection.'

(Jung 1953: 29)

In looking at the picture in the context of a therapeutic relationship and in talking about it, Louise started to tame her image, and to bring it into her world rather than rejecting it. The aspect of herself that this image revealed was externalized in a way that harmed no one. The image mediated, and allowed the manifestation. Words mediated also, but only after the image had been exposed for a while. Subsequent images developed from this one, revealing her destructive, persecuted, and feared internalized world. Each new image was, initially, similarly fused but each one was a progression. They were like stepping stones towards owning and facing the shadow with its feared and demonic aspects.

There is little question that there was ambivalence in her anticipation of my rejection of her. It is also possible that I was identified or incorporated with the dream image; there was possibly a genuine fear of me. There were indeed transference elements in her relationship with me. At the time, however, this did not feature centrally. In such a community there are many staff involved with each patient, and Louise's main transference was to the staff member who ran her closed group. Her feelings were powerfully engaged with him, whilst my role, as the art therapist and a woman of a similar age to herself, seemed much more that of companion or guide on a journey. She used the art making, and me, to try and make sense of her feelings. Rather than working *in* the transference, we were engaged in a therapeutic alliance, which allowed for a transference to the picture to take place. Art therapists often find themselves in such a situation, whereby they are not in a sufficiently well-defined position, in relation to the setting, to clearly see the transference in operation. This can lead to a situation in which a split transference develops, all the good being invested with one therapist and all the bad with another. As far as I can know, this did not happen in this case. The point is that, within the space and relationship provided by the art room and my presence, Louise was able to work on facing her inner, conflicting images. She was able to project them, not on to a person, but on to an object, a piece of paper. Here they could not be denied. They had to be owned; no one else could be responsible for that image. For someone whose world was very fragmented, it would be possible to imagine that I had made her make the image, or in some magical way intervened in the process. In the sense that the picture was created in the context of a relationship, the picture could be seen as 'ours'. However, what was significant was that the picture offered a unique opportunity, within the therapeutic relationship, of containing the transference and simultaneously exhibiting it as an aspect of the artist.

Disposal in this case was not destruction of the image. Here destruction would have been, if not inconceivable, certainly a very negative act. Louise needed to live with, stay with this image; to destroy it would have been an attempt at denial, an attempt to push the image back into the darkness.

After the session described, we put the picture away in her folder, on the shelf with her other pictures. There it was kept, out of sight but accessible. We both knew it was there to be referred to and explored when she was ready. In putting it away safely, guarding it, we gave it a home, a place where it could be kept, out of sight, but not completely out of mind. It was still powerful, still a talisman, but by looking at it and then putting it away Louise had accepted some dominion over the image which she had created. She had claimed some power in relation to it, rather than being, as she had been at first, overpowered by it. If such an image is kept, it can be hidden away for weeks, even years, but its role as a talisman may continue until the person who made it feels ready to work with it. Each time the image is looked at by the artist it reflects its content back to her.

Each time we look at an image we have made, we feel slightly different about it – we see it in a different light. In this way the image interprets itself back to its maker, reminding her of how she felt, or what she experienced in making it. In evoking these feelings the picture is rather like the therapist who repeatedly brings the patient back to the painful area which she may wish to avoid. This usually takes place with the mediation of the relationship, and in the context of past and present images. The pictorial image formulates the feeling, bares the phenomenon, and brings it to light, but finally it is words which bring it to conscious acceptance. The timing and choice of words, as in all therapies, is crucial. As we have already seen, they must not intrude on the natural process of separation.

Summary

The scapegoat picture, in addition to its other qualities, allows for a physical enactment, as well as an internal assimilation – one for which there is no equivalent or substitute. In each of the two examples that I have given, the picture was more closely identified with its maker than a mere representation. In each case the picture was initially fused, the phenomenon was bared, and the picture became a scapegoat. It became a scapegoat in the sense that it was invested with power, and was then dealt with by disposal. Sally's scapegoat picture, invested with the power of her infantile and unacceptable aspects, was burned. The emotions linked with it were gradually assimilated, the process continuing long after the act. Louise's picture was less dramatically disposed of, by gradual familiarization, and then by keeping it stored, hidden but accessible. It was disposed of in the sense that it was given a place, both literally and metaphorically. As we saw earlier the therapist can never be disposed of, so the pictures played a role which no therapist, no person, could ever take on – a role for which there is no substitute.

As will be seen from Weir's description of Kleinian analytic theory (Chapter

4), there could be an analytic interpretation of both the cases which I have described. The meaning Hanna Segal (1981) makes of the process of symbol formation is very similar to the understanding which I have derived from Cassirer's philosophical approach. My reservation regarding psychoanalytic interpretations of art is what I perceive as the inherent assumption that ultimately the art process and the art object can be explained as mere symptoms of the artist's pathology. To follow such a theory to its logical conclusion, we might assume that in a perfectly analysed world there would be no art, and that mythical thinking would be seen as pathological and to be cured. The approach with which I am more in sympathy sees these phenomena in a different way. Here mythical thinking contains the seeds of self-healing. The image is accepted as needing space to live. The image is not so much analysed as *amplified*. The aim is rarely to reduce or stop the image, rather to permit it, to stay with it, in uncertainty, and to let it grow. This approach is closer to Jungian attitudes to imagery and is described by Avens:

> 'In contrast to the Freudian approach, Jung gave attention to the images in their own being. For example, he considers the dream imagery not so much as created by the censor to disguise the wishes of the unconscious, but as fully meaningful in its manifest content. Elaborating on this stance, archetypal psychology regards the image as "an irreducible and complete union of form and content . . . ". The inseparability of image and its content is described by Jung in these words: "Image and meaning are identical: and as the first takes shape so the latter becomes clear. Actually, the pattern needs no interpretation: it portrays its own meaning."
>
> Hillman suggests that the first rule in psychotherapy should be: "'stick to the image' . . . in its presentation" because "an image is complete just as it presents itself. (It can be elaborated and deepened by working on it, but to begin with it is all there. . . .)"'
>
> (Avens 1980: 37)

Magical thinking and fusion are not necessarily symptoms of pathology; although in certain cases they may be evidence of infantile processes. They are also a part of all embodied image-making. We may hypothesize that most artists may go through a similar process. First an image is powerful and private. Later it becomes public and separate. Eventually it is disposed of, kept, or abandoned, sold, or given away. Thus the most recent picture is usually the one with which we feel most identified. This is a healthy and adaptive process.

*

The talisman: a transference within a transference

Earlier in this chapter we saw how the picture in art therapy may become empowered, a talisman. We saw that the talisman may become a scapegoat, subject to a process of disposal. In this last part of the chapter I plan to explore disposal of the talisman in more detail.

Both Sally and Louise, described in the first part of this chapter, worked mainly in a therapeutic alliance (Greenson 1974). The role of the therapist was that of guide or companion on a journey. The therapist provided a safe environment wherein the client could enact her transference to the image and explore its meaning. In the three examples which follow, the therapist's role was more central. The pictures incorporated aspects of a transference relationship to the therapist, which evoked a corresponding counter-transference. My aim here is to show how an embodied image, made within the context of an empowered relationship, affects that relationship. This parallels psychotherapy without pictures, but is also distinct from it. One distinction is in the physical act of disposal.

We have seen that prior to the scapegoat is the talisman. The disposal of the scapegoat is only meaningful if the image disposed of is empowered. The making, the investing of the talisman picture, is the first stage of the process. The second stage, explored here, is the subsequent disposal of the picture. To dispose of a thing is not only to 'get rid' of it. The *Oxford English Dictionary* definitions of disposal include 'settling', 'dealing with', and 'bestowal'.

If the picture is kept or guarded within the setting of therapy, the therapist will, consciously or unconsciously, be incorporated in the decision. Frequently the therapist is active in keeping the work. One of the first things I do with new clients is to provide a folder, on which they write their names. This sets an expectation that their work will be kept together, safe and private, in the art room. It is common practice for art therapists to assert the value of the pictures in this way. In Chapter 2 Case refers to keeping a child's work on the blackboard during breaks, and the importance to that child of finding is still there on returning. In this way even in absence a part of them remains, ensuring that they are not forgotten. This is no less important with adults. People readmitted to a psychiatric hospital are reassured to find that the art therapist still has the folder containing their art work, even when the previous admission was many years ago. In this way the art therapist actively places a value on the work, the person, and the relationship.

The psychotherapist is said to 'hold' aspects of the client during therapy. This denotes a symbolic holding (Winnicott 1965, 1986). The art therapist also holds aspects for the client, as a person. In addition, she may literally hold something real and tangible. When the picture, which is experienced as a talisman, is left with the therapist, there may well be considerable significance in this holding for both people. The consequence of safekeeping the picture has, potentially, profound transference and counter-transference implications.

Counter-transference

The empowered relationship in any form of psychotherapy demands an ability in the therapist to enter into the imaginal space created between the participants – the two in individual therapy, the several in the group. The 'real' world is shut out, and the forces at play are experienced, responded to, and observed. When this is not fluid we look to the client to see what she may be experiencing in the transference. First we need to know, as well as we ever can, that it is not something in us, in the therapist, which is stopping the flow. When our own resistance is stopping us moving in a fluid matter, then this is for supervision, or our own therapy. This may seem obvious, but in this chapter I will be discussing my own responses and actions, as a therapist, in relation to people with whom I have worked. For this reason it is important for me to clarify my position regarding counter-transference. For the sake of argument I will artificially polarize the theoretical distinctions. There are two ways of regarding counter-transference: the first is to see it as a block, indicating the need for further analysis in the therapist. A therapist who is well enough analysed will be able to deal with the transference, reflecting it back, but remaining relatively unaffected. The second stance is to regard the counter-transference as the total experience of the therapist in the therapeutic relationship. This will include the feelings evoked by all the verbal and non-verbal messages from the client. The counter-transference in this case is the therapist's main guide to under-standing the transference. Feelings, attitudes, even fantasies which occur in the therapist, in the therapeutic relationship, are considered as potentially evoked as a response to the client's transference. This is not to blame the client for the feeling, but rather to attend to unconscious communication. Accepted and acknowledged, rather than acted upon, this deepens our understanding, and in turn deepens the client's relation to her unconscious. The latter is the approach to which I am closer. Rather than try to summarize such a vast topic any further, I refer the reader to some of the many sources: Fordham (1978), Greenson (1974), Langs (1974), Kernberg (1975), Racker (1974), and Searles (1979).

If it is the case that all the messages from the client affect the counter-transference, then the painted messages will be no exception. In art therapy the counter-transference is influenced in several ways by the pictures. Dalley (Chapter 1) refers to Kuhns (1983) and Wood (1984) in this regard. In the following material I will focus on an aspect of the transference and counter-transference, to the art object itself, and its influence on the therapeutic relationship. We have seen that the therapist needs to be fluid in approach, to move through different levels of experience. For the artist/therapist resources include, in addition to our life experience, our personal history of art, and our knowledge and appreciation of, as well as preference for, certain types of art. Our response to the person may sometimes be influenced by our aesthetic appreciation of the picture; our appreciation of the picture is at other times influenced by our appreciation of the person; the effects of the imagery work both ways. Consequently, it is possible to see that there will be times when the image itself may provoke strong feelings, even occasionally mythical thinking, in the therapist. The pictures in therapy may be experienced in a wide variety of ways. They may be felt, more or less consciously, to be an attack, a seduction, a shared joke, or a decoy. They may feature as an aspect of the transference, or as an enactment of it. They may be empowered by both people, or one, as a talisman or charm. When so much is potentially invested in them, it may be understood how at times the therapist can be drawn into a picture, in more than one sense.

In the following pages I plan to focus on three incidents in therapy. In different ways each picture was a talisman, and each revealed the incorporation of the transference relationship in the solution to the problem of disposal. The first was a container for unwanted projections, the second a link between sessions, and the third a gift.

The talisman as a container for unwanted projections

It is the integrated function of a talisman that it in some way benefits its possessor. It may have this effect by keeping the good powers invested in it safe. This will be pursued later. It may benefit its possessor by carrying the bad, the ills, away.

In a section of *The Golden Bough* entitled 'The transference of Evil', Frazer (1922) gives accounts of evil and sickness being transferred to objects, which then become scapegoats. In some such cases the objects are placed in the path, where some casual passer-by will inadvertently contract the affliction, and thus take it away. Others are more personally intended:

> 'To cure toothache some of the Australian blacks apply a heated spear-thrower to the cheek. The spear-thrower is then cast away, and the toothache goes with it in the shape of a black stone called 'kariitch'. Stones of this kind are found in old mounds and sandhills. They are carefully collected and thrown in the direction of enemies in order to give them toothache.'
> (Frazer 1922: 539)

He describes leaves and stones being used in similar ways to dispel fatigue. The traveller who is tired strikes himself with leaves or stones and then disposes of them, in a place set apart for the purpose. These eventually become cairns or heaps of sticks which mark a place as significant. Frazer makes an important distinction in this passage. He makes it clear that this is not a religious ritual, explaining that 'the thing thrown on the heap is not an offering to spiritual powers and the words which accompany the act are not a prayer. It is nothing but a magical ceremony for getting rid of fatigue' (Frazer 1922: 540). It seems that, for Frazer, the distinction between magic and religion is related to the level of ceremony to which the empowered object is subjected in the process of its disposal. Perhaps we could equate the ceremony of the religious empowering with a conscious act; and the more magical empowering with an act which is less conscious. This distinction might help in understanding a process in art therapy, illustrated by a man I shall call Gary.

Gary did not empower his talisman picture in any conscious way. There was no ritual involved. His talisman became empowered in spite of himself. I suspect that Gary empowered his picture unconsciously, and then, rather like the incidents described above, attempted to dispose of it without acknowledging it. Unconsciously, he attempted to pass the unacceptable contents of his picture to me – to get me to take on, and take away, the disease. This evoked a counter-transference response in me.

When Gary was a patient in the psychiatric hospital he came to me twice a week for art therapy, as a member of a group. During this time he made many pictures which did not affect him in an important way. They described his conscious feelings. Then one day he made a picture of a face, painted in red on black paper. It was looking out of the paper, like a reflection. Such a position is common and often indicates an unconscious need to 'face' something. This was a picture he was quite unable to look at, and it was quickly despatched to the storage shelf. He was discharged from hospital after a few months, continuing to see me on a weekly basis, individually. At this time he took all the pictures he had made – all, that is, except one. This one I found when tidying the shelf some months later. It was the one he had feared when he made it. I told Gary I had found it, and he asked to see it. When he did, he recoiled in horror; he had forgotten it and didn't want to be reminded. In my view this was his most important picture emotionally, and his best aesthetically. Inadvertently his power had leaked into it, and it had tapped the source of his genuine creativity.

For Gary his creativity was frightening, bound up with his fear of violence. In the time I worked with him, he was never able to face squarely this aspect of himself, the demonic, the dreadful. When he dreamed of violence he asked, 'Why do I dream such violent dreams? This is not me, I am a gentle person.' Unable to face what his dreams and this picture revealed, he rejected a part of his own nature. He had difficulty in owning the attacker in himself. The picture embodied this rejected aspect; in it I suspect he saw both victim and attacker, so he ran from it, leaving it with me. One day sitting with him in silence, I had a fantasy in which I felt him leap across the room to me in violence. Momentarily after this he announced that the previous day he had been interviewed by police investigating a violent crime. He was flattered to have been considered capable of, as he saw it, so powerful an act. The power of his repressed sexuality and violence was expressed in his pictures, his dreams, and even in the images he evoked in me. While he worked with me he never admitted his power. He came to see me regularly for more than two years, then one day, without indicating his intention, he left. It is possible that he was experiencing bad feelings for me, which he dared not face. In a similar way he had left his picture, in the hospital. He did not take it with him this time either.

My observations above, although elaborated by hindsight, indicate the type of verbal interventions I made. The picture, as well as embodying a transference itself, was also one manifestation of the transference relationship. The picture, the dream, and the relationship to the therapist were all indications of the same psychic process. There is much I could explore in this incident regarding Gary's history, my interventions, and, retrospectively, what I consider to have been my mistakes; but this is not my purpose. My purpose is to point out the specific role of the pictorial image within the psychotherapeutic relationship – to distinguish what it is that is special about art therapy.

Earlier in the chapter we saw that for a picture to be an effective scapegoat, the empowered nature of the image must be acknowledged. Gary's picture became a talisman in spite of his conscious resistance. This is common for if we let go we cannot tell what will appear on the paper in front of us. For Gary 'the phenomenon was bared', the image was visible, but he didn't want to see it. In some layer of consciousness, Gary experienced his picture as having 'taken on' his harmful aspect. This was not consciously acknowledged, nor was it assimilated. It was actively rejected. So whereas Louise (see p. 91), whose image was similar in many ways to Gary's, became gradually familiar with her image, Gary could not allow a process of familiarization, and so the image continued to have dominion over him. In the sense that it was empowered and that it 'held' the split-off aspects, this picture was an object of transference.

Gary's talisman was not, I think, left with me for safekeeping, rather it was surreptitiously deposited on 'my' art room shelf. It may be of interest to examine the counter-transference evoked by both the image and the treatment of it. When the image was first made I felt neutral. It was a picture which was put away to be reclaimed later. It is common for this type of image to be unacceptable when it is first exposed. When Gary rejected it a second time, many months later, I felt at a loss. The decision about disposal was left to me. I still kept it; the alternative would have been to insist that he make some other decision. This would have been analogous to imposing an interpretation. I kept this unwanted interpretation, and waited for the time to come when he might recognize a need to look at it. I do not remember whether I interpreted verbally my feeling regarding the meaning of his leaving the decision to me. In retrospect this seems important. By this time he had stopped making pictures. Both these incidents could be seen in terms of veiled aggression, towards me, an art therapist. Not to paint, nor to own the existing pictures are effective ways of de-skilling an art therapist (see Chapter 7 by Diane Waller). They also reflected Gary's very real inability to move. I no longer wanted this one lost image. Keeping it served no useful purpose if he had truly abandoned it. My own magical thinking was evoked, and I now saw the picture as dangerously powerful. This I see as a counter-transference response on many levels, the most obvious being the message which Gary was giving – that it was dangerous, and *I* should keep it – a message not stated, but implied. If Gary had been able to work with this picture, it is possible that these negative elements could have combined with positive ones, so freeing his inner world. But we were stuck, and this image indicated where.

When I began to think about writing this, I thought to seek out this picture, to look at it again. I cannot find it, and suspect that eventually I did destroy it myself. This is most unusual, for I keep pictures for years after people leave, in case they should return. Interestingly, too, I don't remember doing it. I see this as a revealing unconscious counter-transference, acted out in relation to the image. It may have been that I acted out my anger at the way Gary left, feeling that he had passed his unwanted image to me. Without him to work it through, my having or keeping his picture was pointless, but I suspect my feeling was more complex than that, and stronger. There is a link here with Frazer (1922), and his description of the transference of toothache to an enemy via a stone thrown, or strategically placed. A similar unconscious process could be seen in the disposal of Gary's picture – an object experienced as holding the 'bad', abandoned unceremoniously, in a place which presumably was seen as mine. This could have similar implications, and would account for some of my discomfort in relation to the image – something I very rarely feel, no matter how disturbing the content of a picture. Here then, the problem of disposal of the scapegoat was solved by leaving it to the therapist. If this talisman benefited its possessor, it was by a disposal into another person, who was not just a casual passer-by. This picture and its handling was an integrated aspect of the transference/counter-transference relationship.

The talisman as a link between sessions

A talisman which is invested with good may also benefit its possessor. In this case it is experienced as precious and special, and it must be guarded. Should it be lost, destroyed, or even merely carelessly neglected, the good power it holds may be damaged or it may evaporate. A talisman's power must be kept alive. A good luck charm must be kept safe for its properties to remain effective.

> 'In connection with Egyptian coronation ceremonies we have exact instruction governing transference of the gods' attributes to the Pharaoh through the regalia, the scepter, the scourge, the sword. These are looked upon not as mere symbols but as true talisman-vehicles and guardians of divine forces.'
>
> (Cassirer 1955: II, 56–7)

Here the investment in the talisman has a profound religious significance, which is conveyed to the objects through a ritual. The benefit of the empowered objects will be derived if they are carefully kept, and valued as carriers of the invested powers.

In western culture we might see the wedding ring as a talisman empowered in one of the few ritualized ceremonies still accepted. The ritual empowers the ring to 'stand for' the marriage, even when the ceremony is devoid of a religious service; but only if the people involved in the ceremony choose to see it that way. If such a ring is lost, or mislaid, there may ensue fear that the marriage will suffer. A person who attaches great importance to the ring may feel desolate at its loss. Another person, perhaps more practical, will see it as merely a replaceable object. It is, then, the attitude of mind of the possessor that makes an object into a talisman. We transfer power to objects by permitting ourselves to attach magical or emotional significance to them.

In art therapy the picture may be invested with magical or emotional significance. This investment may be made by the possessor alone or by both the people involved. At times it may be invested by a group. An object or picture created in art therapy may be a talisman which functions as a charm, a link between sessions. A picture may be experienced as unfinished, not yet assimilated, and left with the therapist for safe-keeping.

A student art therapy group was coming to an end. With five weeks to go, considerable ambivalence (as well as sadness) about ending was expressed. In this session Sarah made three clay models which were obviously important for her personally. They were also clearly significant for other members of the group. This was not unusual in this group. On many occasions one person's very personal image took on significance for other members. In this way the transferences and counter-transferences to the images were echoes of the multiple projections within the group. Frequently the pictures revealed the complex, inarticulable levels of the interactions, and subtly influenced them. When Sarah spoke about her objects she handled them, with great care. It seemed that they were very much part of her, that she felt identified with them. There were several layers of significance in the role of these objects. First, they were invested with power by Sarah in a very personal way. They had meaning for Sarah in the context of current group themes, to which they were an indirect response. Sarah's models also had considerable significance for other group members, some of whom admitted to feeling identified with them. So, these objects were invested with power by Sarah, by other group members, and I suspect, also by me. When the session ended Sarah asked me if she could leave them somewhere to dry. The room we were in was used for other purposes during the week, so they could not be left there. Half consciously aware of the significance of my offer, and half unconsciously, I suggested she leave them in the office I share with two other people. (Here I must point out that the students usually look after their own work. The therapist/tutor is not identified with a particular studio. The shared office would be seen as my space, and my desk the only part of it which is wholly mine.) I would not have suggested this earlier in the group's life, but, now, as the end was near, it seemed appropriate. Intuitively I allowed this flexibility of the group boundary. It was a way of relinquishing the previously structured boundaries, a way of preparing for ending. Perhaps too, it was a way of revealing something of my own involvement in the group. When I entered the office I found the models placed, not just anywhere, but on the corner of my desk. Although I had suggested my room, Sarah had (I think) solicited this suggestion and selected my desk.

> 'It has been suggested that mythical thought functions according to the principle of *pars pro toto* (a part can stand for the whole): the image or the thing (for example, a lock of hair) is experienced as a genuine presence containing the power, the significance and efficacy of the whole (the man). The meaning of images dwells in the images themselves as life dwells in the body.'
> (Avens 1980: 60)

Sarah had left something of value with me: a talisman. Perhaps unconsciously she wanted to maintain a link with me/the group during the week, and to ensure that she was remembered. I did nothing with the models. I could have moved them to a less prominent place, but I chose not to. They were just there, on my desk each day, a reminder of Sarah and of the group. I was living with her objects, getting to know them. One evening, before the group session, as I was falling asleep, they flitted into my awareness, and their meaning seemed to become clearer. They were working on me, deepening my understanding of their role in the group. At the end of the following week's group session Sarah reclaimed her sculptures. She realized that there were other places she could have left them, and that she had chosen to leave them with me.

Sarah's talismans were not empowered in a conscious ritual. Instead they were unconsciously endowed with meaning. 'The meaning of images dwells in the images themselves as life dwells in the body' (Avens 1980: 60). Sarah was identified with her objects. The talisman was, I think, felt to be literally a part of her. The meaning and the images were fused. The process of separating, of acknowledgement and conscious understanding, was to grow. Asking me to hold them during the week was the start of this process. They were, perhaps, too important and unresolved to leave uncared for at this stage. There was another aspect; the images were identified with the group, so leaving them with me stood for leaving them with the group, keeping it alive during the week. This was intensified as the group was soon to end. The need to separate was not only the need to separate from personal images, but for the group members to separate from a state of identification with each other, and each other's images.

For my part, I was aware that my holding Sarah's images might affect other group members, but it felt as if I was holding this talisman, not just for Sarah, but for the group in which it had been created and empowered. For me it was not only Sarah's talisman, it was the group's talisman.

This incident illustrates how the empowered object may become a way of keeping 'in touch', of maintaining a process and of affecting the transferences and counter-transferences in a group, as well as in individual therapy. In the group this will involve a more complex set of interactions, which will include all the participants and the therapist. Here again, the role of the art object is far more potent than a mere aid to communication. It actively affects and influences the process.

The talisman as a gift

A gift may have a multitude of meanings and functions. It may, for example, be seen as giving of oneself, as standing for affection, respect, or love. Usually it is associated with positive feelings. There is pleasure in giving pleasure. It is enjoyable to bestow on another something we have made or chosen to give them. This is not a totally unselfish act – we get a return from the other's pleasure. The act of sex is the ultimate example of this, where two people give and take simultaneously. We learn the pleasure of giving from the earliest stages, if all goes well. Earlier in the chapter we saw that for an infant its faeces may be such a gift. The pleasure in the act of giving is nurtured by the first parental figures, by their genuine delight in receiving. A child's first attempts at art are a good illustration. We see the child grow in spirit before our eyes, when its gift is well received by adults. Here the gift is more than the mere thing, it is an object through which a child's worth is symbolically affirmed. The child interacts with the adult world and in return receives something back from that world.

There are ritualized forms of giving which have more archaic significance. There is, for example, the offering of the first fruits of the harvest, as thanks giving, and in order to ensure the abundance of future harvests. This gift has magical significance. There is an investment in performing the act of giving, which is propitiatory. The gift is an appeasement of the powerful spirits or the god. Embodied within this positive act is an acknowledgement of the dangerous implications of not giving. These two forms of giving, although apparently different, are also profoundly interlinked – giving as a token of friendship, and giving as an insurance against reprisal, in the form of future paucity.

The pictures made by Alex demonstrated both these forms of giving. When he became an in-patient, Alex made numerous pictures. These were certainly acceptable as pictures in their own right, and his friends and the nurses appreciated them. He gave them away to all who requested them and to some who didn't, willingly dispersing them. One day, only a short time after his admission, I was surprised by his gift to me of a picture. A very sunny and light image, it incorporated my name. I have mentioned this elsewhere (Schaverien 1982: 11). This picture was in direct contrast to other images he was making at the time, which exhibited his depression and distress. At the time, I was confused by this gift, but accepted it, keeping it carefully in the art room. He told me he had made similar pictures for his mother and his aunts; clearly I was in the same category in some way. When I realized that his pictures were all disappearing, claimed by family and friends, I intervened. I asked him to keep the originals of all his pictures for the duration of his treatment. The pictures were small, so he was able to photocopy them, which meant he could give them away, as well as keeping them. This solved the immediate problem, and later he no longer wanted to give them away.

Alex's disposal process changed. His initial method of disposal of his empowered images was as gifts. This was a way of pleasing others – an offering to his mother, family, friends, and myself; a token of quite complex feelings. If 'a part can stand for the whole' (Avens 1980: 60), Alex could be seen to have been giving parts of himself away. My early intervention, asking him to keep his pictures together for the duration of his treatment, was based on a feeling that Alex was dispersing his power. I was later to learn that this graphically illustrated one of his relationship difficulties. At the time I knew that, in order to work with his pictures, we needed to assemble them all in one place. The pictures embodied his inner state and were beginning to reflect the therapeutic relationships he was making. His inclusion of myself, in with his mother and aunts, indicated that this was happening. In order to understand the transference, all the feelings need to be centred with one therapist. Otherwise, the transference becomes indistinguishable from the reality situation. The dispersal of Alex's pictures was an analogous lack of containment. I asked Alex to keep all his talismans, his transference pictures, in one place, accessible to him and retrievable. Pictures are rarely isolated. They usually follow each other and link in a meaningful sequence. If they are prematurely dispersed this meaning is no longer accessible in this embodied form. By my intervention I gave Alex permission to keep his pictures for himself. Symbolically I was valuing Alex, taking seriously the painful content of his pictures, and temporarily disregarding the fact that they were well executed. In this case this was important, because all the world responded to the surface quality, but ignored the pain they revealed. This is the visual equivalent of responding to the superficial smile, without realizing that behind it the person is in pain. In aesthetic terms the visual impact of a work is dependent on the emotional content – they are inseparable. This was the case with Alex's work but it was responded to without cognizance, on the part of his audience, that there was a process involved which related to his hospitalization. In this sense, the art therapist teaches her client to stay with and value his work, giving weight to its unconscious meanings.

Alex did value his pictures at the time, and his giving them away was evidence of this. His way of valuing them was as a way of pleasing others, an expression of affection for his mother, aunts, and me. In the main the recipients were women, which may well have indicated his need to appease the 'great mother', in archetypal terms. By this I mean his internalized image of 'mother'. He may have feared that if she was not kept 'good' her awesome power, wrath, and sexuality would be unleashed and would overwhelm him. I do not have space to pursue this in depth here, as it would mean considerable discussion of Alex's presenting difficulties. The main point I wish to extract is that the gifts, although consciously well intended, had a negative aspect; the need to keep the women, who were important to him, good, idealized, and controlled. The good was split off from the bad and attributed to the women in his life, particularly his mother, who was over-idealized. In asking him to keep his pictures I was asking him to keep his projections for himself. Once he did so it was possible for him to work with them and recognize the split. In our work together he faced some very painful realizations which included accepting the opposite side of his mother, the aspect he feared and even hated. The picture he had given me was a manifestation of the same process. While he was feeling in the depths of despair and depression, he gave me his good. Towards the end of his time in hospital he made another image, which exhibited all the elements which were displayed in the picture he had given me. This time he didn't give it away. He was able to keep the good, and recognize it as belonging to himself. He was also able to see how important it had been for him to keep his pictures.

Alex's pictures were talismans, in that they were embodied images of his inner world. He was engaged in them from the beginning, as if he knew intuitively what he had to do. It was in the process of disposal that significance of the talisman changed. From an offering to appease and please others, they became containers of his own power, so that when he left hospital he took them with him and was able to value them.

Conclusion

In this section I have attempted to show, by examples, three ways in which the art object in the therapeutic setting was simultaneously both an object of transference and counter-transference itself, and an aspect of the transference and counter-transference relationship with the therapist. In this way the transference in art therapy is a transference within a transference. There are two transferences – linked, but also separate. The first is to the picture itself, the second is to the person of the therapist; these overlap, but are slightly different in effect. The transference to the picture is, in essence, a dialogue with the self, a reflection of, and on, the inner world. The transference to the therapist may well be incorporated in this, but it is also inter-personal. There are times when transference to the picture features very centrally without a strong transference to the therapist, as we saw earlier in the chapter. There are also times when the transference to the therapist is exhibited and incorporated in the picture; the picture here becomes an integral aspect of the transference and counter-transference. I hope that this has been illustrated in this last part of the chapter, in which I have selected three enactments of disposal of the talisman picture to demonstrate how the process of disposal extends therapeutic possibilities. The physicality of the object adds a dimension to therapy – which can take no other form. This distinguishes art therapy, in emphasis and in practice, from other forms of psychotherapy.

© 1987 Joy Schaverien

References

Avens, R. (1980) *Imagination is Reality*. Dallas: Spring.

Cassirer, E. (1955 and 1957) *The Philosophy of Symbolic Forms*. London: Yale University Press. (1955) *Vol. I: Language*. (1955) *Vol. II: Mythical Thought*. (1957) *Vol. III: The Phenomenology of Knowledge*.

Fordham, M. (1978) *Jungian Psychotherapy*. Chichester: John Wiley.

Frazer, J. G. (1922) *The Golden Bough* (abridged edition). London: Macmillan (1959).

Freud, S. (1912) The Dynamics of Transference. Standard Edition (1963) Vol. 12. London: Hogarth Press and the Institute of Psychoanalysis.

Freud, S. (1915) Observations on Transference Love. Standard Edition (1963) Vol. 12. London: Hogarth Press and the Institute of Psychoanalysis.

Gellner, E. (1985) *The Psychoanalytic Movement*. London: Palladin.

Greenson, R. (1974) *The Technique and Practice of Psychoanalysis*. London: Hogarth.

Hillman, J. (1972) *The Myth of Analysis*. New York: Harper Row.

Hillman, J. (1979) *The Dream and the Underworld*. New York: Harper Row.

Jones, E. (1953/1955) *Sigmund Freud: Life and Work*. 2 vols. London: Hogarth.

Jung, C. G. (1953) *Psychology and Alchemy* (CW: 12). London: Routledge.

Jung, C. G. (1956) *Symbols of Transformation* (CW: 5). Princeton: Bollingen.

Jung, C. G. (1959a) *Archetypes and the Collective Unconscious* (CW: 9). Princeton: Bollingen.

Jung, C. G. (1959b) *Aion* (CW:9). Princeton: Bollingen.

Kernberg, O. (1975) *Borderline Conditions and Pathological Narcissism*. New York: Aronson.

Klein, M. (1961) *Narrative of a Child Analysis*. London: Hogarth.

Klein, M. (1980) *The Psychoanalysis of Children*. London: Hogarth.

Kohut, H. (1971) *The Analysis of the Self*. New York: International Universities Press.

Kuhns, R. (1983) *Psychoanalytic Theory of Art*. New York: Columbia University Press.

Langer, S. (1953) *Feeling and Form*. London: Routledge.

Langer, S. (1957) *The Problems of Art*. London: Routledge.

Langs, R. (1974) *Psychoanalytic Psychotherapy*. New York: Aronson.

Langs, R. (1980) *Interactions*. New York: Aronson.

Malcolm, J. (1980) *Psychoanalysis: The Impossible Profession*. London: Picador.

Neumann, E. (1970) *The Origins and History of Consciousness*. New York: Routledge.

Schaverien, J. (1982) Transference as an Aspect of Art Therapy. *Inscape* (Journal of BAAT) September.

Searles, H. (1965) *Collected Papers on Schizophrenia*. New York: International Universities Press.

Searles, H. (1979) *Countertransference*. New York: IUP.

Segal, H. (1981) *The Work of Hanna Segal*. New York: Aronson.

Racker, H. (1974) *Transference and Countertransference*. London: Hogarth.

Winnicott, D. W. (1965) *The Maturational Process and the Facilitating Environment*. London: Hogarth.

Winnicott, D. W. (1986) *Holding and Interpretation*. London: Hogarth.

Wood, M. (1984) The Child and Art Therapy. In T. Dalley (ed.) *Art as Therapy*. London: Tavistock.

Addendum

The ideas expressed here are unfinished and should not be regarded as conclusive in this state. This work is in progress and the chapter indicates the stage of development of these ideas at the time of publication.

Acknowledgements

I would like to thank Dr Anthony Winterbourne and Professor Richard Wollheim for invaluable constructive criticism of various drafts, Peter Wilson for his timely comments on the text and for his continuous encouragement, and Galia and Damien: their humour always brings me back to reality.

4 | The role of symbolic expression in its relation to art therapy: a Kleinian approach

Felicity Weir

In this chapter I will attempt to provide an explanation of how the emotional/ego development of the individual affects his use of symbolic expression. This will be described within a psychoanalytic framework, using the Kleinian approach to psychoanalysis, which in itself, places great emphasis on the emotional attitude adopted by the infant towards his/her environment during the different stages of ego development. I will also illustrate how such infantile attitudes still prevail in the adult, and how they are essential to life's fundamental meaning. I will also show how such attitudes can become cripplingly dominant in the emotionally disturbed individual. This fluctuation will be exemplified by the symbolic relationship which the artist has towards his work, and which both corresponds and is mirrored by the way he relates to his environment. In addition I include some examples of visual expression done within a therapeutic setting which help to illustrate the relationship which the patient/artist has with his work.

The origins of symbolic expression

In tracing the origins of symbolic expression I need to refer to the early stage of infantile development, in order to describe how the infant's emotional and psychological attitude prevents the natural progression of symbol formation. I also intend to explore the various methods of defence employed by the ego which act as a hindrance to this process. But first we need a definition of symbolic expression.

Broadly speaking, the psychoanalytic definition of a symbol involves a mode of indirect and figurative representation of an unconscious idea, conflict, or wish. In other words, the projected and repressed impulses of the psyche, detached from the original 'object' are instead transferred to another. In this sense psychoanalysis holds any substitute formation to be symbolic. It ought to be established that my use of the word 'object' will refer to the Kleinian notion of 'internal objects' which are presumed to be images or ideas of his parents that the infant may construct in his mind. These are introjected, that is, enshrined within the self. Such internal objects may have little bearing on external reality.

The use of symbolic behaviour is, according to Melanie Klein, a necessary development of the ego as a defence against separation. The infant, having internalized an image of its mother, needs to be able to maintain this image in her absence. This image becomes projected on to external objects in order for the child to be able to re-create the mother/child relationship in the outside world, thus enabling him to gradually become more independent of her. This describes Winnicott's idea of a 'transitional object', whereby the child's toy becomes to symbolize the mother, but having been created by the child, it is in fantasy under his omnipotent control.

During the early stage of ego development the mental functioning of the child is governed by omnipotent fantasies which provide a necessary barrier against those disturbing elements belonging to external reality. As a result, little differentiation between reality and fantasy exists. The omnipotent ideas of the infant thus become reality. According to Klein the early stages of emotional development are not only dominated by these omnipotent fantasies, but also by intense emotion of love and hate. This last she refers to as sadism, which is seen to be partly constitutional and partly due to the fact that the infant is in no position to appreciate, and therefore tolerate, the fact that his instinctual needs cannot always be satisfied. Such frustration can only be viewed by the omnipotent infant as a sadistic attack on himself.

Klein places great emphasis on the sadistic drives of the individual, which she considers provide a basis for mental illness. The fact that sadism is present in early infancy, or from birth onwards, helps us to appreciate that the infant would need internal protection from its own destructive fantasies.

The most significant of the defences employed by the ego against sadism is projection. The infant here perceives the object of his projected aggression as the container of aggression towards him, thereby defending himself against the pain of experiencing his own sadistic desires. In addition, the primitive ego attempts to redirect this sadism, so that the loved 'object' will be saved from destruction, through the mechanism of 'displacement', which is a corporal part of 'projection'. Displacement enables the infant's persecutory fears, and the concern for the loved 'object' to be located in other activities and interests. These now become the focus for instinctual drives and fantasies, thereby forming a fusion with the original 'object' and its substitute. Furthermore, when excessive 'projection' persists, the fantasied flight from the apparent source of danger leaves the subject prey to constant persecution. This is due to the fact that the substitute 'object' also becomes invested with the same anxiety that the infant associated with its original. The infant is thus constantly compelled to make new substitute symbols.

The role of projection in art

The effect of excessive 'projection' can be seen in a number of trained artists who went mad, and whose work underwent a significant change as a result. Among them was a German sculptor, Franz Messerschmidt (1736–84). According to Ernst Kris (1952: 128–58) Messerschmidt felt compelled to create agonizing grimaces in his sculptural busts. He believed that they would ward off and intimidate those demons that he thought would come to annihilate him. By so doing Messerschmidt convinced himself that he had achieved miraculous power over them. Here we can see how such works of art are no longer meant to communicate themselves to the minds of the spectators, but are instead intended to gain control over the 'psychotic external world, which contains those persecutory objects' arising from 'projected sadism'. By his creation Messerschmidt commands his persecutors, exercising an omnipotent control. This way of retaliating illustrates a regression in ego functioning to an earlier stage of development, in which projection and omnipotence maintain a dominant role, this in turn reversing the separation of the ego from the outside world. Art in this instance has deteriorated from communication to sorcery, where we are reminded of defensive magic in the rituals of many pre-literature societies. In psychotic art, of the nature just described, the artist speaks mainly to and for himself, but he is held prisoner by his delusions. In this respect one distinction between so-called real art and psychotic art is that the sane artist does voluntarily what the psychotic is compelled to do. In other words, in normal adult behaviour, the cycles of alternating levels of ego functioning are under the control of the individual, slipping in and out of fantasy at will.

Another similar example was found in the once-a-week art therapy sessions I had with a 10-year-old girl called Paddy. Paddy had been referred to the clinic by her school, who had found her to lack concentration in her work. Such under-functioning was in marked contrast to her well-above-average intellectual potential. I first met Paddy in a joint interview involving both her and her mother. I remembered how struck I was by the inhibition Paddy displayed when answering my questions. Instead they were answered by her mother. Paddy seemed only too willing for her mother to speak on her behalf. Her dependence on her mother seemed abnormally strong. They had managed to create a fusion between them where it became impossible to determine their separate identities.

One of the main themes that developed out of her sessions with me was her preoccupation with witches. The witch image would occur regularly, in different forms: there was a witch mother, a witch child, a witch cat, and a witch, all expressing one concept. At root it came from her perception of a split-off bad part of her 'internal object'. In this instance it was Paddy's image of how she viewed her mother, whom she saw as dangerous and persecuting. Such primitive fantasies arise at a time when sadism (projected or otherwise) is at its height. In Paddy's case they were embodied in the symbol of the witch, representing those feelings of persecution which the infant has towards its mother, and which can still be seen to persist in later life. The way Paddy coped with her paranoid anxiety in relation to this image is exemplified by her creation of the 'witch' children. Paddy made them into two free standing figures, and told me that she would like them to cast spells and punish those people whom she felt had been nasty to her. Soon after completing these children, she quite suddenly felt that they had come alive. At this point Paddy shot a fearful glance at me, as if she had just recognized me as the bad witch, and as if she was experiencing me in the same way that the infant part of herself had experienced the persecuting mother. When I put this to her she became quite frightened and moved away to a table at the far end of the room. I then emphasized that she had made me into a bad witch, but at the same time I knew that I was no such person. This latter comment appeared to reduce her anxiety. Her reaction to my interpretation suggests that she not only confused her 'witch' symbol with me by associating me with the 'internal' bad image of her mother, but during such moments the lack of differentiation between the ego's internal image and the symbol it represents caused the distinction between fantasy and reality to become blurred. As a result the witch mother image had been made real. In order to escape these feelings of persecution Paddy's ego attempted to transfer her 'projected sadism' from something of her own creation, which she might have felt to have been too much a part of herself and therefore linked to her own aggression, to someone quite separate, and therefore less frightening. This shift may have been due to her need to externalize her conflicts, so that they could be directed away from the warring internal situation within her. If left in this form they can only repeat a perpetual cycle of self-destruction. Klein sums up the infant's defence against experiencing its own sadism through the mechanisms of 'projection' and 'identification' by saying, that 'such identification, the forerunner of symbolism, arises out of the transformation of interest to less attached and so less frightening substitutes, that establish the foundation of symbolism and from which all sublimations and talents spring (Klein 1975: 220).

However it is important to bear in mind that this description of Paddy's behaviour would also seem to indicate that her ego was operating on a sliding scale of emotional development in the way in which her witches changed from being 'symbolic' to becoming real. During the time that she experienced the 'witch mother' as actual her ego was functioning on a regressed level of emotional development. Such regression is a result of increased persecutory anxiety (projected sadism). Although the act of regression prevents ego disintegration, it none the less means that the distinction between the 'symbol' and the 'persecutory object' is blurred. The point at which Paddy's ego had regressed can be seen directly to correspond with the early stage of ego development in which the infant tends to use 'projection' excessively. This in turn curtails his ability to develop his own sense of identity, preventing him from distinguishing between reality and fantasy. The relationship Paddy had towards her mother exemplifies this. Alternatively, the infant's fear of his projected sadism can cause the symbolic relations he has towards the substitute 'object', representing his feelings for the original, to be denied. This is turn can hamper his curiosity towards the outside world and consequently his own developing imagination and creativity.

A primitive state of fusion

I wish now to return to examine the primitive state of fusion between subject and object to reveal a different example of how omnipotent thinking influences the relationship the artist has with his work. In the egocentric stage of development the child believes he has created his mother, but also belonging to this stage the infant's perception of the world is experienced through his bodily sensations, referred to as the 'body ego', which stipulates that the all-embracing bodily sensations of infanthood are bound up with primitive psychic processes and are the means by which the child experiences and expresses emotions. Indeed, generally speaking all communication is received through the senses. The way in which, for example, the artist uses his material to externalize his thoughts and feelings is physical. Bruno Bettelheim (1967: 106–10) describes this process in his observation of autistic children. He observes how the rich textural effects of the paint and other substances smeared by their hands are reminiscent of the child's earliest preoccupations with the tactile experience of their bodies. It is not difficult to imagine how any mark or line can portray the pressure and tension of the hand holding the brush. In other words a broad sweep of a brush stroke could be seen as a result of a larger action which may have emanated from a tension from within the body of the artist. Likewise Marion Milner, a psychoanalyst with a great interest in art, explains that the medium used in a work of art is derived from stages of interest in different aspects of bodily experience: 'The artist . . . is making available for recall and contemplation . . . what he feels to be the most important moments of his feeling life, his psycho-physical experience. Seen in this way the creative process is partly a reliving of bodily experience' (Milner 1950: 159). For instance a work of art will always portray historic moments of action. Fuller, in his observation of the abstractionist painter Natkin, noticed how the artist's bodily processes manifested themselves in his work:

'He dabbed the pigment layer after layer in the same way as that of a dancer (in fact in adolescence he had trained as a dancer), the rhythms of his body informed the way in which he gradually builds up the image. There is thus a real sense in which every painting he makes is imprinted with his touch and movement; it cannot but stand in an intimate close relationship to his body, and be expressive of the emotions and sensations which he experiences through his body.'

(Fuller 1980: 233)

In perceiving painting in this way we are reminded, on the one hand, of the manifest content, being in this case the public's attitude to the artist's technique, determined by cultural tradition, and on the other hand, of how the psychic state of mind of the artist is expressed through his bodily actions that make the marks on the paper constituting the latent content. In seeing the subtle transformation of an artist's expressive and emotive material, on the canvas, as being determined by a bodily process, we are now in a better position to examine the way in which bodily sensation can be perceived through omnipotent fantasies. An instance of this can be seen in the process of defecation, which to the infant will be an experience of sensory delight. In addition the omnipotent fantasies of the infant will lend themselves to his perceiving the faeces as a gift to his mother, a magical creation from out of his own body.

In the normal development of the child this attitude gradually disappears, so that the child learns that his faeces, for example, are not the most important gift in their own right. Some individuals however remained trapped within this 'narcissistic stage' whereby they attempt to retain omnipotent control over the external world. This we have seen in the psychotic behaviour of Franz Messerschmidt.

The following clinical example of one of my adult patients illustrates how omnipotent behaviour can be a hindrance in the use of art as communication. This particular patient, who was an artist in his early twenties, had decided to discontinue his career because he was unable to finish off any of his work. He felt that what he had achieved was 'absolute rubbish'. However during the art therapy sessions he would often experience intense sensual delight while he was in the process of plastering layer upon layer of painted colours on to paper. Once he had completed his work he would invariably complain that his painting had gone completely wrong: 'I don't want to have anything more to do with it. I can never bear to work on it again. It is such a mess, so that I can never refine what I have done. Objectively it has lost all meaning. It has nothing to do with what I had intended.' This feeling of disillusionment with the finished work of art in this instance was considered to be due to the patient attributing his faeces (for this artist represented by his paint) as being imbued with magical powers. Marion Milner explains this concept by saying that such disappointment occurs once the artist realizes the harsh reality that the finished work does not hold or evoke the excitement and meaning that the artist experienced whilst doing it. The beautiful mess does not stand up as a picture in its own right. Here we can see that the artist would appear to suffer from a catastrophic disillusionment in the ordinary discovery that his faeces are not as marvellous or as beautiful as his feelings had led him to believe.

By equating the magical power of faeces with the finished work of art in this way we can deduce that there is no discrimination between the feeling of giving and the actual product given. The denial of reality thereby lies in the nature of the mess, not in the nature of the psychic experience of which it is the symbol. The realization of the discrepancy – between the objective reality of the finished product or gift and the subjective involvement and importance of it – does seem to be one of the most fundamental problems that the artist has to grapple with in order to communicate his inner feelings successfully. The problem would therefore appear to arise over the agony of disillusionment in giving up the belief that everyone can see in it what the artist experienced during the process of doing his work. In the symbolic functioning of the artist/patient we encounter, although in another guise, the fusion of the identity of the symbol with the thing symbolized. In this instance the symbolic fusion was in the artist's use of form, which constitutes the style, medium, and technique he uses. It must be emphasized, however, that the stage of omnipotence is a necessary prerequisite for symbol formation.

Winnicott's concept of merging and differentiation

Here we are reminded by Winnicott (1958) of the necessary subjective illusion that the infant needs to develop so that he can create an image of his mother, which is part of himself. This is achieved through the mother's interaction with the child where the infant's ego attempts to introject idea/image of the breast/mother in his mind and later other objects within the surrounding environment. In being able to identify with her in this way the establishing of an internal object is facilitated. In order to establish a sense of self-identity the same process of introjection is involved, based on the internalized mother figure. When the mother looks at her baby, for example, her expression is related to the impression the baby is giving her. This in turn feeds back to the baby an image of himself perceived by his mother, which he takes into himself. In other words, the baby's self-image is reflected back to him via his mother's interpretation of the impression the baby gives her. A more complex picture emerges where not only is the image/idea of the mother contained within the child, but also embedded in his image of her is her perception of him. This concept delineates the beginning of personality and identity. Winnicott describes the process of differentiation of the self from the environment in the following way:

'I am proposing that there is a stage in the development of human beings that comes before objectivity and perceptibility . . . a baby can be said to live in a subjective or conceptual world. The change from the primary state to one in which objectivity is possible is not only a matter of inherent or inherited growth processes, it needs in addition an environmental minimum. It belongs to the whole vast theme of the individual travelling from dependence to independence. This early stage of development is concerned with tentatively ambivalent feelings about merging and separation; about being confused as to the whereabouts of those boundaries, as to what is inside and what is outside, and the limits of containment. While the infant is beginning to recognise autonomous objects, he still feels mixed up with them. This reality confronts him throughout his life, requiring constant resolution.'

(Winnicott 1971: 151)

Winnicott uses the phrase 'transitional object' to describe the illusory state and the infant's awareness of another person simultaneously, a sort of half-way stage betwen fusion with the mother and differentiation from her. The transitional object is usually depicted as a doll, or a piece of cloth, which a child treasures and uses as a comforter, but the element of omnipotence still plays an important role, because the child uses any such thing without the consideration which would be appropriate to a person. Here we see the transitional object as a possession of the child, which describes the process of the child separating itself from the environment, which later becomes the adult's concern. Winnicott refers to the transitional object as creating a 'potential space' where the merging and separation of the baby is defined in relation to its mother, and where illusion can be seen as both real and unreal simultaneously. This stage of transition is seen by him as a process in which the ego not only creates a denial of separation, but also acts as a constructive defence against the earliest anxieties of abandonment and annihilation. Without this healthy transition no emotional maturity can occur.

Klein's view of infantile sadism originates in such primitive anxieties. Through knowing how to use this potential space the individual can come to trust his environment and as a result he can explore the interplay between himself and the outside world. The transitional object acting as a vehicle for the realizing of this potential space is originally created from the interaction of mother and child. According to Winnicott it is from this relationship that cultural pursuits develop symbolically, through artistic expression. The art critic Peter Fuller shows how the basic ambivalence between subject, object, figures, and environment (object relations), can be seen to manifest itself in the subjective spatial representation that is often seen in the 'form' in art. Fuller in his analysis of Cézanne's paintings notices a particular ambiguity between the foreground and the background. He describes how a branch of a tree in the foreground of the picture seems to be depicted only feet away from the others. However at another moment it appears to touch the slopes of the mountains far away in the distance. Fuller goes on to suggest that the ambiguity depicted in Cézanne's paintings becomes more prominent in his later work. This can be seen in *Women bathing*, which was done within four years of his death. The ambiguity in the foreground and background is encapsulated in the naked figures painted within the landscape. Fuller, in looking at these figures in their groupings, experiences them retaining their own autonomy, but becoming simultaneously indissoluble from their surroundings. He denotes how there appears to be two kinds of aesthetic emotion, one derived from separating out, and the other embodying a fusion between the separate parts. From this it is logical to conclude that Cézanne's creative perception of the external world could be seen to contain both the acceptance and denial of separation. This being symbolizes in Cézanne's art (his transitional object) through the spatial relationship between objects, which could be seen to stem from his early object relations, the fusion with (and separation from) the object.

Marion Milner was perhaps one of the first psychoanalysts to realize that an important aspect of artistic expression was that the artist's feelings could be conveyed through spatial representation. From her own personal experience of painting, she considers the importance of space:

'If one saw it as a primary reality to be manipulated for the satisfaction of all one's basic needs, beginning with the babyhood problem of reaching out for one's mother's arms, leading through all the separation from all one loves, that the business of living brings, then it was not so surprising that it should be the main preoccupation of the painter. . . . So it becomes clear that if a painting is concerned with the feeling conveyed by space then it must also be to do with the problems of being a separate body in a world of other bodies which occupy different bits of space; in fact it must be deeply concerned with ideas of distance and separation, and with having and losing.'

(Milner 1955: 92)

From this discussion Winnicott's theory of 'potential space' can be seen to have an important influence on the understanding of artistic expression. The infant's first contact with reality is in moments of illusion, when he sees himself as an extension of his mother. Therefore there must be such a time during the creation of a work of art in which there is experienced a feeling of being at one between the artist and his work. Gradually and continually until its completion the part elements of his work of art are given separate form. It thus seems to me that an individual's potential for creativity lies in the area between fusion and separation. In other words, the more an individual can willingly fluctuate between the two areas of fusion and separation (and at times contain both of these elements simultaneously), the more creative he can become.

All forms of symbolic expression produce different kinds of relationships from those involving external reality. For example, the child can manipulate his play materials according to his desires, and although they are external to him he does not have to believe in their own separate or objective existence.

Marion Milner adds to this discussion in reference to Winnicott's notion of transitional phenomena, by adding a further dimension in the use of play and art:

'In play there is something half way between day dreaming and purposeful instinctive or expedient action. As soon as a child has moved a toy in response to some wish or fantasy, then the scene created by play is different, and a new situation sets off a new set of possibilities; just as in free imaginative drawing the sight of a mark made on paper provokes new associations, the line, as it were, answers back and functions as a very primitive type of external object.'

(Milner 1955: 92)

I take Milner to imply that any sort of contact with external reality, even if it is only an extension of the self, creates a dialogue by means of the subject's manipulation of that reality. This, simultaneously with the fantasy, contains a separate identity. It is therefore in a position to dictate certain demands. To put it another way one could say that the external activity involved in image-making expressing a dream of fantasy can come to provide a link connecting our understanding of the subjective world of fantasy with the outside world of everyday life and culture, thereby creating a permanent oscillation between and fusion with reality and fantasy.

In relation to this idea, Winnicott introduces another factor that helps to create a distinction between reality and fantasy. He suggests that the infant's destructive attacks on its 'object' can be used as a constructive force to enable differentiation between self and 'object' to occur. He postulates that at a certain stage of ego development the child comes to realize that his fantasized attacks on his mother or 'object' do not actually destroy the 'object' in external reality. Out of this realization a new relationship is created, whereby the 'object' can be objectively perceived as a separate and independent entity, outside the subject's omnipotent control. The essence of this change of attitude lies not only in the 'object's' survival, but also in the subject being able to make use of the 'object' which has survived destruction. By placing the 'object' outside the self, the individual is able to absorb and learn from it, according to its own properties.

'Without the experience of maximum destructiveness the subject is unable to place the object outside, and therefore can never do more than use the object as a projection of part of the self. The very act of destructive fantasy plays a part in making the individual experience reality.'

(Winnicott 1969)

It is interesting to note that Winnicott's hypothesis runs contrary to orthodox psychoanalytic theory, which considers sadism to be a reaction to the encounter with external reality. However it must be stated that the infant's response to this whole area of emotional development depends on the externally perceived object surviving those destructive attacks which the infant makes on it. Only then can infantile omnipotence become modified. The subject is never free from its object, within the area of subjective reality. Winnicott's idea of the constructive use of aggression, involving the consideration of the nature of the object as part of an external reality, corresponds to his idea of the infant's use of a transitional object that represents the in-between stage of the subject's relation to an 'object', as being a creation of the ego as well as having separate existence. For example, a firm belief in the reality of a work of art can coexist with the certainty that it is only a painting.

One can therefore surmise that the individual's ability to differentiate between reality and fantasy reflects the true meaning of sublimated symbolic expression. An example can be seen in the artist's use of symbolic content as well as in his use of media. For Winnicott, symbolic/artistic behaviour, related through cultural experience, can be seen as a reproduction and transformation of the mother/child relationship. In addition, I have attempted to describe how the infant's interest is transferred from an original object to a secondary one, and how the identification of the primary object with another is established.

Sublimation

I wish now to pay attention to another task that contributes to symbol formation, and which confronts the developing ego. One of Freud's greatest contributions to psychoanalysis was the discovery that sublimation is the outcome of a successful renunciation of an 'original object'. This involves the resolution of conflict between those forces forbidding interest in the original object, as well as the actual loss of the object. Such renunciation, according to Klein, following up Freud's formulations on the subject, can only occur through the process of mourning. She states that mourning, as a natural part of the child's emotional development, reaches its climax with weaning. At this stage the child experiences the painful realization that his mother is no longer available to him in the same way, namely the breast-feeding relationship which incorporates those aspects of love, goodness, and security. The infant, still governed by his feelings of omnipotence, experiences this loss as a result of his own uncontrollable, greedy, destructive fantasies against the mother's breasts. That is to say he may feel that the breasts have taken revenge, and are punishing him by their limited availability or with-drawal. Generally speaking, by the time the weaning process begins, the infant, according to normal ego development, has reached the 'depressive position'.

This earmarks the change in the whole climate of thought. The child begins to show concern and guilt for the object, in that he is able to acknowledge that his feelings of both love and hate are directed towards the same person. This new attitude is in contrast to a previous way of functioning, which kept such opposing emotions apart. For instance the hateful and persecuting mother was projected elsewhere, so that the infant's love towards his mother could be preserved and split off from his destructive feelings – thus making the benevolent mother all loving and bountiful. We come to realize that this new feeling of concern belonging to the 'depressive position' arises from the sense that he has lost the good object through his own destructiveness. He remembers that he loves his mother, but he feels that he has destroyed her, so that she is no longer available in the external world. Klein stipulates that the loss of the loved object leads the child, through the process of mourning, to reinstate the lost loved object in the ego. In other words, to internalize the good object by making it part of the self, helps the child to repair and restore that which has in his fantasy been damaged by his destructive impulses. Thus, the process of mourning can be seen as a result of the child's ability to renounce his forbidden object (the mother's breast), which instead he installs in his ego. This process of internalization allows the individual to 'project' his now internal object, a symbol within the ego, on to other things or people in the external world. These represent a symbolic relationship between the subject and the original object, child, and mother.

Every aspect of the object, every situation that has to be given up in the process of internalization, gives rise to symbol formation. We are once again reminded of Winnicott's concept of 'transitional phenomena' which provides a prime example of the renunciation of the lost loved object. This concept succinctly illustrates man's need for fusion and his experience of belonging, in contrast to his need for separateness. The individual ability to create a symbolic relationship allows him to make a distinction between psychic and external reality. Furthermore the symbol differentiated from the object is felt to be created by the ego and can therefore be freely used by the self, permitting greater freedom of expression. In other words, the individual is protected through the process of internalization from the fantasy of an irrevocable sense of loss and damage to his loved object as a result of his destructive impulses. The sense of security and autonomy, achieved through the assimilation of the loved object, can, therefore, be seen to be responsible for all symbolic elaborations that form the very essence of artistic expression. Conversely, Bowlby (1971: 319–79) has written about the difficulties of mourning, and the renunciation of the original object which the individual encounters. He suggests that the infant who feels insecure in his relationship with his mother develops an excessive resistance towards internalization, so that his capacity for differentiation and separation between self and object is impaired. Such resistance results in the use of denial as a defence against the pain caused by the loss of the loved object. This implies that the relationship with the loved object is lost, and being thus unavailable to the symbolic process, a new relationship with it cannot evolve. Perhaps an adult example of the denial of separation could be seen in the artist who isolates himself from his environment and denies the relevance and value of tradition. Instead he becomes trapped within the state of fusion and identification in which primitive omnipotence is at its height. As a result he comes to deny the reality of the external world and can no longer see himself as a person within it.

Out of this discussion we come to recognize how in the making of art the development of symbolic formation plays a crucial role in the individual's shift of attention, from the original object, on to the ego, and by means of projection, on to a work of art. However, I feel it is important to bear in mind that this same shift could occur without the intermediate stage of internalization. Here we discover that the original object has not been given up but still lives on in a projected form. This produces a situation where the work of art gains a permanent place in the artist's life, making it difficult for him to part from what he has created. We witness yet again the theme of over-identification. This shows how the artist's attitude to his work becomes invested with those same feelings that he originally possessed towards his object, and they therefore preclude the possibility of his being able to experience emotionally feelings of mourning and of loss for the loved object itself. In order to understand how the development of symbolic expression is influenced by the individual's ability to renounce and mourn his lost loved object, it is has been necessary to review both the problems and benefits that accrue from the process. What is constructive in creating symbolic expression will provide the substance of the last section.

The final illustration depicts how symbolic fusion results in a displaced object retaining the same primitive intensity of feeling that the artist felt towards his original object, due to a regression to an earlier stage of ego development. This relationship is in direct contrast to true sublimation, involving a mature level of ego functioning that enables the process of neutralization of primitive drives to occur. Arthur Koestler (1974) in his book *The Act of Creation*, calls 'bissociation' the individual's capacity to make rapid, or at least appropriately rapid, shifts of level in ego development. He considers this to be an essential ingredient in mental functioning, through which mankind can come to an understanding of himself in relation to the outside world. The individual can thus use bissociation to gain easy access to id material without being overwhelmed by it, or having to maintain control over it.

Ernest Kris's notion of 'regression in the service of the ego' mirrors Koestler's idea of bissociation. Kris (1952) considers there to be two stages in the ego functioning involved in creating a work of art. The first is during the period of inspiration which can only occur when the ego's control is relaxed (regressed) and thus provides a way to an interplay with the id. During this phase the artist and his work are one. In the later phase the ego asserts its position in what Kris calls re-creation, so that instinctual drives are fashioned and contained within the framework of 'aesthetic illusion'. The controlled and temporary ego regression, which occurs during inspirational creation, was described by Plato as a 'productive insanity'. Perhaps the same could be said about Abstract Expressionism. Adrian Stokes, for example, quotes Herbert Read on the later paintings of Jackson Pollock: 'of symbolism there is no suggestion: on the contrary there is a desire to destroy the image and its associations. . . . His aim was to get inside his own painting rather than his own painting should represent what was inside him' (Stokes 1961: 169). Here we could consider Pollock's art as achieving a symbolic representation of symbolic fusion, under the dominance of ego control. Thus, only in the more 'narcissistic regression' of the psychotic is it a pathological process. It is now apparent that in emotionally mature adults the close fusion and extreme identification with other people and objects is never completely lost. From this early stage of symbol formation springs the adult's capacity to enter into the bissociative process or – according to Winnicott – a 'transitional phenomena'. We are already aware of the early stage of ego development of the infant who cannot contain the ambiguity of fantasy and reality, and this finds its adult equivalent in the psychotic whose mental functioning is reduced to a state in which it is impossible to maintain such ambiguity. In both instances their thinking is fixated in a world where illusion becomes reality.

Ego regression

I would now like to draw attention to an aspect of ego functioning in diametrical opposition to that just described, namely 'regression in the service of the ego'. This does not readily occur, and concrete reality is here the only possible reality. This is a very literal interpretation, with no imaginative connotation. In this situation the ego is unwilling to surrender to its more primitive levels of thinking. Such a shift evokes a temporary loss of the sense of self, inducing a feeling of insecurity in the individual, owing to the fact that while the lessening of rational control increases, the discriminating function of the ego is reduced. Koestler reminds us of the ego's need to regress by saying,

'The mind needs freedom to act as an anaesthetist who puts reason to sleep and who restores for the transient moment the innocence of vision . . . without the art of forgetting, the mind remains cluttered up with ready made answers and never finds occasion to ask the proper questions.'
(Koestler 1974: 190)

The ability to achieve this state he calls 'snow blindness', the 'mental eye cataract'.[1] However, he describes it as providing a dual role. On the one hand it prevents the intrusion of novelty and accounts for our mental inertia, while on the other it is equally responsible for our mental stability. The inflexibility of the ego can often be attributed to an overwhelming fear of the fantasies attached to the id, which in turn prevents it from regressing to earlier and therefore more primitive stages of development. One recalls Klein's theory of the infant world dominated by sadism which ultimately inhibits internalization of those projected and instinctual emotions belonging to the id. Likewise Klein has shown that the individual's inability to renounce the lost loved object also hampers the process of internalization, leaving the individual with an empty view of the world. Hanna Segal (1955: 390–91) in her paper 'A psychoanalytical approach to aesthetics', demonstrates how an impaired capacity to internalize the object leads to an inhibition in artistic expression. In a clinical example she describes how a young girl patient with a definite gift for painting could only produce decorative handiwork in preference to what she sometimes called 'real' painting. The girl was, however, aware of the fact that though correct, neat, and pretty, her work failed to be moving and aesthetically significant. Segal claims that this patient's work demonstrated manic denial of an overwhelming fear of reinternalizing her projected sadism embodied in her father. This led her to make believe that all was well in the world, by creating an effect of superficiality in her work, where ugliness and depression and conflict were denied existence. I am once again reminded of a recurring theme in this thesis, namely the need to 'regress in the service of the ego', or, according to Koestler, 'bissociate' between two levels of ego functioning. In relation to this, the subjective world of the id's omnipotent fantasies, in which there is a fusion and identification with the object of inspiration, is essential to the making of a work of art. Milner, writing about her own painting of people, confirms this idea. She states,

> 'In order to realise other people, make them and their uniqueness fully real to oneself, one has in a sense to put oneself into the other, one has to temporarily undo that separation of the self and other which one has laboriously achieved. To break down the barrier between self and other, yet at the same time to be able to maintain it. This seems to be the paradox of creativity.'
>
> (Milner 1950: 11–12)

One could go on to describe the individual's avoidance of the state of fusion from the standpoint of Kleinian theory, where the fear of our aggression is one of the reasons for the ego's avoidance of its instinctual drives, which are dominant in the early stages of ego development. Another defence against these primitive impulses is for the immature ego to force itself into a premature position, into a state of pseudo-independence. The ego, having skipped over its earlier phases of development too soon, becomes aware of its separate identity. Thus the necessary subjective illusory state that earmarks the infant's fusion with the object is no longer maintained.

Continued growth of the ego, leading to its gradual ability to differentiate between its subjective world of being mixed up with its object and external reality, allows the child to relate to his environment as well as feeling free to re-enter the stage of being at one. What happens then, when regression is prevented from occurring with sufficient frequency, or at the right moment? The good early mother/child relationship permits the infant to experience the necessary blissful feelings of fusion, felt most intensely by the infant through being fed, and having intimate bodily contact with his mother, from which he derives his fundamental sense of security. If however this relationship is not sufficiently sustained, then the infant's frustration will lead him to experience such closeness as evil and persecuting, further accentuated by his projected aggression returning to him as an evil harmful force. This situation compels the infant to turn away from intimate contact. Such a level of frustration is therefore held responsible for feelings of abandonment and annihilation. From this position the infant feels the illusion of union to be a catastrophic chaos rather than a blissful state, resulting in his giving up the illusion and prematurely establishing ego development.

Here separateness and the demands of necessity may be apparently accepted, under the auspices of the ego's rational and intellectual thinking process that delineates the 'secondary process', but the child's needs can never be properly satisfied. In other words, the secondary process becomes a cage for the individual rather than an area of functioning that has great value when it is in collaboration with the unconscious. The realization that premature ego development occurs when the external object has not been sufficiently introjected leads us to another problem in object relations.

Pre-mature ego development

According to Esther Bick (1955: 484–86) this involves the mother's function of containing those primitive anxieties of her infant which cannot be of use to the child if the mother has not been introjected. The need for containment produces a frantic search in the infant for an object, which can hold the attention and thereby be experienced, momentarily, at least, as holding the unintegrated parts of the personality. Replacement of dependence on an object – a pseudo-independence – by the inappropriate use of certain mental functions, is thereby installed for the purpose of creating a substitute for containment.

An example of a pseudo-containing function was evident in my patient Paddy, who had suffered quite extensive maternal deprivation in her first year of life. This false independence revealed itself in her therapy sessions with me. She was a physically aggressive child, who took great pride in her muscular strength. This showed itself to have a mental equivalent to a corresponding verbal muscularity, in which she would vehemently defy whatever I had to say. However, when she was not responding in a defiant manner it was painfully obvious that she had very few opinions of her own. In connection with her defensive attitude she drew an image of a horse-chestnut complete with bristling prickles. Her association in relation to this image led her to perceive the spiky case as being a 'suit of armour', to protect the baby chestnut. She was able to equate the chestnut with the vulnerable part of herself and its case with her strong muscles. Here we can see that she was using her verbal and physical muscular strength as an external container in order to defend herself from deep-rooted anxieties of disintegration. Her metaphoric use of a 'suit of armour' provided her with an external frame of reference. This was particularly reflected in her attitude towards art. The first painting she did with me was made by moistening the tablets of paint, which she used as a printing block. I commented on how she used the shape of the tablet to provide her with a ready-made structure, rather than creating one for herself. She told me that she preferred mathematics as a subject because it provided her with the figures for her to play with. She continued, saying that English was more like art, because the paper was blank and you had to fill it with your own ideas. This is much more difficult. Paddy clearly found subjects requiring imagination more threatening, which would eventually expose her to her earliest feelings of extreme frustration, disintegration, and chaos.

In addition, this would also make Paddy aware of a profound feeling of emptiness through having deprived herself of developing a rich interchange between the internal world of fantasy and the external reality. We can now more readily appreciate that her need to manipulate facts and figures and ready-made structures, was made to bolster up her protective defence. Such a shell provided her self with a false independence and pseudo-self-containment.

I would like to end by saying that this chapter has concerned itself with the problems and difficulties associated with the relationship the ego, in its many varied states, has in its involvement with symbolic expression. I have also explained how this in turn determines the quality and meaning of such expression. In addition I have attempted to illustrate how visual expression, or a work of art, is affected by the artist/patient's inextricable and overall involvement with his work. This has been understood in terms of the individual's relationship with his internal 'objects', that inevitably become externalized and thereby embodied into any creative process. One particular aspect of this creativity has been examined in this chapter through the use of visual expression.

© 1987 Felicity Weir

Note

1 The fine example of this is Freud's blindness to one of the implications of his own work. Ernest Jones (90–107), in his biography of Freud, points out that the great man heard about some Indian tribes who chewed coco leaves (cocaine) to enable them to overcome deprivation and hardship. Freud thus decided that cocaine was the magical drug with which to combat depression and various neurotic disorders. However, the man who tried to benefit humanity and created a reputation for curing nervous diseases was soon accused of unleashing evil on the world because his patients became addicted to cocaine. One should perhaps note that at the time of this discovery Freud was studying neurology in Vienna. His snow blindness prevented him from seeing his discovery. He wrote about the effects of cocaine in nervous disorders, and as a footnote added that it could be also used as a painkiller in local infections. Its use as an anaesthetic in minor surgery never occurred to him.

References

Bettelheim, B. (1967) *The Empty Fortress*. New York: Macmillan.
Bick, E. (1968) The Experience of the Skin in Early Object-Relations. *International Journal of Psychoanalysis* 49.
Bowlby, J. (1971) *Attachment and Loss* Vol. 1. Harmondsworth: Pelican.
Freud, S. (1963) *The Standard Edition of the Complete Psychological Works*. London: Hogarth Press and the Institute of Psychoanalysis.
Fuller, P. (1980) *Art and Psychoanalysis*. London: Writers and Readers.

Jones, E. (1953) *The Life and Work of Sigmund Freud.* Harmondsworth: Penguin.

Klein, M. (1975) *Collected Works Vol. 1: The Importance of Symbol Formation in the Developing Ego.* London: Hogarth Press.

Koestler, A. (1974) *The Act of Creation.* London: Picador.

Kris, E. (1952) *Psychoanalytic Explorations in Art.* New York: Schocken Books.

Milner, M. (1950) *On Not Being Able to Paint.* London: Heinemann.

Milner, M. (1955) The Role of Illusion in Symbol Formation. In M. Klein (ed.) (1977) *New Directions in Psycho-analysis.* London: Maresfield Reprints.

Segal, H. (1955) A Psychoanalytic Approach to Aesthetics. In M. Klein (ed.) (1977) *New Directions in Psycho-analysis.* London: Maresfield Reprints.

Stokes, A. (1961) *The Critical Writings of Adrian Stokes* Vol. 3. London: Thames & Hudson.

Stokes, A. (1963) *Painting and the Inner World.* London: Tavistock.

Winnicott, D. (1969) The Use of an Object. *International Journal of Psychoanalysis* 50.

Winnicott, D. (1971) *Playing and Reality.* London: Tavistock.

5 | Peak experiences: the individuation of children

Diana Halliday

Introduction

In these pages, I shall try to recapture some of those 'peak experiences' which emerge from my years as an art therapist in a child guidance clinic. To be a member of a psychiatric team whose support and understanding were invaluable and to enjoy a one-to-one relationship with children were privileges I can never over-estimate.

The clinic was a place where children had the space to be both seen and heard in the presence of one concerned adult. In an atmosphere of privacy and trust, the therapy room became a play room, studio, shop, battlefield, nursery, office, home. It satisfied a multiplicity of needs, where these could be described, enacted, and contained.

However sad, mad, or bad children may have felt themselves to be, creative art and activities have enabled change to come about. Inner worlds have been expressed; fantasies and feelings have taken shape and colour in the magic play of art. The 'Wendy' house has been a sanctum – a house within the room; a stage-set for a drama, which I could either watch or share – or a wholly secret place.

A Wendy house is made of wood or plastic. Under 5 feet high, it is large enough for an average 8-year-old to sit and stand in. There is room for a small table and chair; it has a door and a window or two.

As well as paper, paint, and oil pastels, plasticine and clay, balsa wood and Lego lead the way to creative and expressive play. Permitting both regression and aggression, hammer and pegs and punchball, sand-trays, forts, and farmyards are essential. Equally so, are uniforms and helmets, puppets, doll families and dolls' houses, life-size baby dolls, trains and tracks, telephone (toy) and typewriter (real), blackboard and mirror; all are means of communication.

Sometimes the mirror was imaginary; we would pin a strip of paper to the door and I would ask the child to paint what he saw in it. Mostly we sat side by side, doodling, squiggling, playing games, or modelling. While the children 'worked' I would often draw them. To see themselves through my eyes might be reassuring; it could counteract a poor self-image, and draw me into sharing the activity. When children paint or model without fear of criticism, works of deeply felt emotion may result. In the course of time, I have seen the healing, integrative power of art and learnt each one's special language from the signs and symbols they devise. In this process, awareness of themselves and others often comes about.

Many years have passed since I was last a member of the clinic team. Employed as a child psychotherapist, I had weekly hour-long sessions with each child. The consultant psychiatrist would interview the family or parents, and the mother would usually attend weekly, seeing the psychiatric social worker. The educational psychologist tested the child and liaised with the school and the psychiatric team. Remedial teachers worked with children in the clinic. Initially, a file giving medical, family, social, and school reports was shown to me for assessment of those who might be suitable for art therapy. Additional reports went into the file during the course of treatment; these kept me in touch with relevant information. Weekly meetings were also held between the team and others concerned with the child. Looking back may seem self-indulgent but my wish is to encapsulate some of those flashes of insight which illuminate the search for meaning. They occur at many points in time, not only during the process of treatment, but sometimes long after it has ended. At this moment, I have become aware of the meaning of a brick wall which often appeared in the paintings of a young girl many years ago (see *Plate 4*).

Tina

I shall briefly describe the treatment of Tina, a 14-year-old girl who had been very ill in early childhood. At 18 months, she had been thought to be autistic, but had greatly improved. She became anorexic at the age of 9 and spent a year in hospital. There, she had made great progress, spending much time on the ward sketching. On leaving hospital, she was, to everyone's surprise, able to attend a normal secondary school. But she was extremely timid and withdrawn, afraid of other children in the playground.

Described as seriously disturbed and maladjusted, she was referred to me for art therapy. At the first interview, she showed me a book of cartoons she had done. These described her 'inner playground' and a sequence of adventures. Her imaginary playmates, I soon realized, reflected conflicting facets of herself. They all remained stuck in early childhood, at about the age of 6; she was terrified of growing into adolescence. We decided she would paint these large. A series of almost life-size portraits were produced in eighteen months. The brick wall which appeared in some of her pictures always puzzled me. I knew it was symbolically important, but did not perceive the message until now. When painting from imagination lately, I found that I had placed myself in front of a brick wall, just as Tina had done. Seeing how it was blocking my own freedom, the need to move away was imperative. I could then relate it to Tina's brick wall; it was a defence protecting her from the dangers of the outside world. It was both metaphor and reality. (I had learned from her teachers that she actually stood facing the brick wall in the playground during recreation, to avoid the rough and tumble of her peers.) What she feared most of all was growing into adolescence. She hid her changing body under childish clothes, socks, and shoes, just like those she painted for her playmates in her pictures and cartoons. My own unconscious choice of the same metaphor (enabling me to move beyond it) also brought about a flashback. She had not needed my interpretation at the time. Our relationship had enabled her to paint her feelings and her fantasies while telling me her thoughts. Through this process, growth and change came about. In the course of time, she painted true images of her adolescent self; a gradual emergence – the relationship was safely based on art. We shared, as equals, our delight in practising our art together. The creative act inspired us both with awe. Most importantly, Tina became aware of and could paint the changing form of her own body: she could articulate her fantasies and feelings and could integrate these with her conscious self. The frightened child who first crept fearfully into my studio left after eighteen months, knowing she would cope well with the adult world.

There is a line in Romans which reminds us that 'we do, not what we want, but the very thing we hate' (8: 15–16). Bearing this fact in mind, it helps to understand the problems of certain children. It is at the root of many conflicts and much social maladjustment. Lennie (13) who only beat up children smaller than himself typed the following statement: 'I hate people who bully little children.' Exactly the same message was typed by John (10) whose explosiveness caused his referral to the clinic. Tom (8) could describe his conflict in a drawing. Five squiggly loops were filled with five different faces (see *Figure 11*). Four of them were ugly, bad. The fifth was different. He turned to me and pointing to the last (an angelic, funny one) he said, 'You only know this one face of mine.' It was the opposite of all the other faces he had drawn.

My role has always been to follow, not to lead, but all too often I lagged

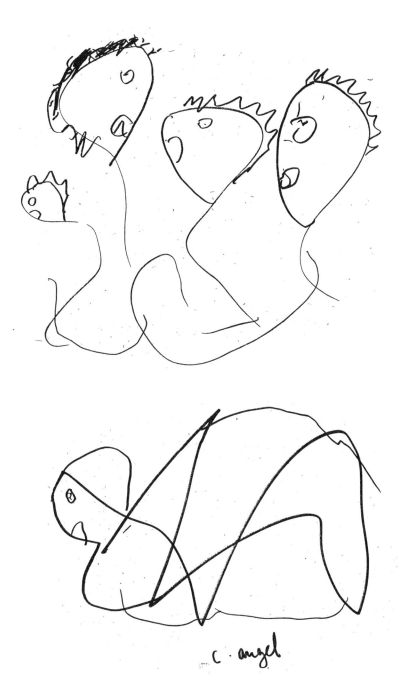

Figure 11 Tom: Five faces

behind. I tried to accompany the children on their inner journeys, to intuit their moods and meanings. But sometimes these escaped my grasp.

Sunita

In the course of eighteen months of art therapy, Sunita had handed me a message. It was obviously of great importance, but what this was eluded me. For years, I have puzzled over the metaphors she used. Referred for 'disturbing and obsessional behaviour', she was 13 years of age. Tall, dark-haired, her eyes seemed not to focus, and looked slightly wild. Adult requirements filled her with alarm. Immature for her age, and of limited intelligence, she felt stupid and bewildered at her school, among her rough and teasing classmates. She wanted to conform, but to which world did she adhere? The Asian or the western one, each with its very different mores? Much of her life had been spent in India; in England she felt lost. At home, she was unhappy: not bright enough for her father, she feared his disapproval, was tormented by her little brother, and only felt secure with her mother.

Asked to make three wishes at the clinic, hers displayed the conflict. Unable to relate to children of her own age her first wish was 'to have friends', her second 'to be very clever', and her third 'to have lots of toys'. (She would only play with little children, much younger than herself.) Her fears were greater than her wishes. She was terrified of blood, of water, and of hair. Blood she saw as sickness; water – she was afraid of drowning in her bathwater, or the swimming pool; hair – her long black tresses might choke or strangle her.

She told me of a morbid fantasy about a woman who swallowed a spider which wove a web in her throat; the woman choked and bled to death. In the dark, she saw ghostly demoniacal eyes. (The fears stemmed from her own sickness in early childhood, and from her mother's chronic bronchial condition.) Sunita was a famished and insatiable child, forever craving sweets. She would be a shopkeeper when she grew up, to have all the sweets she wanted. (Or else, she'd be a doctor and keep herself and her mother well.)

During three years of weekly sessions at the clinic, I saw little progress, though I now perceive I underestimated what was going on. She loved colour but lacked the power of visualization, as her paintings and claywork demonstrated. But she would try to tell me all her dreams and nightmares, and the worries that tormented her. (Her problems caused sores around her mouth and she tore strips off her cuticles.) Sex and marriage were unreal to her, although she day-dreamed of a nice, polite young husband whom her mother would present. I thought I felt unreal to her as well; she once described me as her 'interviewer'. (But there were also good days when she would bring her guitar to the clinic and would sing to me.) She seemed always to need filling; her models were of empty vases, boxes, jugs, bowls, baskets, even a tomato-tin – always that great void inside her needing to be filled. One day she made a candy-dish with her open mouth painted on it, ready to be stuffed, she said (with almonds, sweets, and potatoes).

During the second year of therapy I heard that she was doing better at school than I thought. Her teacher said she no longer needed to attend the clinic and her parents wished to terminate the sessions. I learned that this provoked a passionate outburst from Sunita. No matter what her teacher said, she cried, she was coming to the clinic; she loved the 'interviewer' who knew how to help her. Clearly she was still in need of my support.

At this time, she handed me a message which was obviously important to her in a way I failed to understand. I've kept it all these years and still am puzzled. This was the message:

> ON COLOUR
> E is for RED, crying for help.
> E is the bank or a bridge.
> E is green, is a field of grass.

Red and green are opposite colours – red for danger and a STOP sign. Red stood for blood – pain and suffering in her mind. She would be standing in water – and was afraid of drowning. The cry for help was to me.

The second E seemed transitional – she may have crossed over the bridge and climbed up the bank to the field of grass, unaided by me. Green was the GO sign. In a field, green grass grows. So there are growth, movement, and now, out of danger, 'green peace'? Had she worked through her paralysing anxiety and found some stability? Had the middle E bridged the gap between the Unconscious and the Conscious? Was she now ready to relax, to enjoy growing up? It had often seemed to me that Sunita saw the world but dimly through a clouded mirror – a sense of unreality diffused her vision. Reading the following passage, I understood her better:

> 'We see the world only through the mirror of the mind. But when this, the mirror in us, is broken on account of the disturbed harmony of the organism, then the mind and soul think without the mirror image, and then thought is present without an inner image of itself.'
> (Plotinus (AD 204–70) in Whyte 1960)

Could this explain her confusion? She lacked a true sense of self; having little ego-strength, she sought a pattern of behaviour that would somehow see her through. Yet, although I felt depersonalized when described as her interviewer, it was as accurate a definition of our actual relationship as the dictionary could provide: 'a meeting between two persons face to face'.

She was, at this stage, in touch with her feelings and her thoughts, and could assert her needs. Perhaps her message meant that our meetings had served their purpose – I shall never know for sure. At the final session her farewell gift to me was a wooden casket, leather-bound and studded, but empty ('of all ills and joys' I wondered?). Pandora's Box came to mind; the third casket which discharges storms, devastation, death – to do with the unconscious and her turmoil. Good that it was empty!

Con

Con was difficult. For most of the eighteen months of therapy, he tested me to the limit; knowing he was 'bad', he tried to make himself obnoxious. In this he ultimately failed.

Aged 9 on referral, he was two years older than his little brother, Greg. Con was bitterly jealous of the baby who replaced him in his mother's affection; Con could do no right. From the moment of conception, Con had given trouble. Nine months of agonizing pregnancy had been followed by a fifteen-hour labour. His mother was ill after his birth, and could only feed him for six weeks; all the love she had was lavished on her second baby, Greg. Con was enuretic from that time on.

He was not considered bright; at the time of referral, he had been accused of lying and stealing (a sixpence from his mother's bag). School phobic, he felt sick every morning and was aggressive to other children. It was recommended that he should be transferred to a day school for maladjusted children, but this proved unnecessary.

His mother feared that his violence might stem from hereditary mental illness in her family. Con could never please her, never win her love. He was in despair and had made two or three suicide attempts. His one ally was his father. Though he was too easily provoked by Con, he saw clearly where the fault lay and could identify with him. At the clinic, Con soon discovered he could safely work through his anger. It was not an easy process; the therapy room became a battlefield at times. Week after week, he flung paint, clay, paper, anything he could lay his hands on that would cause mess and trouble. He would destroy his claywork and mine, as well as that of other children. But also he would paint, construct Lego models to perfection, and make clay objects with great care.

His first painting was of a dream about a fire which killed his father and his cousin (*Plate 5*). That night, his father asked him what he had done at the clinic and was furious with him when Con innocently described his picture. Next session he was miserable and swore he would never paint with me again. But eventually he did – and his next picture was a solemn one. It was of a church in a rainstorm – perhaps a symbol of his father. He tried to paint a roof to protect the church from the rain and the rain resembled tears. This picture seemed to me to be about his hurt and vulnerable self. It seemed also, in some way, an act of reparation. He felt so much better after doing it that he told me there was nothing wrong with him, why did he have to come? The first assumption was correct. He had to come to prove it for himself; and this was hard.

The next few sessions were filled with violence and aggression. He tried to get me to reject him. He spoilt his paintings, threw clay at me. He hissed and grunted as he worked. He farted to annoy and laughed uproariously. He told me he deliberately farted at school to cause trouble. All but violating the unwritten rules (not to harm himself, the therapist, or clinic property), he worked his way through his anger in the course of time. He painted a portrait of me and flung gobs of paint at my painted face. I felt that was progress indeed. From throwing varnish, paint, and clay all over the room, he was at last transforming his violence into art.

Jealous of Charlie (my next patient) who waited at the door for him to leave, on two occasions Con twisted his arm, pinched him, tweaked his elbow, and tried to kick him as he left the room, leaving Charlie in tears. Charlie was used to being hurt and stood there waiting for the blow to fall. After a while Con ceased to feel threatened by Charlie and once invited him to play with us for a few minutes. I could have discouraged such a gesture, but at once, intuitively, I knew it was too important to dismiss. Playing together was healing for them both – no longer needing to be victim and aggressor. Con began to notice other children at the clinic – at the beginning he would destroy the clay models they had left in the therapy room. Now this yielded to a sympathetic interest.

He was beginning to value his own work and no longer had to ruin it. But when things went wrong at home or at school, this would always be reflected in his behaviour at the clinic. He would splash paint (describing it as shit) all over the place. However, change was sometimes visible. He modelled a large, angry head with sharp teeth, tongue poked out, large ears, and a big hat. It was his 'bad' self. But praise delighted him; he needed nothing more than encouragement and to know that he was understood and not rejected.

The next development was 'could he bring his little brother to the clinic?' It wasn't fair to leave him out! I explained that really the sessions belonged to him. Gratified, on leaving he took my hand and shook it solemnly. Next time, Con wanted to atone to Charlie for his meanness, and could we ask him in again? For five minutes the three of us played cowboys and Indians, and Con was at his charming best.

The following session he was quiet and happy. His mother being ill, Con had cooked for the family and taken her hot drinks. He felt 'good' at last. The next session showed an important difference from previous ones. Instead of the physical discharge of anger, he worked his violent feelings out with puppets – his was a fierce, aggressive tiger; he gave me the kitten and the monkey. The tiger savagely grabbed their tails and choked the kitten. He then turned to the dolls' house. He locked the doll up in a room. It was made to open a window, to climb out and hang on the sill. Without a word, he smiled and left abruptly.

He had found a way of telling me what he could not have uttered. I heard later that he had been locked in his bedroom as a punishment and had tried to throw himself out of the window. For this dangerous attempt, he was deprived of his birthday party. He regressed, but contained his rage within the sandpit and in total silence. Then, Con mothered the large baby doll. He fed her a bottle; she could shed tears, and he asked me if they were real. He undressed her to dry her clothes on the radiator and remarked that 'little girls were flat in front'.

This was both a manifestation of his anima, and a boy's natural curiosity about a little girl's anatomy. He had spent the afternoon with a girl of 9 that week, and was exploring the doll's body as a safe substitute for the real thing! Above all, he gave her the tender, loving care he longed for himself.

Time passed. He had modelled an ashtray for his mother. Sweets were not acceptable to her. When he bought her candy, she had merely scolded him for wasting his pocket money. Into the ashtray he had incorporated a head, the image of his own (*Plate* 6). What more could he offer but himself? I saw it as an effigy-bowl, an offering to propitiate the angry goddess. It was the ultimate expression of his love.

The making of it, watching it grow before my eyes, and the absolute devotion it expressed and symbolized became a peak experience for us both. When he had painted it and put the final coat of varnish on, he ran wild with delight. The room became too small for his high spirits. Our clinic was close to the cattle-market – we both needed air and respite from the intense emotion he had generated. We went out into the sunlit farmyard with its lambs and piglets at one end and the horses at the other. We walked around the shed and Con gently stroked each horse's muzzle. I bought him monkey nuts and he saved them for his mother.

There had been another time when his violence had almost overwhelmed me. We had needed to escape the confines of the room and to get into the open air. It was autumn. The brown-gold leaves shimmered in the sun. He ran ahead and kicked the twigs and fallen leaves, but playfully. We walked and talked and were relaxed and friendly. Later I heard that he had told his mother he had taken me to the park. Hearing that little bit of role-reversal made my day. Not long after this, he typed a poem for his father. Where the poem came from I never knew – the poem, he said, was about himself.

> A tall dark stranger rode into town
> a weary stranger whose head hung low
> as tall as timber and eyes of fire
> a man in danger, a gun for hire.

Mine was a hot young heart who saw him there
a man who needed someone to care
but in that moment he caught my eye
he smiled to see me, then passed me by.
But in the night by an open tavern door
he saw me there and he seemed to draw me across the floor
a thrill of danger led me astray
I lived a life-time in just one day.
But I still love him till years may go
but my tall dark stranger will never know
he will never know.

Con had been described as 'deep and secretive'. Indeed, he was. These were his secrets – from the depths of his loving heart.

The following year, Con was able to go to a mainstream secondary school. No longer a candidate for special education, he could join his peers. He came back to see us and proudly showed off his school tie. He looked clear-eyed and radiant. Two years later, when he was 13, we saw a familiar face pictured in our local paper. He was the youngest person to take part in a walk across Israel. He had gone with his father; it was hoped that next year his mother would join her husband and son.

Charlie

Charlie was always waiting at the door when Con emerged from the therapy room. We have seen that Con had tried to hurt him. Tears came to Charlie's eyes. He had been described as an 'elective mute'. Charlie had one of the saddest faces I have ever seen – he had known nothing but pain, both physical and emotional, since babyhood. He seemed doomed to suffer. At 10 months he was ill with kidney trouble and spent nine months in hospital. By the time he was 2, he seemed better, and his mother left him with his grandmother in the West Indies and came to England. He was 4 when she went back. She stayed nine months and returned to England again, leaving him behind. Most of that time, he had refused to speak to her. Charlie was 8 when his older sister brought him over to England, a few months before he was referred to me. He had always wet the bed, and his well-intentioned mother beat him every morning when he woke up wet. He was so accustomed to this treatment that he would not speak at all until he was beaten. Charlie spoke to no-one but his older sister. Words could not reach his lips. When he tried to speak at school his mouth turned down in pain. Though learning was a problem, he was friendly and quite popular. Despite his inability to talk, his teachers found him easy to manage. A gentle child, he wanted to please them and be liked.

One day, Charlie had missed the school bus. He was afraid to go home and just stood in a doorway in the street from 9 a.m. till 2 p.m. Someone noticed him and took him to the police station. He was taken home. When his mother came back from work at 10 p.m. that night, she went straight into his bedroom and beat him with a slipper for not having come straight home. Finally, the child cried out 'Oh God, oh God' and her husband told her to desist.

It was this story which Charlie told me in a series of paintings at the clinic. He seldom uttered more than a whispered 'yes' or 'no' during our twenty-four sessions, but we communicated somehow through our art games, his play with puppets, and the typewriter. He even typed a poem one day. A favourite game was Snakes and Ladders, climbing to the top of the ladder and then falling to the bottom. That was like the pattern of his life; he was doomed to fall. Another favourite game was Noughts and Crosses. We turned them into comic strips. That was how the story about missing the school bus was recounted to me. He turned the noughts and crosses structure into the school bus and the noughts became the children's faces in the bus (*Figure 12*). Next he painted himself standing in the doorway and a big policeman (*Figure 13*). Our second painting of the bus, we did together.

Figure 12 Charlie: School bus

Figure 13 Charlie: Policeman

It was a saga without words. I knew it was important to him but I did not fully understand till I heard about it later. Without the painting, he could not have told me. Our baby doll could shed 'real' tears. One day, just as Con had done before, Charlie fed her, made her cry, wiped her tears away, loving her in silence as he needed to be loved. Con and Charlie were alike in this.

When Charlie first came he was too terrified to smile. I noted that his mouth looked like a scar or a downstretched gash – a pathetic noiseless cry. Never have I seen so sad a mouth. I used to drive him home. One day I drew a car with myself at the wheel. He promptly drew himself beside me. (That clinched our relationship and our roles.) Then we took the puppets – Tim the monkey and Grumpy the tiger – and we wrote a dialogue about ourselves.

ME: I like you, Charlie, do you like me?
CHARLIE: No, no, no, you a nut!
ME: Don't you want to come back next week?
CHARLIE: Yes, yes, yes!

He looked up at me, grinning broadly. Despite his silence, the sad little boy was doing much better in school and did not need to come back. He was altogether happier (his mother no longer beat him and could show her love in other ways). It was I who might have needed comforting; I missed his solemn little face and would have liked to hear his voice.

Gina

Gina was 9 when she was referred to art psychotherapy. She was the only child of a very young mother and much older father. The problem was seen as one of a mother and child relationship. Dissatisfied with her family, it was aggravated by the fact that the mother was under stress. About to sit her finals at a teacher training college, she had little time or space for Gina.

It was felt that help was needed for each to become a separate person in her own right. Temperamentally, Gina's mother was volatile and highly critical. Gina, at the receiving end, was desperate for approval. She was in a state of conflict between feeling unwanted and unloved, needing to placate her mother, and denying all her pain and resentment.

Gina's despair showed itself in constant nightmares and a fear of sudden death, and in nervous tension and anxiety which made her dangerously accident-prone. She was clumsy, always punishing herself and identifying with every victim of disaster. Beneath all this was the fear of being sent away to boarding school.

She was babyish at home, yet oddly precocious and adult in manner outside the home. She seemed out of touch with the outside world. This was partly due to her poor self-image and loneliness, and partly to her insecurity. Between moving house, changing schools, the threat of boarding school, being sent to stay with friends or neighbours, she never knew what the future held for her. Basically a healthy, happy child, she could form loving trusting relationships with other adults when away from home. On the way to stay with friends in Scotland she enjoyed the flight. It was only coming back that she became apprehensive once again and felt airsick. It took some time before she could admit her feelings to me. To trust me with them threatened her defences and her loyalty. She would cover up and pretend that all was perfect. In art and play she worked through many of her traumas. During sessions, despite her continued resistance and her denial of these problems, changes did occur. They were enacted in the dolls' house, the Wendy house, and the sand and water trays. In make-believe she mirrored or confronted her two selves: the symbiotic relationship with her mother, the clinging baby self, and the bossy, 'adult' self. So intense was this experience that she made her own doll families, down to modelling their eyeballs and their lids in plasticine. She dressed them and made the furniture and furnishings in a mixture of plasticine and bits of cloth. She was creating her inner world as vividly as she experienced it. Often, my part was to play herself, while she played the part of her mother. This role-playing enabled her to express a great deal of her own anger and the tension of which I (as Gina) was to be the victim. A complex process of dual mirroring and role-reversal was going on. By identifying with her mother she could now externalize her own violent feelings which had always been repressed. In punishing me she was projecting her anger away from her own mother on to me. Our make-believe relationship enabled her to take command both of herself and me in the only way which satisfied those needs.

As make-believe it was less threatening than creating a picture or a model where spontaneously she did express her true feelings, but had to cover up the evidence by blurring all the images. Hers was 'performance art', ephemeral and therefore safe.

I would sometimes see her from the window; her mother in a hurry, fearing to be late, would pull up in her bright red car, decant her daughter on the way and speed off to her college. Ejected from the car, Gina would race up the stairs, rush frenetically round the playroom on Hornbeam, the inflatable rabbit, holding on to his ears, bouncing wildly about. (Or, to punish me, if I were not quite ready for her, she would hide sulkily behind her comic in the hall.) She could not stick with any one activity for long but would paint a bit, play a bit, do some claywork, or type – yet could seldom get beyond her name and address. 'What shall I write?' she would ask. 'Something about how you're feeling?' I might reply, and cleverly she would type 'I feel . . . very typish', and evaded such a leading question.

Her fears about death and dying were too terrifying to conceal and these she would confide to me. Her uncle had been found dead in bed, she told me. She had nightmares about dying. A boy in her street had been run over, and had died. The funeral had been only yesterday. Gina was dangerously accident-prone. Yesterday, too, she had nearly drowned in the swimming pool. In too great a hurry to breathe properly before diving, she had choked and swallowed water. She had to be fished out, and fainted in the cubicle. When she wasn't scratched by accident, she was constantly scratching herself. When there was talk of sending her to boarding school, she told me that her friend's brother who was away at boarding school had got a javelin stuck in his neck and had died. These were some of her many fears of accidental death. And Gina was being sent to boarding school. She even sprained her ankle while skipping. Her death wish/fear was symbolized in a piece of claywork. She had set out to model a horse. Too depressed to finish it, she turned it into the dead body of a horse, dented it, and pricked it. It was put away reflecting her dejection. She had just been turned down by the school of her choice. She repressed her tears and fears. Her mother was going away on holiday and she had to be 'placed' somewhere. Again, she angrily denied the hurt. Her real bitterness and pain at feeling once again unwanted and unloved had to be buried away with the dead horse.

The next session, she announced one day, was going to be her last. She and Mum had decided. It was followed by yet another accident – she had fallen off her bike and she showed me the huge bruise; and she had almost gone to hospital to be operated on for appendicitis. A sore throat had delayed it. These were some of the many near-disasters she recounted. One day she made an ashtray for her mother, like many children make as gifts to parents. But this ashtray became a house and the house became a face (*Figure 14*). Roughly modelled, she painted it in black and burning red. It seemed to be herself and possibly her mother too, since she could scarcely differentiate between the two of them. It was an unconscious image of their anger and depression. Although she also did one portrait of her podgy, freckled face. On another occasion she did a blackboard drawing of the school hamster, which they were looking after at home. Her mother was furious with the creature which had eaten holes in all their clothes. Gina empathized with it, she felt like the hamster in the home. It seemed to symbolize her clumsy, jerky self. She would draw birds with muffled claws reminiscent of her nails which self-punitively scratched her own cheeks, arms, and legs. Still, she had a lively sense of humour. Making a six-legged monster out of clay, she observed that a dachshund needed an extra pair in the middle. We could laugh at this, but not at her next 'accident'. Gina's arms and legs were covered in bleeding scratches. She had fallen on a rosebush and had bled profusely. It was not her mother's fault if she had turned the hose pipe full on Gina and made her lose her balance. Anyway, Gina had felt no pain (she swore), and they had both laughed at the incident. This was indeed one of her patterns.

She had begun two books; the titles were significant. One was called a book about 'Something or Nothing' which exactly described her need to pretend and cover up what was really important. 'Something' was very much the matter – to feel yourself unwanted, a trouble-maker in your own

Figure 14 Gina: Ashtrays

home is no laughing matter. But always her line of defence was to pretend that it was 'nothing'.

The other book was a book of 'paturns'. This was an attempt to create some sort of design of her own. It expressed a fundamental need for order and stability. Both books were an attempt to understand herself. She wanted me to explain what they were about. She would paint spontaneously, often making what can only be described as meaningful marks. Some were about the fall into the rosebush. Others were about running and falling over. Another pattern was an attempt to paint the week. It consisted of alternating patches of light and dark colours, like her alternating feelings. They were placed on top of each other. Scratched into the patches of colour with her nails were the words 'This is me'. The patterns went on, blotches and blobs, streaks of paint, and dots and splodges. They told of her many accidents, of her swallowed tears, and her troubles with Mum. She painted herself as a pin cushion, again writing her name on it. In both books, she covered up the evidence with a flat wash of paint. Knowing what her pictures were about, she was too disheartened to go on with the books, and then was too disturbed for anything but finger painting.

Six months went by. The insecurity of her daily life, never knowing who she was going to stay with, or which boarding school she would end up in, conflicted with her loyalty to her mother, and stifled what complaints she might have uttered. None the less there were certain happy times. Acting out her relationship with her mother, painting and modelling her confused and hidden feelings – these were surely cathartic experiences which needed no discussion. At her final session she shut herself in the Wendy house, made a plasticine cake and cut just one slice for herself. I was excluded, since I was no longer her partner in either art or drama. It felt like a punishment, as if I had let her down. She was her mother; I was still cast in the role of Gina. I may have felt sad at losing her, but that act of making and eating her slice of cake was symbolic of the long process of maturation, of gradually becoming her own person, having to take responsibility for herself and to fulfil her own needs, though lonely once again. At least she was suffering less, and enjoyed creating what she wanted.

Some time ago, I heard how well she had done academically. With a boyfriend of her own, Gina was now transformed into a slim, good-looking teenager. To her I can now apply the quotation with which Dr Malcolm Pines began his paper 'Reflections on mirroring':

'A woman has two images. There is a magical person seen or remembered by those who love her, her finest qualities are flesh and spirit illuminated. She herself knows this ideal self; she projects it if she is confident; or she daydreams her ideal self; or she recognises it with gratitude in the admiring eyes of others.

There is at the same time a second image: the woman as seen by those who dislike or fear her. This cruel picture has an all too powerful mirror in her own negative idea of herself. She sees with fear her own ravaging impulses and, most painful of all, a graceless, freakish and unlovable physical self.'

(Glendinning 1981: 35)

Gina had let the second image go.

Danny

Danny was a sturdy little boy with a glint of humour in a solemn face. Referred for therapy at 7, he was the second of three boys, the oldest being 8 and the youngest 6.

His mother had been in her teens when she married. Her husband turned out to be a drunken bully, and he picked on Danny. He would throw things at him when he was learning to walk, to make him fall, like a little human ninepin. His mother said he was a healthy, happy baby whose problems apparently began when he started school. But, from being her favourite child, he soon became the family scapegoat. Sandwiched between his two brothers, he hated them and they hated him. There was no room for him within his family; unwanted and unloved, he made himself unlovable. Not unnaturally, his resentment was soon projected on to boys at school.

His parents' marriage ended when he was 3. For some time the family had no settled home and Danny's mother had a breakdown. When she finally remarried, her husband could give some stability but no affection to her children. Danny knew he was rejected, aware that his mother could no longer bear him. A loving child, whose feelings were intensely strong, he needed to be kissed and hugged. When he wanted to be cuddled, he was pushed aside. He soon learned not to show his feelings, but his behaviour became much worse. He was depressed and dangerously accident-prone. Desperate for attention, he alternated between violent and aggressive behaviour and making reparation. The struggle between his 'good' and 'bad' self was more than he could cope with. He felt suicidal at the age of 6. He would walk along the balcony ledge, or fill his mouth with marbles and, when reproved, he would say 'I'm glad it's dangerous, I want to die'.

At the first session he preferred to come up the wide staircase to the therapy room by himself, rather than be brought up by his mother. He knew the sessions were for him alone. Gratified by the serious attention that was concentrated on him, he inaugurated them by typing his name with great care – an important affirmation of identity. He then began to paint, mixing the colours with deliberation. He drew a large lorry, placed the wheels correctly and filled in the spaces with rectangles of colour. Behind it was his brother and their yellow dog, and a large bird which flew above the lorry.

This was about a most important memory of leaving their first home. Their pigeons had been killed and eaten; only one bird had remained, the one that flew above the lorry. His stepfather was in the lorry and he sat behind. They were going to visit his father in Dartford. This was a moving blend of fact and fantasy; both significant and symbolic of a crisis in their lives. Then he had to tell me of his bad self; how he frightened his little brother on the way to school, threatening to push him into a hole dug in the roadside. He went on telling me about life with their real dad . . . time was up, but he wanted to stay on.

At the second session Danny had a go at the punchball. It was his older brother's head. He didn't mind the younger one, but wished they both were girls. He could then have been the only boy in the family. 'But I have four girlfriends', he told me proudly. Again he told me how much he liked his dad and how he wished he could see him more often. Then he confided that he had tried on his mother's rings and couldn't get them off; his fingers were fatter than hers. Meanwhile he was modelling a girl with arms outstretched – his mum – and making clay fingers and clay rings to fit them. One of them he turned into a cross, and stuck it on a bracelet. Talking all the while, he handled the clay like a workman. His voice was intimate. He was letting me into his private world. The session was not long enough; he wanted to type, and to play with sand and all the puppets.

Danny spent the next three sessions acting out the family relationships. The scene was first set in the dolls' house, but home was more a battlefield and he transferred it to the fort, making hideouts for the soldiers. From time to time he would pause to take a swipe at the punchball. With his sense of justice (it was, after all, his brother's head), he put on the policeman's helmet and made the punchball hit him back. At this point he asked if he could go to boarding school. Now he was making a ladder to reach his mum; she was in a turret on top of the fort. But first he had to make a roof to keep her dry in her turret. He climbed up the ladder, but wanted his mum to bring him down. He turned to me and asked 'Why doesn't she love me?' (Much later, we had a one-off art therapy session together with the family and the social worker. Such a session was very unusual. It happened only once in my experience, and Mum, in fact, had drawn herself at a top-floor window, wanting to be left alone and looking at her mirror.) The play-acting was getting more impassioned and intense, but by the end he had calmed down, having worked it through.

In the clinic Danny was insatiably hungry and thirsty. For many months he continued to fill yoghurt cups with sand and water. The mixture had to be exactly right in texture and consistency to simulate the yoghurt. He would fill eight pots within the hour. It became obsessional, but he was fulfilling his primary needs and could not be stopped. He was asserting his self-sufficiency and independence, but this had its negative aspect. (He was gradually enclosing his needy baby-self within an even harder, tighter cast.) Thus, suppressing his own feelings made him indifferent to the feelings of other boys. Particularly, he hated his brothers; they stood between him and his mother. They were less demanding. She could cope with them, but she had neither love nor patience left for him. He became increasingly aggressive with the boys at school.

Danny would tell me about his cold bedroom and how much he wished he could get into his mother's bed. This was not allowed. 'Only girls kiss and cuddle', she asserted, 'not boys.' 'Why not boys?' he asked me. And his stepfather wouldn't let him sit on his lap – he was too big for that. '*Why* am I too big?' again he asked me, and then frustration would take over and he made the puppets fight. I made a clay monster and he attacked and broke it up. When this was worked through and his anger exhausted, we played at making up words and he displayed his gift for language. And always the yoghurt-making, on and on. 'I'm thirsty, give it to me', he cried, as if it were the breast; and then sourly 'I don't want it any more.' He drew a circle, turned it into his own head, smoking a cigar – vicarious satisfaction: 'If I can't be a baby, I will be a man.' When the session ended, he hid in the Wendy house and refused to come out. It was becoming more and more difficult to persuade him to leave. Finally I left him. He came bounding down the stairs, noisy and high-spirited.

But the anger, hunger, and despair were always there. He fell on to a piece of glass and showed me a big cut in his groin. He didn't cry (he said), and he made himself a mask. He made a base to keep it vertical, to show that he stood on his own two feet and would not display his wound. Then he typed some words which were, in fact, his credo: 'FIGHT, LOVE, HURT, JOKE.'

Another time he drew a cuckoo; this was mum, laying her eggs in another bird's nest. The other bird was his stepdad. That was how he told me she was pregnant. It was his stepdad's home. Reflectively, he thinks he can't like either of his dads; only his mum. But *he* doesn't matter. Angrily he shouts, getting wilder. No-one loves him.

Next time, calm and self-contained, he is concerned about his mother's pregnancy. 'She must have a girl this time.' Danny has had enough of boys. Talking of babies, he reminds me that he was once a lovely baby – and how much he hates his younger brother, hurts him, breaks his toys, makes him cry, and then says 'serve you right' – meanwhile mixing yoghurt in the sink, his special recipe. 'Mum only buys two pints of milk a day for the six of us!' 'The six?', I ask, 'Who's the sixth?' 'The cat', he says, 'I gave him some of my yoghurt once.'

He now struts into the clinic masterfully. Now he is a tough little guy. As he makes me an ashtray (chopping the clay like a butcher chopping meat) he tells me he hit a boy's head, so hard that he had a headache later. No remorse; he didn't care. He gets hurt as well; a boy punched his nose. He didn't cry but simply went to First Aid. Another kicked him in the mouth. All the others were against him except his teacher. This time, he felt glad to be the injured party rather than the criminal. At this point he donned the policeman's helmet and hit the punchball hard, again and again. It was always someone's head. He represented Law and Order, and that gave him the right to punish in his turn.

He was feeling more accepted in his home. A family outing, all together – a rare event – made him feel much better. His mother talked to him about the baby. This was now reflected in his painting. He typed patterns, needing a design in his chaotic life. We did squiggles together. He insisted on doing his with two pencils and then four pens tied together. It was a trial of strength and he felt triumphant at succeeding.

It was June. Instead of staying in the clinic, we walked in the park. He took me to the playground and we read a book on babies. He had to know the facts. Later we talked about what we have in common with other people. I said 'but also we are different from each other. Each one of us is unique.' '*I'm* not unique', he argued. 'There's my shadow and there is me in the mirror.' I was awe-struck by this observation, but continued. 'I only like people who like me', he intimated – the self-same words as other girls and boys have used, who felt unloved and unlovable.

When Danny wanted to tell me about his secret feelings, he enclosed us both together in the Wendy house – it felt womblike in its intimacy. At home, things were going badly once again. He was bitterly jealous of his brothers, and his parents were at the end of their tether – though they admitted he was calmer on the day he came to the clinic.

Lately, the typewriter had been the means of self-expression and communication. He was typing 'just like Mum' and then he typed a letter to me. He modelled a figure of myself, before returning to his yoghurt-making, but it became just like Mum. More and more, he longed to be her only one.

He had a dream about a robber knifing him in the back, and was reminded of his dad, who had thrown cushions at him when he was a little boy. He got angrier and worse – he refused to wash and went berserk. He said he'd kicked his mother, because she'd made him lumpy porridge; he saw no reason to apologize. This was serious. We talked about the baby inside him, which always wanted its own way and was resenting the baby inside mum.

On the other hand, he was finding solace in religion, going to church with his next-door neighbour. He modelled a pulpit and spent the session trying to create some order once again. Symbolic of this need was turning all the dolls'-house family out into the 'garden' and arranging them sitting at a table. (He wanted his own bit of garden to dig in – knowing intuitively that that would have provided the safest outlet for his violence.) Now calm and happy, he enacted a tea party, making little breast-shaped cakes, smothering them in sugar; these were for us both. In the sand, he wrote 'I like you'. Next time, he cut up plasticine, like Mum baking a cake.

He confessed: 'I always wanted to be a girl!' 'You don't always know what's you and what is Mum, do you?' I reflected. 'I don't always', he agreed. He kept quiet while I drew him, and then he made a model of himself in plasticine. But the top half was a girl. He said 'I wish I was a girl. I'd like to have a baby, just like Mum!' 'Do you wish you were a baby, inside Mum?' I asked. He nodded.

There was a significant change. He modelled heavy saddles for elephants and rhinos. They were all to build a castle. The biggest elephant – himself – was not wild but tame. Perhaps this had to do with his mother's pregnant body and the need to control himself.

Next time his stepdad brought him to the clinic. Danny was glad to have him there. He was still obsessed by the fantasy of being Mum. In the clinic, he was warm and trusting, but at home things went from bad to worse. I suggested that if he was no better at home, his mum might stop him coming; he countered quickly: 'If I am better, she will stop me' – it seemed we couldn't win.

Some weeks went by before he came again. His mother had a job and nobody could bring him to the clinic. We picked up where we had left off. He was still an elephant; he made a pond for two thirsty elephants to drink in. Animals now fought men. Apes, elephants, and bears pounced on men and knocked them out. Primitive 'id' triumphed over 'ego' in his play, but at home he was trying very hard. He asked me how to change from being the 'worst of all' to 'good enough'. He role-played his good and bad self. The good one told the other what he was not to do.

But at the following session the elephant ran wild. In a rampage, he created havoc all around him. He stamped a dead buffalo into the ground. Danny then became a boy again and wanted a reward for being good. A month later he was punishing himself and told his mother he would bring his sessions to an end. He drew that day to a dramatic close. He took all his wild animals, put them in a truck, and covered them with sand. He picked up a tin soldier (himself) and made him aim a gun at the animals and shoot them dead. He then drew on the blackboard, rubbed out picture after picture, dropping all the chalks, one by one, on the floor. With the blackboard rubber he drew a Union Jack, put a roof on the flag, and wiped out the pole. It then became a house. Then finally the house became his mother's face. Feeling stunned, I drove him back to school. He waved goodbye. We stared silently at one another. He ran off.

Four months later, he was back. He was quiet and subdued. All he wanted was to cut and do woodwork. He declined to paint or play. An hour was spent on cutting balsa wood.

Next time he was more forthcoming. All the pain came out. They were underfed at home. Food was carefully apportioned, and anything left over on their parents' plates, they could have. But Danny was hungry all the time. The three boys had to act and share as if they were a single being (this was Mum's idea of justice and fair play). Things were also bad between their parents. The boys would hear their quarrelling and this too was unsettling. Danny was the scapegoat. He had to fight for territory (like his animals had done), he got smacked and sent to bed. He felt miserable and guilty. He'd come back to us against his mother's will. He dug deep graves in the sand and kept on burying and unearthing all the animals. There was no need to interpret. We both knew what was going on.

He became apathetic. Mum was now working full-time. He showed no feeling; he tried to type, but jumbled all the letters up. Finally, he typed a formal message: 'I hope you are well today.' He cut out a huge circle and made it smaller and smaller, a mandala[1] for himself. Pale, dry-eyed, and withdrawn, he said he didn't care whether he came or stopped.

The following session he was very unhappy; isolated, pent-up and dejected he denied all feeling and reality. He was in trouble with his teachers and told me 'I don't want to work or try any more'. Finally, he worked through his feelings in the sand. 'People' were put on horses and into the truck. They were attacked by soldiers. Pouring sand on the soldiers from high up above, he fought them back. Danny let me know how bad he felt. He now knew he was a loner. It was no use coming to me. Just the same, he didn't want to leave when the time came. He preferred to miss his dinner.

The next session was even worse. Danny was sad, bitter, apathetic. He said Mum didn't like him any more. She said he was worse. He would go off by himself all the time to the park, alone. Coming to the clinic was no good any more. He hated himself. None the less, he did three squiggles: the first, formless; the second, a clown; the third, large and free. But then he flung paint all over it and wrecked the lot.

Danny refused to talk. It was our final session. I was to take leave of absence from the clinic. We were by no means finished with each other; I wanted to go on, but it was impossible. He now had to cut me out, as he had cut out all feelings for so long.

On arrival, he entombed the action man, who had carried out his fantasies, his magical 'superman' self, under a mound of sand. He quickly nailed together two small pieces of balsa wood to form a cross, wrote his name on it in small letters, and stuck it on top of the burial mound. Then he made another, larger sign, wrote his name in capitals 'MR DANIEL JONES' and nailed it to the door of the Wendy house. We talked about the child Danny and the cross under which he had buried him, and the 'MR DANIEL' who had taken his place in the Wendy house. I said this was fine; there was now a man inside him who would grow stronger all the time and would help him to do good things for himself and others. He relaxed and could agree with this. I said we would always be friends and we might write to each other sometimes. He asked me for my full name. Danny's last session ended as his first one had begun – by writing his own name – but ending as a man: 'Mr Daniel Jones (aged eight).' What I felt I had witnessed was an act of death *and resurrection*. The child whose inner self I had known, was buried in the sand.

He went into the Wendy house to type, but the ribbon had run dry. Frustrated he banged the keys up and down, getting them all tangled up. He refused to come out, so I went in. He whispered – the keys were like the kids at school, rushing for their dinner and hammering at the door. He was the one in front, always first, always hungry. He grew alarmed, looked at the clock and thought he would be late for dinner. Then he refused to leave the Wendy house, let alone go back to school. After several minutes he came out sullenly. On the way back he relapsed into silence, waved to me as he left, but had cut off before he ran into school.

Two years later, I saw him at a day school for maladjusted children I was visiting. He was alone, sitting in a box, wrapped up in himself, solemn and withdrawn. He looked at me with no apparent recognition. I asked him if he could make me a replica of the cross and the sign, which I feared I had lost. Within two minutes, he had duplicated them and handed them to me, his face expressionless. I found the originals later, the copies were identical. He had not forgotten.

I heard no more of him till I came to write this account, ten years later. The years between had been troubled. Continually rejected at home, he had been disruptive at every school he'd attended. But when he left his final boarding school at the age of 16, it was the man 'Daniel' who went into the world. He had done well in every way. 'In every area, he has given of his best . . . his wit and cheerful disposition have made him many friends. Daniel is a "winner"' said his school report. It was filled with eulogies from all his teachers. It seemed almost too good, but it was true.

Micky

Because of the exceptionally sensitive nature of this case, I present these extracts from my notes verbatim, with as little intervention as possible.

Micky was referred by her mother at the age of 9 for disturbed behaviour. She had lit a fire on the living-room floor and had thrown some money out of the window, in an outburst of distress. Fires are frequently a cry for help (and an effective way of drawing attention to the urgent need for something to be done). Fire-raising may also draw attention to parental strife.

An only child and highly intelligent, she felt inextricably involved in her parents' marital problems. Micky was a buffer between them – especially at night, when she would hear them quarrelling. Aware of the sexual struggles she would rush into their room to protect her mother. Her father had been in and out of mental hospitals for many years. Paranoid about his wife, he believed she had affairs with other men. Her mother had previously had a nervous breakdown and was under dreadful stress, unable to leave her husband for economic reasons, although she knew how damaging the situation was for Micky and how serious it could become. Micky knew that her father's caresses had sexual undertones and was torn between her natural love for him and her hatred of his madness. He teased her cruelly. She feared him and longed to get away. She had, in fact, decided she would run away. She had packed all her things to take refuge with an auntie, but had to unpack them. 'Where could she go?' she asked me. She didn't want to leave her mummy – she might die and Micky would have to stay with Daddy. All the while, she was painting jellyfish, snails, starfish, sea urchins – all creatures she would hate to touch. She yawned wearily as she finished talking.

At school she could cope, and no one would have known how unhappy she was. To at last have someone she could trust and talk to at the clinic was a continual relief and she understood this very well. 'Nobody knows what Daddy's really like', she told me, 'He hurts me all the time. He teases me – he quarrels. Then Mummy shares my bed.'

10 May: She was more relaxed and happier next time. 'I wonder why I hate Daddy so much? I don't understand Mummy – your own flesh and blood and yet you don't *know*' – she turned to me – '*You* help me', and she played with clay for a solid hour.

24 May: Two weeks later she seemed less afraid of him – they were to go away together for a week. She told me, not that she had in fact already lit a fire but that she wished she could – she loved fire. She had just put a fire out in her bathroom curtains — I forbore to ask her how they had caught fire.

24 June: Micky was relaxed – thinking of her mother – M for Micky, Mo for mother, interwoven, describing while she dribbles paint – 'this looks like a snake' – 'this like No. 2'. She mentioned Dad's wet kisses on her mouth and covered up her painting with thick muddy paint.

5 October: Obsessed with fear and hatred of her father, and identifying with her mother, she painted lips – Mummy's, Daddy's, hers – and covered up the lips with black – nobody must know!

12 October: Painting fireworks led again to talk of setting fires – she could now tell the truth, although all the fires were accidental, she assured me.

26 October: She told me about a letter she had sent her mother two years ago – 'Dad is trying to kill me – I don't like him – wish you were here'. But he read her letter – again she covered up her painting.

2 November: Full of doubts about her feelings: 'Am I happy? Do I really want Daddy to go?' (She liked him tickling her arm!) Her ambivalence became a revolving circle in bright, clear colour, quickly covered up with muddy paint.

She was beginning to censor her free spontaneous talk, especially about sex. She identified with her mother, yet was more tolerant of her father.

16 November: Her father was demanding love from both his wife and daughter and provoked only rejection.

6 December: On a red background, she painted a netball game in black and yellow – yellow was herself. She won against the black – happiness versus misery. She saw then how she could be happy on the surface and angry, hurt, confused, chaotic on the inside. She had to cover up those feelings. Baffled, she asked me why does love turn to hate? Did I love my husband when I married him? I said being in 'love' was more like having a temperature, loving was different! She nodded sagely: 'Like me wanting Mummy when I've got chickenpox!'

11 January: Micky gave a vivid account of Dad and Mum struggling in bed – Micky remarked that she liked them fighting; wanted them to go on. 'Dad's like a 2-year-old. Some people like him – but he's mad.'

18 January: 'I hate red – red comes between Mummy and Daddy – red is danger and death'. (It seemed he was ill again and might go to hospital 'for a rest'.) Micky thought he would take her mother's love away from her if she gave in to him. She was suddenly afraid of boarding school. 'I love my bed, my room, the house, Mummy – I wish Dad would go away and marry some other woman.'

24 January: She was happier today – able to assert herself at home. Her mother had made her take a bath against her will. Angrily she told me 'I wrote Mum a letter: "You have got two lives. I want mine back."' She painted spheres – earth, sun, moon, planets, monsters.

15 February: This time she painted a storm – a great black sky. She painted a house and then blacked it out. Great pink stripes of rain, whirling grey winds, a big, black tree, a streak of lightning cracking the tree. She wrote the word 'cracked' on the picture. 'It's Daddy and there is no *home*.' She then painted two burst balloons – Dad and Mum – on the ground, and a third balloon – herself. She painted over it all, again and again, and scrawled: 'Daddy angry. Mummy – love' (*Figure 15*).

She was afraid of marriage. Nobody was happy. She only trusted Mummy's love.

8 March: Micky was much happier this week. She had changed towards Dad; she loved him. She drew two pairs of lips.

Figure 15 Micky: 'Daddy angry. Mummy love'

15 March: She announced on arrival 'Mum can't have any more children – I have a baby growing in my tummy!'

19 April: Unhappy holidays – daily quarrels again and she wanted to get away.

26 April: She had decided not to have a baby through her tummy because she was afraid of injections! She would adopt one instead. She composed a song:

> 'Love is a very funny thing
> You can't play around with it
> It always backfires'

3 May: She was disturbed now by the truce at home – she mistrusted it and knew that scenes would break out again.

10 May: 'I hate Dad. He's like dirt. Mum is a clean window. One could see through it, if it weren't for him. Wipe him out – destroy him! If only they'd split up.'

17 May: She was desperate for Mum to get a divorce. Dad's kisses were hateful. 'I am grown up enough to understand.'

14 June: She was calm, but fearful that calm at home precedes a storm. I suggested that she must make her own life!

21 June: She asked me seriously, how she could live alone. Painting a river winding its way through countryside, she said, 'This is like my life. I can make it myself!'

5 July: She was afraid of Dad, and afraid for her own sanity.

19 July: Micky was again involved in their sex war and took refuge in playing with the dolls' house.

30 August: She said, 'No rows, Mum and Dad talk gently to each other.' The moment there was peace at home, she reflected it – looking fresh and lovely: 'I don't want to paint, only draw with coloured pencils – I'll do modern art.'

'What's that?'

'It's putting yourself – what you feel, rather than what you see or know – into a picture.' She swished paint around – till rainclouds or lightning appeared – then she pressed tissues on to the wet paint.

'The storm is over – here's a duck – it's coming out to play.'

'Like your life at home!'

'It always turns out like that!' she said sceptically – yet with a little more perception.

11 October: She told me once again about a row overheard at home and she commented, 'They've made their bed and chosen to lie on it.'

'Very well put!' she considered, pensively.

18 October: Micky seemed increasingly indifferent to the quarrels – she didn't understand her mother's ambivalence. As she came in, she asked: 'What's it called, a penant? – no, a penis. Mummy says we ought to talk about things like that!'

22 November: A dream had made her aware of her father's incestuous kisses – 'I said "*Don't!*" – just like Mummy does. He does the same thing to us both.'

10 January: Painting! A sun, a wind – herself alone, like a flower with petals. She now understood that she would have her own life, her own decisions to make. What would she be? She might teach in a nursery school.

29 May: She had been away at camp and had grown much taller. Her mother had been ill. She 'gets everything she wants and comes first'. Micky was indignant to discover that Dad was much fonder of Mum than of her! Her mother was going into hospital and Micky was to stay with an aunt.

Her painting began with a great purple patch and a black, swirling circle – 'That's the world. It's being swamped' (*Figure 16*). She stuck tissues on it, and poured more paint and water. 'Red like blood! The world is being taken over by life and life kills the world! That's death.' Her grandparents were

Figure 16 Micky: 'The world being swamped'

dying; her periods had begun; she talked. of dizziness and blood, earth, water, the universe, and spilt the water jars all over, splashing walls, floor, self, and me – a global, elemental picture of her overwhelming body/soul upheaval.

12 June: Micky's mother was quite ill, and rather sharp with her. She was losing weight and appetite and was going into hospital. Micky felt worried – where would she stay while her mother was away? Perhaps she could be with me? This fantasy gave her comfort. The future looked tragically uncertain. She was painting great dark masses – like constipated faeces – out at last. This gave her great relief; she 'doodled' a clay half-human figure and she analysed it, 'It has no sex, neither bosoms, nor penis!'

10 July: Next time, hot and red-cheeked, she came bouncing in and beamed with pleasure. The hour was taken up assembling the plastic female figure, complete with reproductive organs. She still did not know who would have her – Mum's or Dad's family. She sought my support against her dad – 'he doesn't like me coming to the clinic – Mum does'.

30 October: Three months later she came in to report on both her parents.

Her mother was very depressed and felt she had nothing to live for. Daddy looked at Micky all the time and this made her uncomfortable. She was remarkably objective now, detached from the family situation, and eager to go away to boarding school – could it be arranged?

Her visits were spaced out. To her intense satisfaction she went to boarding school. She did extremely well there, coming top in every subject, and she became Head Girl. She was able to cope with her parents during the holidays and she visited the clinic, full of her new life. She had learned to ride – was popular with staff and had many friends at school.

Gina and Micky, both only daughters, both basically healthy loving children, were distraught by their parents' unhappiness. While Gina covered up her paintings, as a denial of her pain, Micky worked through her feelings and covered up as part of a self-healing process. She would often cry while painting and would mop both her tears and her wet pictures with the tissues.

Despite their different personalities and life experiences (it must be remembered that Gina felt unwanted by her mother and Micky, who both loved and hated her father, felt protective of her mother), both girls emerged successfully from their painful childhood.

When I began to write, I found I had no choice at all. These children, one after the other, simply surged up from the past, as peaks emerge into the light from enshrouding mists.

© 1987 Diana Halliday

Note

1 A mandala is a Hindu term for a circle. In Jungian psychology, it contains the totality of the self. Danny's unconscious use of this symbol showed how his former 'self' was shrinking. He had buried his libido in the sand-pit – it was the 'action man' – dead – a symbolic suicide.

References

Glendinning, V. (1981) *Edith Sitwell: A Biography*. London: Weidenfeld & Nicholson.
Whyte, L. H. (1960) *The Unconscious Before Freud*. London: Julian Freedman.

6 | Art therapy: a way of healing the split

Patricia Nowell Hall

There seems to be a paradox in *writing* about art therapy. Much of its essential healing power lies beyond words – experiencing is perhaps the best way of understanding. Art therapy can offer a way of exploring and expressing areas of ourselves that lie beyond the reach of words, and can create a bridge between inner and outer, towards greater integration of the two. In practice, the people best qualified to comment on the effectiveness of art therapy, and the only people who can really understand, are those who have directly experienced it. And as art therapy claims to be about psychic growth and in-depth long-term change, they cannot know it at the time; they can only really begin to know something afterwards.

With this in mind I carried out a study based on the words and images of patients and ex-patients who experienced treatment in a therapeutic community. I wanted to explore the value of art therapy; and attempt to find out whether it could be useful not merely as an adjunct and catalyst to the verbal and group psychotherapy, as practised at that hospital, but also, and more powerfully, useful as an alternative and complementary, non-verbal way of therapy, thus redressing an imbalance within the intensely verbal, analytic, and group culture of the therapeutic community.

The study was carried out by gathering the patients' comments and images, both during their time of therapy, and more importantly in lengthy interviews between seven and ten years after their experience of therapy. They looked again at their pictures and talked about their experience. The images evoked memories and many feelings, and they talked often with extraordinary insight and honesty, and in great detail. Images can hold their meaning, and reveal more only when the person is ready to see. Words, in contrast, are easily forgotten and denied. Let me say at once that I considered at the time that the heavy emphasis on the verbal, interpretative, and group approach to therapy at this hospital created an unhealthy imbalance, and denied much of the potential for the non-verbal and more creative attitudes of the patients, and that art therapy offered one way of beginning to redress this imbalance.

The implications of this study may have a far wider significance. In *Modern Man in Search of a Soul* (1961) Jung claimed that many of the psychological ills that afflict 'modern' people are due to the one-sided rationalism of our culture. And Irene Champernowne suggests that 'Perhaps even more today when the intellect and cerebral activity is too highly valued to the exclusion of feeling, man is turning for very life to the means of expression in the arts' (1969: 2). In 1986 Patrick Pietrone, Chairman of the British Holistic Medical Association, asserted that 'The search for a balance is also a search for wholeness. It is a search for the connections between the disparate bits of ourselves.' It is interesting that it is now, against this background, that art therapy is emerging.

The setting

I was working at a day hospital, run on 'therapeutic community lines' (Jones 1953). Patients came voluntarily and were expected to come for about nine months (a significant length of time?) though they could negotiate to stay longer. All were expected to attend for five full days a week. There were on average between twenty-five and thirty patients attending the hospital at one time, aged between 20 and 40 years old. All attended voluntarily and were thought to be able to benefit from the verbal, group analytic mode of treatment. There was a large psychotherapy group daily for the whole community. Patients were also allotted to a small psychotherapy group, run by their 'principal' therapist, and a co-therapist. This was seen as the focal point of the treatment.

There were two art therapy groups a week led by myself: one open to everyone, the other an 'intensive' art therapy group for six to eight people, with a commitment for a fixed length of time. I was also a co-therapist in the 'dream group', thus working closely with dream images in relationship to those arising through spontaneous painting in art therapy. (Throughout this chapter I shall at times be referring to 'painting' as shorthand for all the different sorts of media used and creations made in art therapy. I shall also be using 'he' rather than 'she' when referring impersonally.)

There was a wealth of art materials, and people had the chance to paint outside as well as within official group times. The space we used was in the occupational therapy area, which also included the patients' kitchen (described as 'the heart of the hospital'). Paintings from the 'open' art therapy group were put up in the large psychotherapy group room for the following morning's meeting, where they might be looked at and commented on, usually more within the perspective of emerging communal, rather than individual, themes. Series of paintings would also be shown at review meetings of individual patients.

The art therapy groups were structured in three stages: (1) people would come together for a short general discussion and a chance to say how they felt, (2) they would find a space and paint, usually working alone (for about an hour), and (3) they would come together as a group, with a turn for each person to show and talk about their painting if they wished. Sometimes exercises were suggested – generally designed to facilitate self-exploration rather than to prescribe areas to explore. More often the sessions were 'open' and relatively 'non-directive'.

Sometimes a session would begin with 'centring' or relaxation exercises, meditation, or yoga (like looking into water – one can see into the depths and at what lies below more clearly when the surface is calm). Sometimes we would begin with techniques designed to heighten sensory awareness and help energy to flow.

After painting, people were encouraged to look at what they had created, to contemplate it, and to allow it space to 'speak' back to them. Paintings were kept in individual folders. People were encouraged to look at them again regularly in the following months, individually and in series.

As the art therapist in the groups, I aspired, as Champernowne (1969) said, 'to provide the protective conditions to let things happen', and to enable the ideal that Carl Rogers (1957: 95–103) claims as 'the necessary therapeutic climate'. This would be one that 'allows both psychological safety and freedom – through unconditional positive regard, warmth, genuineness and accurate empathy' thereby maximizing the chance of openness to play, to experiment, and to change and for constructive creativity and growth to emerge.

The role of the therapist

In trying to describe the role of the therapist, three images leap to mind. One, as a patient described it, is that of a 'psychic midwife' – helping to bring things to birth, aiding the transition between inner and outer. The second image is of a kind of 'gardener'. In the lyrical words of another ex-patient 'it's a question of enriching the ground to help the seeds to grow'. In both cases, it's a way of assisting a natural process. (According to the Greek derivation of the word 'therapy', a therapist is 'one who waits on, attends'.) Healing is an organic process. There is no magic or scientific formula for 'cure' or 'growth': each person must find their own way in their own time. As Auden (1956) has said, 'the art of healing is not so much a science, as the intuitive art of wooing nature' – and waiting.

But perhaps the most powerful guiding image for me in my work as an art therapist arose when I was intensely and unexpectedly moved upon first seeing and experiencing the huge unfinished sculptures by Michelangelo which stand in the Academy in Florence – huge powerful figures of slaves struggling with great force to release themselves from the stone. Michelangelo had described the process – the figures had been buried and trapped in lumps of stone before he began, and his job as a sculptor was to carefully chip away the stone to help them fight free and emerge. It can be a deeply moving process to see people fight free and emerge. And both client and therapist are changed through the process and the relationship.

The approach of the therapist inevitably influences how patients work with the material that arises, and much of my approach will become more apparent when considering the images themselves later in this chapter. Working at this hospital was very formative for me both personally and for my subsequent work as an art therapist. My approach developed, paradoxically, more in complementary relation to the central mode of group analytic therapy rather than as a technique within it. I had a growing conviction about art therapy, and a growing conviction that its power lay most centrally with the 'art' and the creative process. And I began to see that it could have a more powerful role to play in fostering individual growth than merely as an adjunct and catalyst to the verbal group psychotherapy. I felt it could offer a separate and alternative kind of therapy. Art therapy can be, for some, a profoundly significant experience, and very much more powerful and 'therapeutic' than it is generally given credit for. It must be lifted out of the 'Cinderella' role and awarded the respect and acknowledgement it deserves.

At first I worked intuitively, but as I gained experience and read more widely I discovered my ideas and feelings crystallized around the ideas and techniques of Jung, who places the arts firmly at the centre of his mode of therapy. Working also with the techniques and ideas of Gestalt therapy, particularly as described by Fritz Perls (1971) and Janie Rhyne (1973), the combination seemed to be, potentially, a very powerful one.

Put simply, Gestalt techniques (as I have used them), especially with the emphasis on body awareness, can be useful in releasing the unblocking feelings and creative energy, and in offering ways of getting more in touch with split-off and projected areas; these can be particularly useful in relating to an image. Jungian principles and techniques give a sense of direction and meaning as an explanatory model, and offer ways of 'mobilizing inner psychic resources through the transcendent function of symbol-making' towards greater integration and individuation. Jung believed that creativity is a basic instinct, and that the releasing of creativity and creative energy is essential for mental health. He talked of psychotherapy as 'less a question of treatment than of developing the creative possibilities latent in the patient himself' (1966: CW 16, para. 82). He claimed that the human psyche can be viewed as a potentially self-regulating, self-balancing organism, capable, given sympathetic and conducive circumstances, of healing itself. He saw symptoms essentially as signs that the psyche is struggling to grow, and illness as psychic blocks and splits needing release and integration. One is reminded of the image of a stream that is dammed up. He saw that within mental illness or breakdown there is a creative process at work, trying to 'heal the split', struggling to bridge unconscious and conscious, and working towards new integration and resolution, and which, if understood and assisted, could enable the person to find their own solution and their own balance. He saw all human psychic activity as working towards 'self-realization', 'individuation', and 'wholeness'.

Jung believed there were two basic approaches which, if used in parallel, would help to bring about greater balance, and greater integration of unconscious and conscious, ego and self. These he called 'the way of creative formulation' (i.e. fantasy, dreams, 'active imagination', symbols, and art) and 'the way of understanding' (i.e. intellectual concepts, verbal formulations, conscious awareness, and abstractions) claiming that 'one tendency seems to be the regulating principle of the other, and both are bound together in a compensatory relationship' (1970: CW 14, para. 706).

This would tally with the ideas of Karl Stern, who, in his book *The Flight from Woman* points out the basic duality of knowing – that of 'poetic knowledge' and that of 'scientific knowledge'. He equates one with intuition, empathy, and femaleness, and the other with 'discursive reasoning' and maleness. He stresses the need for respect for both. He argues that 'human knowledge seems to have the greatest chance to arrive at truth when the two . . . are in perfect balance' (1966: 42–3); a view compatible not only with the findings and theories of Jung, but also with the truths of ancient Taoism.

Jung believed that symbols are a natural mode of psychic expression, and the natural language of the unconscious (as opposed to the Freudian idea of 'manifest content' which conceals latent or repressed desires). Symbols arise spontaneously – they cannot be produced intentionally. He recognized the living quality of symbols, and the healing power of the symbols and symbol-making. Symbols are living and personified aspects of the psyche. They are charged with psychic energy – with numinosity – and are thus dynamic, have driving power, and will produce consequences. Jung recognized their role in activating inner psychic resources together with the compensatory, homeostatic potential of the unconscious. 'A symbol represents and is also a part of a larger whole. It throws together (*sym, bole*) what is known and what is (as yet) unknown', thus it 'discloses (however dimly) new levels of meaning both in the external world and in the personal psyche. It is a bridge that joins "inside" and "outside" whilst retaining a distinction' (Hobson 1985: 111). As Paul Tillich puts it:

> 'Every symbol opens up a level of reality for which non-symbolic speaking is inadequate . . . . But in order to do this, something else must be opened up – namely levels of the soul, levels of our interior reality. And they must correspond to the levels in exterior reality which are opened up by a symbol. So every symbol is two-edged. It opens up reality and it opens up the soul.'
>
> (quoted in Hobson 1985: 111)

Fritz Perls, described as 'the father of Gestalt therapy', believed that the verbal and psychoanalytical approach was in danger of perpetuating the neurotic split between the intellect and the emotions, thus inhibiting the ability to assimilate and make use of insights. How can the insights and interpretations be integrated, made real – 'real-ized' – and used?

Jung argued that neurosis was self-division, 'the suffering of a soul that has lost its meaning', and that the purpose of therapy was to heal the split. 'To heal is to make whole', and the way towards that was not so much understanding it with one's head but experiencing it, and feeling it:

> 'The needful thing is not to know the truth but to experience it. Not to have an intellectual conception of things, but to find our way to the inner, and perhaps wordless, irrational experience – that is the great problem . . . nothing is more important than finding the way to these far-off goals.'
>
> (Jung 1953: CW 7, 67–91)

Some patients and staff realized, from their experience, that there was a real need to redress the balance by finding a complement to the verbal, analytical, and more problem-centred approach; a need to help synthesis, to integrate more effectively the intellectual understanding and meaning with the feeling and experience, the verbal with the non-verbal, and to re-establish the natural dialogue between conscious and unconscious, between the ego and the self, towards the integration of the personality as a whole.

This point was illustrated by one of the first images that emerged in an art therapy group. It was an image, powerfully painted, of a head, described as having a mask for a face, which was cut off from its body, which was depicted with powerfully muscular limbs. The patient described the image as showing the split she felt between her 'head and body' – her 'thinking' and her 'feeling'. She claimed at the time that this was because of 'all the words and insights that I don't know how to use', and felt that the verbal–analytical style of therapy was not helpful in taking her further. She accused the therapy of 'left hemisphere domination'.[1] At a later stage she realized how she had been able to hide behind her words, and by encapsulating the insights within intellectual concepts, she had been able to defend herself, in some measure, against the pain of allowing herself to feel. It is interesting how the making and contemplating of the image had been vital steps in helping her to confront herself with this, and eventually to realize it. For some, it seemed, words were not enough.

The drive towards 'healing the split', towards integration and wholeness was beautifully exemplified by a series of paintings, described as 'Body, Mind, and Spirit'. The three images were painted in the same session, and facilitated by a guided fantasy. They were painted by someone who had great ability intellectually, and had achieved great academic success and respect, but nevertheless found herself rather depressed – feeling somehow 'out of balance'.

The first image represented the thinking, cerebral side. She had painted a black outline of a large static figure, without hands or feet, and with a huge head. Inside the head was a grey brain, with a small black figure standing inside it. She said she felt she was seen as 'just one big brain'. In the fantasy 'I was stuck in my head', and 'I got lost inside my brain'.

The second image was the 'feeling emotional and creative side'. It was a figure, painted in green, with an undefined face, painted in large flowing brush strokes, with feet half planted in the brown earth, and daffodils growing out of the raised hands. This, she said, is how she wanted to be – 'out of her head and into her body, and of the earth'. She described how she wanted to 'get more in touch with her creative side'.

In the third image, she had painted 'expanded lungs, full of air and light' filling the paper, reaching beyond the bounds of the paper. She said she longed for 'space to breathe' with perhaps an acknowledgement for something more spiritual. In the centre of the picture, she had written 'I am the void – the space between – the breath of life – the inexpressible'.

The art therapy group: the patients' comments

For some, art therapy played a synthesizing role, acting as a vital complement to the verbal group therapy in various ways. It seemed to have a particular importance at the beginning, as a way into therapy. Many patients were severely depressed, and insecure, and lacking in confidence and a personal sense of self when they first came to the community. For some it seemed to offer an area of extra safety – and the activity gave it a more permissive feel.

The structure of the art therapy group provided an opportunity for everyone to be seen and heard. The situation was less threatening for some than in the talking groups, because everyone was working at the same time (rather than taking it in turns), because they were 'doing something' (painting can be easier for some than talking), and because there was no obligation to talk at all – about their paintings or themselves. One patient commented: 'It was a gentle way in a rather violent and aggressive culture – but no less powerful because of that.'

Several talked of the 'unfreezing' or 'freeing' nature of the activity and the group – the beginning of letting down defences, getting involved, and experimenting. One former patient explained:

'It wasn't seen as so threatening or challenging as the psychotherapy groups . . . not so serious . . . painting wasn't a formal activity, and anyway there wasn't the feeling you were going to be stripped to the core two minutes after you'd done something – so you could relax controls and play around a bit.'

Then he insightfully added:

'and so what did come out, paradoxically, was often more authentic . . . it all seemed more important in retrospect. . . . It was the first group I talked in . . . and laughed in . . . you could make a mess.'

Another patient summarized its importance to her – especially at the beginning – as 'safety, play, and sympathy'. Several also mentioned the energy-releasing effect:

'It was good to *do* something about your feelings – and good to use your hands and body.'

'It was generally releasing, and at the end of a session you usually felt more positive and had more energy.'

The art therapy at the hospital seemed to have offered an opportunity and the permission 'to play and explore through playing'. The majority of those interviewed mentioned the importance of the playing – many fully realizing its significance and seriousness only in retrospect:

'It was alright to regress and play in art therapy . . . someone needs to consider the therapeuticness of enjoying something versus being stirred up and antagonized.'

'There was a chance for the child to play. It was good to have the chance to let our fantasies fly and explore them.'

Of course, play and fantasy – helping people release their creative 'child-like' selves – are central to art therapy. They are two of its most valuable aspects, working together with respect and trust in the healing power of the imagination. (Coleridge (1802) talks of 'the shaping spirit of Imagination'.) As Champernowne (1969) said, 'play and fantasy can be a preparation for life – rather than a path away from it'. And Jung said, 'while at first glance

Plate 7

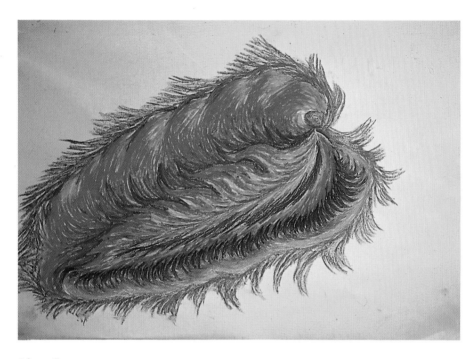

Plate 8

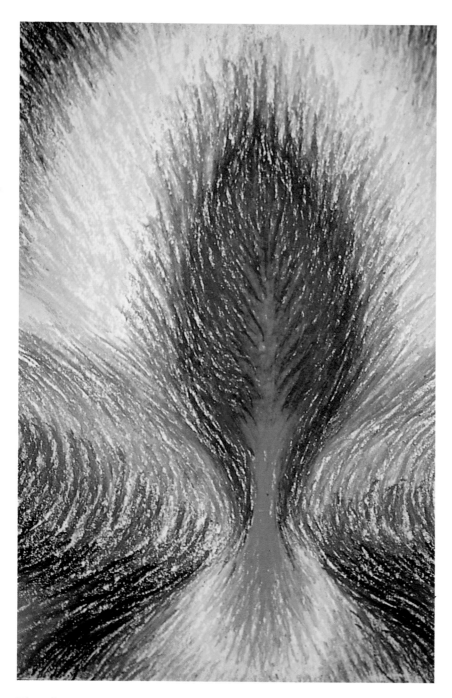

Plate 9

Plate 10

playing might look like a regression, the constellation of the child archetype represents potential future . . . in playing lies our greatest potential for growth and development' (1930, as quoted by Schwartz 1978). And as one ex-patient so beautifully explains: 'Art and play are inherently positive. They provide the tools for health.'

It seemed important for some in providing a way of beginning to make contact with others, to share, and to begin to build the necessary trust and social support towards facilitating the individuation process.

'Doing something was important, and doing something together – or anyway at the same time as other people – it brought people together.'

'It's easier to make contact or break the ice if you're all doing some activity. You can say "can I borrow your pencil?" or something.'

And as another person succinctly explained:

'One of the strongest things going for the art therapy was that it offered a less rigid way of relating to people and made genuine contact possible. . . . And everyone had something definite to talk about, whether it was a squiggle or a finished painting.'

At the same time it was felt that in the art therapy group there was a chance for some 'personal space' while being together with others – space and containment – 'being with people, yet being private and alone' and a chance to 'go into oneself and fantasize'. The group exerted its healing power indirectly:

'It was alright, in fact expected, to be quiet and private – you have to be if you're painting anyway, you didn't have to interact or feel you had to.'

Another person said:

'Painting is like a modern sort of prayer – and it's easier to do it with other people even though it's essentially private. It's like in a Quaker meeting, or in church when you are together yet alone.'

The art therapy session offered a balance of privacy and sharing: first, to withdraw, reflect, and explore, through the art materials, alone, intra-psychically and silently; and then to 'come out' and come together with others for showing and talking – each with his own individual and unique creation to show and/or talk about. In this way the private world of painting became linked to the public world of language, and with an intermediate stage of being able to communicate with and confront oneself first, before sharing with others. This was commented on as very important, especially in a milieu that was in a sense based on a more extroverted and interpersonal group therapy culture.

In this way, the art therapy activity offered an opportunity to begin to develop the vital capacity to be separate and alone (all-one) in order to be healthily together with other people. Developing this capacity of 'alone-togetherness' and 'creative aloneness' is a central task of therapy. 'I have a basic need for relations with others . . . and yet to remain alone with my own middle.' Aloneness and togetherness are interdependent. Robert Hobson, in his paper on 'Loneliness' explains it well:

> 'I can be alone only in so far as I can be together with others. And I can be together with others only in so far as I can be alone. That is what it means to become an individual with an identity and be a member of a community.'
>
> (1974: 77)

Of course this applies not only to the hothouse of this community, but also to living creatively in the world outside.

It seems that the art therapy not only helped people with talking and 'learning the language of therapy' but it also had particular importance in the initial stages of therapy as a way to begin the journey. In various facilitating ways it provided an area of extra safety, and an easier way into self-exploration, through play and image-making, releasing feelings and tapping energy – a place for easier and more genuine contact between people, a way of learning to be an individual yet part of a group, a way towards building the trust and social support needed to explore and use all the therapy.

The official language of the therapeutic community was words – with the expectation that patients would explore and share through talking. But for some there was a need for another form of expression and communication. While some people found it easy – at times too easy – to talk, there were others who found it difficult to find words for their feelings or difficult to talk at all – especially the more naturally introverted or those in particular crises.

> 'The expectation to talk, meant an expectation you could think fairly straight – and to think at all, rather than just have feelings, you had to have your head pretty together. We were there, most of us in the first place because we'd fallen apart and were pretty confused, and our heads weren't together.'

When one is feeling too overwhelmed to find words for feelings, and too fragile to be able to try, the demand to do so can be frightening. One person quoted at length from her diary written eight years before, during her time at the hospital, giving a graphic and moving description of one of her first experiences in a large psychotherapy group, and the threat to her sense of reality and identity. It may help to understand from the inside:

'If people's eyes rested on me, I felt attacked, almost obliterated with the terror that I would be obliged to speak. The horror of having to find words from nowhere terrified me. Caught between not existing, and existing as pure feeling, I had to struggle to hold on to both sides of myself, consciously keep drawing back the thinking self which threatened to flit up to the ceiling, detach itself, leave me forever. . . . I physically found I was clinging on to the seat – almost pinching myself. . . . Whose feelings were whose . . . where did people begin and end? Were there any boundaries?'

You need a sense of self from which to find words and talk. But as she later said: 'Some things are beyond words. . . . Painting gave me something definite and concrete to hang on to' – a proof and reinforcement of her own boundaries and identity, and a way to communicate something of her feelings.

The beginnings in art therapy

Many would spend the first art therapy sessions playing with and exploring the media. Some would, relatively consciously, use it as a chance to factually portray through their paintings, information about themselves, their past, their background – any information they wanted others to be aware of. Some would use it as an opportunity to 'make and express mess', to express something of their inner chaos – and the 'prima materia' from which new patterns can emerge. All would consciously or unconsciously portray something of their emotional state, not only in what they portrayed, but how they portrayed it and made their image. And a first image could be like a first dream in therapy, and show not only their present state but also their potential.

But it can be difficult to allow oneself to begin, to make the first mark, the first image. It involves having trust enough to begin to 'let go' and allow things to happen. It involves having what Coleridge (1817) calls 'poetic faith', together with a 'willing suspension of disbelief'. An ex-patient described the process:

'The important thing is to let the thoughts float to the front of your mind, and catch the images as they float by, just letting it happen without doing anything about it . . . and when you paint the image, there's no doubt about its authenticity – you feel a sudden release of energy, like a sexual thrill.'

The 'art of letting things happen' is how Jung described the process of 'active imagination'. He felt it was vitally important. Basing his views on his own inner explorations, he said: 'the act of letting things happen, action through non-action, letting go of oneself became for me the key opening the door to the way. We must be able to let things happen in the psyche' (1962: 93). The Taoist phrase is 'wu-wei' – action through non-action ('wu' = not; 'wei' = action, stirring, straining). As the images will show, people can be surprised by what they produce when they 'let go'.

Some of the images I have described in words, and words, though inadequate, can convey something of the images' message. Others must be seen and experienced – perhaps those that carried numinosity, i.e. were charged with psychic energy, and those that were particularly alive and dynamic for the person who made them.

Michael, who painted *Figure 17*, explained: 'This is me and this is really where I want to be – safe and secure in the womb!' Later he said: 'Paintings can get you to a place where you can start.' This picture, generously painted in shades of green, with firm black outlines, began as a 'doodle'; he surprised himself by what appeared.

Some patients, particularly at the beginning of therapy, were in quite a regressed state. Art therapy offered permission and a way of exploring and expressing their feelings more 'acceptably'. The language of images seems more natural to those in a regressed, often pre-verbal state. Perhaps by taking himself 'back to the womb' this patient was making a necessary step – finding a starting point so that some sort of rebirth might happen. (He, it was, who later talked of the therapist's role as a 'psychic midwife'.)

In talking about the image, and being back in the womb he later added wryly: 'but it might be rather uncomfy – like being a square peg in a round hole!' Confronting this image he began to feel not only a sense of security, but also a sense of uncomfortableness and claustrophobia. The image holds the polarities. In this he aptly demonstrated the archetypal life tension between the urge for security and fusion, and the urge for individuation. The ambiguity of the image has a vital purpose in the understanding of its meaning. It also allows the expressing and holding of the polarities simultaneously – facilitating integration. As Jung said: 'Symbols are natural attempts to reconcile and reunite often widely separated opposites' (1967 CW 5: 259).

Wholeness is about transcending opposites. I would argue that this potential for the holding and communicating of polarity and ambiguity is one of the therapeutic strengths of art therapy. This image and his comments about it are also an example of how something profoundly serious can be expressed, and presented in a playful and jokey way. It was painted in a quick 'throw-away' manner as a way of making it more palatable, to protect the artist against possible criticism or ridicule. People did laugh at it but he later agreed that 'it was serious too'. It led to some important discussion and insight.

Figure 17

Diana's first image emerged after a period of feeling excruciatingly paralysed. She had been coming to the art therapy group for some weeks, but had found herself unable to begin, to make the first mark. She would take some paper, but would quickly leave it and wander round or sit and watch others working, seeming very uncomfortable with herself. When we looked again at her image, which had many layers and frames, she very clearly remembered doing it:

> 'I remember sitting looking at the paper. It seemed very white, and frozen and empty, and I noticed the sharp corners and regular edges. It looked cold and critical, and suddenly I felt angry, and wanted to mark it. I wanted to dominate it, and with a pastel I drew a slow deliberate circle, and then a square around it. Then the energy came, and I quickly drew another square within the circle, and a circle within that, and a triangle inside that, and at the centre I put a dot. Then I surrounded it all with curling sun-rays. It looked fairly pathetic, but felt very good. And I felt a huge sense of relief, and energy.'

At the time, she explained it merely in diagrammatic terms as being about the psychotherapy and art therapy groups, and her within them: 'The art therapy is like a circle and the psychotherapy group like a square.' And she talked of the extra safety and containment the art therapy area offered. Later she said the image became 'a symbol of safety and security' for her, and 'a way of getting centred', a way to 'enable her to carry on'. It also appeared as a symbol of integration – she had created for herself extra framing and protective boundaries.

She kept the image beside her, where she could see it, before going on to explore more obviously vulnerable and unknown areas. She said it enabled her to begin. In a sense she had created her own alchemical vessel, a vessel to begin her journey.

In her following picture, she chose a square bit of paper and, again finding it difficult to begin, found a washing-up bowl and drew round it to form again a firm circle within the square. Then she could begin painting; and she began right in the middle. She painted in hot, fiery colours, at first tentatively, her strokes gaining in confidence as she expanded outwards. She travelled outwards in a 'Catherine-wheel' motion until she had painted over, dominated, and in a sense taken control of the boundaries of the circle, to touch the edges of the square. She said that she felt she had 'grown herself' out of the need for the extra boundary – the containment and protection of the art therapy group. Her autonomy was growing. Now she was pushing against the boundaries of the square.

'I couldn't talk, I couldn't scream, but I could paint'

Jan had been in a state of frozen silence and deepest despair when she first arrived at the hospital. Unable to communicate, she was cut off and unreachable. There are no words when one is imprisoned and paralysed in deepest loneliness and fear. She couldn't talk, or scream, but eventually she could paint.

Her first image, painted apparently without emotion, was of a tiny black figure, falling headlong into a huge and seemingly bottomless abyss. On either side were huge thickly painted black oppressive cliffs. Its effect was stark and shocking. When she had finished, and as she looked at it, she began to cry. She was beginning to let go and 'unfreeze'. 'I felt I was falling and falling through some sort of abyss. . . . Some images don't need words.' There are some states of feelings that are far beyond the reach of words. How can one penetrate the core of loneliness and speak to that – or out of it?

Perhaps for some, sometimes, making an image can create a bridge and a way of 'speaking' out of states of being that might be described as the depths of despair, 'naked horror', 'psychotic loneliness', or the 'frozen isolation of no-being' (Hobson 1985: 267). It can begin to make a bridge between inner and outer worlds, enabling the first steps to be taken – away from this prison and towards reaching another person. It can begin to allow other people in. By giving external form to a measure of these feelings, it can be a step towards gaining some control over them, by creating boundaries for them.

Later she framed the painted image further by mounting it on a sheet of black paper. In doing this she sealed the abyss.

'Art therapy can be a way of giving expression and description to the unspoken and the unspeakable'   (Halliday 1980)

The following examples that I am going to present will illustrate some of the ways in which people use this language of art, giving form and voice to the inner world of images. In this way they can create a bridge between the seemingly irreconcilable worlds of inner and outer reality. It can provide a way of healing the split.

I have particularly selected the work of three people to look at in more detail, in order to highlight some important aspects of art therapy. (Of course, the different aspects of art therapy are intricately bound up with each other, and any attempt to highlight and categorize them must inevitably be superficial, as it will deny the richness and importance of the interconnections. Art therapy is a far more powerful and mysterious process than the sum of its parts.)

At one level, images can be considered as a powerful form of *symbolic speech* – with or without consideration of the archetypal component. The series of five images, the first two of which are shown here (see *Plate 7* and *Figure 18*) were consciously intended expressions and communications from a patient to his therapist. They were used as an alternative mode of expression and communication to words. John's images show clearly how he had transferred on to his therapist aspects of his relationship with his mother. They also show how he was able to express powerful – and dangerous – feelings more safely through pictures. He said later how he was also using the pictures defensively – as a way of avoiding direct communication and the feared confrontation with his therapist. This avoidance may have contributed to a lack of resolution of the transference, as the final one of the series suggested.

Marion had been the patient's doctor. She ran the small psychotherapy group of which he was a member. The relationship with her had become explicitly a tripartite one, of patient–image–therapist, with the image not only as the embodiment of feelings but also as the mediator and container of them. The pictures also exemplify a kind of *symbolic acting out*. As he said, 'I had quite a wild sexual time with Marion on paper', and his paintings (of which these were only a few) were, he claimed, 'an expression of my relationship with her'. He said: 'I used painting as a secret language to people and especially to Marion – a hotline of communication, which others might see but might not understand.'

It also created a feeling of uniqueness and specialness of communication and relationship for him with her. (He found the group situation and the fact of having to share her attention very difficult.) He said that this was a safe way of 'saying' things, giving messages out, but at the same time he 'never knew if they were received', but 'thought she would understand'. He also felt that by communicating in this way he was providing an element of protection for her. She needed protection because he imagined that he destroyed those with whom he became emotionally involved. He added that he valued the element of ambiguity and obscurity because to an extent he could hide behind it. 'I'm let off the hook a bit, I've said things but they can be disguised. . . . I couldn't say it directly to her and anyway there wasn't an opportunity' (except in the group which he said was unsuitable). At the same time he got the feelings out, and publicly, for all including Marion to see if they could. By expressing and giving form to these feelings and fantasies, he was also communicating with himself, confronting himself with his own feelings, ordering and exploring them and thereby monitoring his own experience. This points to the two stages of communication within the art therapy process.

He called the whole series 'An expression of my relationship with Marion, my therapist.' 'She was the only one who could see through my defences. . . . I was the baby that had never been born, and I wanted Marion to be the midwife.' His feelings for her were intense, and were reflected in his images. The first (*Plate 7*) he called 'The good nourishing mother' or 'The good cosmic breast'.

'That's Marion's huge breast . . . every time she spoke I felt I was underneath receiving these life-giving forces and getting inspiration from her. I couldn't be a man to give sperm – unless I was getting milk from the Eternal Mother. Only then could I ejaculate and fertilize.'

In referring back to the picture, some time later, he agreed that he seemed to be bathing in her milk, rather than actually taking it into him – which was a way of fusing with her, rather than achieving separateness or autonomy. On the other hand he also saw her (*Figure 18*) as 'The bad devouring mother' or 'The bad breast'.

> 'Every time Marion took a bite of her apple, I felt it was my head. She became the mother rat that was destroying the child. . . . I thought I was either going to faint or freak out in that group.'

The third image in the series he called 'Contractacus'. This was a boldly painted picture of a marriage ceremony. The two figures, somehow suspended, were painted in black, white, and red – the man in formal morning dress, and the woman, significantly smaller, in a red dress and framed within the black outline of a coffin. They were holding hands. The whole scene was framed by a heavy black line, doubling the framing of the edges of the paper.

> 'It's Marion and I getting married. I wrote our names in a language that no one would understand – I showed my secret claim on her – at the same time I had made it public. But I thought the only way I could marry her was by killing her and putting her in a coffin. In that way I could keep her. I felt I was a destructive force and it was because I was close to her, it was making her leave the place.'

(Marion was temporarily leaving to have a baby. John had been extremely angry and jealous of the baby, saying that he was the one who should be inside her. He felt usurped.) He had seriously felt that if he allowed himself to get close to anyone, they would inevitably be destroyed.

The fourth image he called 'Sorry'.

> 'I was very angry with Marion and did a lot of tearing and ripping things. She seemed not to be taking any notice of me, and she was leaving. I really hated her. I ripped up the paper instead of her, then tied the bits together again with string, and wrote "sorry" across it. . . . There was a taboo on expressing violent feelings, but you could do it with art.'

Using materials in this way he was able to symbolically act out his feelings, and not only to 'safely destroy' and express the rage and destructive feelings, but also to restore, rebuild and make reparation, all without risking the retribution and criticism of a direct confrontation with her.

This highlights the great importance of the process – as well as the 'product'. John graphically described what he called one of his most

Figure 18

significant 'breakthrough' moments, which came at another point in his therapy. This came about through manipulation of materials and symbolic acting out of self-destructiveness – which at the same time proved very constructive. It is also an example of the condensation of layers of meaning and significance. He described how he actually acted out the mutilation:

'I did a self-portrait – of tissue paper in layers; they were the layers of skin. I tore the skin off the face – like mutilation.'

He went on to explain insightfully:

'The act of doing it was quite releasing. It was a strong symbolic act with a feeling of satisfaction – a real self-destructive act . . . but at the same time I was making something. It allowed me to look at my self-destructiveness and to look inside. It was like tearing off layers of defences too.'

Then he spoke of the power of the visual image:

'It's all there – *direct* – and so much is compacted in time and space, whereas psychotherapy works more in abstracts, it's not so concrete, and not so immediately graspable.'

The final image in the series he called 'Immaculate discharge'. He had made a representation of an ejaculation, out of paper. He had cut out a coil of paper – with a snake's head. One end he firmly stuck to a sheet of paper, while the coil was made to spring through the gash in a second sheet partially stuck on the first. Later he likened the image to an 'Ouroboros'.[2] Here he had brought about his own 'discharge' in the form of an ejaculation (while still remaining attached). He said about it:

'At this point I had decided I would discharge myself from the hospital. I persuaded myself I hadn't been touched by the place, and I wasn't going to be born out of the hospital. Marion was leaving and there seemed no point in staying.'

By creating his own 'discharge' in the various aspects of meaning that it held, he was gaining power over it, and taking some responsibility for it. At the same time by calling his discharge 'immaculate' and himself 'untouched' he was also angrily denying his involvement and his need for others. In this way he denied the pain of separating from Marion.

The second sequence is called 'The rat/rabbit sequence and the clay models'. I am including Catherine's images, and her later comments, at some length. Not only do they demonstrate something of her tremendous courage and honesty in her inner journey of self-exploration, but also they articulately embody and describe some profoundly important aspects of art therapy and its potential, many of which are central to the message of this chapter. She has taught me a great deal, and the experience has been very formative in my work as an art therapist.

Her images, and her comments later, show an example of symbolic acting out, not so much directly with the materials as in the previous example, but more through the power, clarity, and meaning of the visual images, and through the image-making for the young woman who made them. 'It's all about creativity really – releasing my creative power.' She painted this series (*Figures 19–23*) about four months into therapy. It depicts the killing of her internalized father.

> 'I painted them all in one go – alone in the evening. It was important to have a private but warm and sympathetic space. . . . They felt very important to do at the time, and very urgent. There was a volcanic pressure from inside, and once I began, nothing would stop the flow. It was a very strong experience, and very cathartic. It was a huge release of emotions and physical tension. I knew they were authentic. . . . I knew they were important then, but I wasn't clear why. . . . Ten years later, they make much more sense.'

She 'knew' when the time was right to do them, she 'knew' when she was safe enough, even though it was frightening. It also demonstrates how powerfully images can hold their meaning, and yield it up only when the time is right for the person to 'see'. In this way, through her own creation, the creator becomes her own therapist. Thus we see how the power in art therapy lives first in the relationship between creator and creation.

She gave the sequence two titles: 'Jesus loves me this I know, for the Bible tells me so' and 'My life in thirty years'. And this is what she eventually said about it:

> 'The first painting [*Figure 19*]: a bunny rabbit – vulnerable and soft – was my symbol when I was little, so that's me. The hand is a multiple image. It's a hand that says "hello", but more strongly says "stop – don't go any further". It is also the hand of creativity, creative power – my hand. I had a toy telephone with a dial, and used to spend hours ringing up a secret family called "The Bunnies" – and couldn't understand why they never answered – why there was no one there.'

> 'The rat/rabbit animal [*Figure 20*] is definitely my father. He was a strong personality and a very religious man – dominating and rather frightening. That's my hand, my grown-up hand (I copied my own hand) and he had chained it to him. He'd chained me and my creative power to him. He was putting his values into me. Note the sizes. . . . I think I felt potentially much more powerful than him – I was a bit frightened by this power.'

> 'The severed hand [*Figure 21*] – I was being eaten up, devoured. . . . This related to an image I had done before coming to the hospital, a horrible image – it was a severed hand made of clay and a cheese grater, set in a pretty dish on a clean chequered table cloth . . . a cheese grater with a kind of smile, and I'd cut off the top of the index finger, and was grating it – a

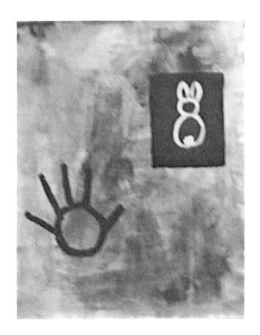

Figure 19

Figure 20

Figure 21

bit of skin hanging down from the smile of the grater. . . . I felt horrified and sickened by it.'

And she made the profoundly significant point for art therapy:

'I suppose one can risk putting one's most horrifying fantasies into an image that's external – it means one is being destructive and creating at the same time. . . . Also you can choose to only share it with yourself – and can show it to someone else only if and when you want to. The hand was always me, and my creativity and creative power. At the same time the destructive rage was mine. . . . It was a way of taking some control over the situation, but I'm not sure if I realized it at the time.'

'This [*Figure 22*] is the picture I remember very clearly – perhaps because it marked a turning point. It was the moment of change. I called it 'Metamorphosis'. . . . It was the moment of getting in touch with the anger, and the power, and the rage. It was murderous rage. Doing it released a huge amount of energy and feeling.'

'This [*Figure 23*] is killing the rat/rabbit, killing the internalized father that inhibited me. . . . I suppose it was killing part of myself in the process, but it had to be done. . . . I had to free myself. . . . Painting allows a safer

Figure 22

Figure 23

way of doing things, and saying the kind of things one couldn't risk saying in words – or doing in real actions.'

By symbolically acting out the destroying of the father's power, she was able to express, externalize, communicate, and eventually own and share more of these feelings and fantasies, and begin to see and explore them more objectively. It gave her a measure of control over the feelings: 'It was important to give dangerous feelings a shape. If you can do something and begin to get hold of the feelings then you're not so likely to get swept away by them.' And thus, despite the fact that understanding the meaning had seemed important from an outsider's view, she was very firm in stating that '*The really powerful thing is the images – and doing them*' – thus reinforcing a central message of this chapter.

> 'It was very important that one's paintings were taken seriously . . . and not necessarily pushed into interpretation. Too much talking about them and interpretation doesn't give the images enough space and power . . . and also all this interpretation took one too deep too quickly sometimes – and there wasn't always the wherewithal to come out – that was frightening.'

After she had painted the rat/rabbit sequence, she made some clay models: images of regression. She showed another side of her rage and pain. 'Usually I come over as very strong – I've never had much trouble showing my anger and confronting people – I'm good at talking and people seem to think I'm strong so they don't see my vulnerability, or my fear.' It had also just been announced that her doctor, to whom she felt very close, was ill and leaving the hospital for a while. Perhaps this intensified the fear of unacceptableness and abandonment, having expressed her rage. She said nothing about them at the time, but did eventually show them, then packed them away again. Later she said they were her needing to find a place to hide – which in a sense she did, by creating it for herself.

> 'I made these clay models – they expressed a lot at the time. I needed to use clay.[3] It looks like a kind of foetus, half formed, terrified, and hiding in half a kind of protective shell. . . . In the last one the shell is breaking open.'

She went on to say how she felt that they were about the need to regress at the time; also about feeling panicky . . . with feelings of neediness and helplessness; and how they were a particular communication to her doctor: 'the concrete images that were important. . . . I didn't allow any of my important work to be displayed. For me, images can express a level and strength of feelings that words can't communicate . . . and images come more easily.'

Just before leaving the hospital she handed me a bag containing the models (there are seven altogether). 'I don't want these, you have them.' Was I to look after them and what they represented? When we met again, some ten years later, she had remembered, and asked me if I still had them (which I had). She made the important point in the interview:

> 'The permanence and tangibility of the art products gives art therapy a dimension that other therapies don't have (especially the talking therapies) – not only can you refer back to your creation and look again later, and it won't have changed, but also you can express things by what you do afterwards with what you've created – that can be very expressive. You could destroy them, mutilate them, hide them prominently, display them, give them to people – lots of possibilities.'

She went on to say 'I quickly lost interest in my paintings, and when I left, I left them all at the hospital.' Perhaps they had done their job. Or perhaps she had chosen to leave that side at the hospital.

The value of chaos

The therapeutic process has been described as having three major stages, working from order, to chaos, to re-order. Without this process there can be no change; without the 'letting go' and breaking of old patterns, there can be no chance of forming new ones. (In ancient Chinese, the word for 'chaos' also means 'opportunity' and 'change'.) Thus a period of chaos and disorganization can herald, and be a definite stage within, deep psychic growth. This involves a measure of trust and belief in the 'spontaneous ordering forces' mentioned by Milner (1950: 71), and a willingness to accept the uncertainty and confusion as a temporary stage, in order to allow the necessary *rites de passage* for the emergence of the new.

It is all too easy for both therapist and patient to fly from the terror and tension of the unknown, with its accompanying fear of, as Anna Freud puts it, 'plunging into non-differentiation', especially if the internal world seems dangerous. It is all too easy to encircle the emergent content of the unconscious and push it into some premature form, being too eager to 'make some sense', and 'gain some control' over it. An over-hasty and premature interpretation by therapist or patient may well 'stop the spontaneous upsurge of unconscious material', and thereby guillotine the natural unfolding of the unconscious healing process, which needs to emerge in its own way and at its own pace (A. Freud 1950: xiii). Even the eminent Winnicott has confessed to it: 'It appals me how much deep change I have prevented or delayed by my own personal need to interpret. If we only wait, the patient arrives at understanding creatively' (1971: 102). This is perhaps a particular danger in a strongly verbal and interpretative culture.

Some months into his therapy, James, who had up to that time painted in a small, controlled, and fairly pre-determined way, suddenly found himself painting in a freer and rather chaotic way. The chaos was allowed to grow and expand within his subsequent paintings, until he painted a large picture, which he later described as 'a wild jumble of paint flying all over the place, like thousands of seagulls flying in different directions'.

He painted with thick paint of strong colours, with power and energy, and at the same time in a way that suggested some essential contact: 'When I was painting, it was like something else took over. . . . I felt panicky and chaotic. I felt I had lost control, I was all over the place. Later I came back and drew a thick line around it.' He had found painting in this way very cathartic, and in the calmer mood that followed he would return to look at his paintings, and contemplate the 'chaos'. He began to see new shapes within the frozen and held mass of paint and movement. 'Things' began to emerge within it, and the next image he made – some days later – was of a 'baby bird', which he painted tentatively and with great care.

He had externalized and given form to his chaotic feelings, and in doing so had not only found some release from the tension, but had also gained a measure of control over his feelings. He had created a focus for them, at a point when he had felt in danger of being overwhelmed by them and 'losing himself'. In a sense he had created his own container for them, reinforced by the boundaries of the material, the line he painted around the 'chaotic painting', the framing of the paper. At the same time he was held within the containing boundaries of the therapeutic relationship between himself and the therapist, a relationship that was itself contained within the boundaries of the community.

Looking back, he said he felt that this had been a period of significant breakthrough for him, and the beginnings of change. He had been able to express, hold, and 'stay with' the chaotic feelings, to allow new patterns to begin to form. Something new had been brought to birth.

This brings us to further consider the healing quality inherent in the art and the creative process itself, irrespective of words and interpretation. Edith Kramer (1971) firmly asserted that it is the 'art' that is art therapy's special contribution – and that 'art is *inherently* therapeutic'. She believed that the experience of art, with its 'inherently healing quality' could lead to change without insight being necessary. And it can lead on to experiences that really lie beyond the grasp of reason. Some of the patients I spoke with felt that the 'artwork' – 'the images and doing them' – had been the basic agent for change, and that interpretation and talking about them had been unnecessary. 'It's like if you keep pulling up a plant to inspect its roots!' These patients felt it very important for their paintings to be given space and validity in their own right, to be allowed to 'speak' and work and develop in their own way, and in their own time.

Plates 8–10 show three pictures from a developing series of five (the second, fourth and fifth), made just before Anne left the community. All she said about the sequence of images at the time was: 'This is a description of therapy. . . . This is what happened to me through my therapy.' They might also be seen as an example and illustration of the creative process.

When we talked again later, she added: 'I have to create in order to know who I am.' Having made these, she took them home and put them up on a wall, and spent time reflecting and meditating on them. She allowed time and space for them to 'feed back' to her, and for the relationship to develop and the process to unfold. She created the images, and they worked with her towards greater integration, growth, and individuation. As Von Keyserling says,

'Man must again and again represent his inner reality in external form in order to progress. . . . [He] begins by experiencing his inward reality as something outside himself and he draws this reality back into himself in the course of integration. It is precisely this mechanism which enables man to progress beyond what he was.'

(quoted in Champernowne 1969)

Conclusion

In this chapter, ex-patients, looking back at their images after some years, have spoken of the ways in which art therapy proved useful to them, in relation to their experience within the verbal, analytical, and group culture of a therapeutic community. We have seen how art therapy is useful not merely as an adjunct and catalyst to verbal group psychotherapy and as a vehicle for words and insight, but how it has emerged as an alternative mode of therapy – a process of healing, beyond words, which puts the image and the creative process in the central position of power.

Some people spoke of the difficulties and frustrations they had found with the verbal and interpretative kind of therapy – especially at the beginning. Some might be described as 'over-verbal' – those who were very able to hide behind their words, and thus defend themselves against their feelings – others as less articulate, or more naturally introverted, and those who were too confused or disturbed to find words at all, for whom interpretation seemed irrelevant. Art therapy could help some people to talk, and to talk about feelings, but for many, words 'couldn't go far enough'. It could also offer an alternative way of expression and communication.

The art therapy proved to be useful 'as a way to make a start'. Many of those who spoke later about it found that it offered an easier way into the journey, and a way 'to learn the language of therapy'. The activity offered a mixture of structure and freedom, and it seemed to provide a way of 'extra safety', in which people could begin to express and reveal themselves, and communicate with others – through images, with or without words. The lack of continuous emphasis on 'problems', the informality yet structure of 'doing' contributed to the more relaxed atmosphere, in which people could 'let go', be more spontaneous, begin to take risks and 'play' – which in turn led to greater authenticity. It offered 'a chance for the child to play' – thus drawing on and releasing more of the healthy aspects and creative energy. 'It's all about creativity really – releasing creative power.'

In this way it offered patients a way to get in touch with their 'creative child-like' selves – wherein lies the potential for growth. The central importance of 'play' and fantasy was recognized much more in retrospect than at the time. As one patient said, 'art and play provide the tools of health'. The art therapy also enabled people to make 'real' contact with others initially, and helped them begin to build relationships and the necessary trust and social support to explore further.

The structure of the activity offered a chance for 'private space' – a chance to 'go inside and reflect' while being with others (particularly important in the group and communal culture) thus helping to develop the essential 'creative aloneness' and the state of 'alone-togetherness'. Within this setting, people created images. This brought with it a sense of achievement. They could help people to find words – especially about feelings that were blocked or at a half-way stage of expression – and thus could lead to greater sharing and insight. The externalized image could act as a focus, and as a mediator or buffer between the creator and others, thus providing a way of communicating more 'dangerous' things to others (and also to themselves) with or without words.

There is also an extra level of safety within the special 'framing' that pictorial expression allows together with the natural boundaries of the medium, thus providing an extra level of 'holding' and containing of dangerous and perhaps conflicting feelings. This can make it safer to express them, without such a risk of being overwhelmed. Thus an overcontrolled person is allowed to 'let go', and a disinhibited person is given limits.

Images can become a form of symbolic speech – a way of speaking with features which distinguish it from words. For instance, using the body in the handling and exploring of materials can draw more readily on the intuitive and emotional sides of people, and can also have a particularly cathartic and energizing effect. Further, it was found that spatial expression and the language of colour and form, tone and line, can describe and communicate profound and complex experiences with an immediacy and impact which words, in their sequential nature, lack.

Art therapy also provides a way of 'symbolic acting out' both through the images and through the manipulation of the media – and can be an explicit way of both destroying and creating at the same time. Paintings can crystallize and fix experience, and can be kept and reflected on. They can create external and permanent landmarks of change. The image will hold its message for days, years, undistorted and undeniable – until such time as the creator is ready to see, re-own, and integrate it into consciousness. There is also the added dimension that the artist can choose what to do with the object afterwards.

The growth in individual people that came about in this process went far beyond their conscious intent. They were often surprised at what would appear on the paper or in the clay before them. Images would emerge spontaneously from the unconscious, and the impact on their creator could be profound. Images and image-making can express a level and strength of experience that words cannot. They could also be the starting point for further fantasy, and lead the person on in a kind of 'active imagination'. The dialogue is both between patient and therapist and, more fundamentally, between unconscious and conscious aspects, between self and ego – through the language of symbols.

The process of 'real-ization' which is art therapy, involves the raising and making of images of the unconscious – the inner psychic resources – shaping them and giving them form, and thus making them 'real', tangible, and external. They can be seen and experienced more consciously. The creator can relate to them and live with them; there is no longer blind identification. By making them, their effect is increased on their creator. By acknowledging their living quality, allowing them space and contemplation, the dialogue can develop and they can work back on their creator towards his 'knowing', and accepting what has emerged as a real aspect of self. Thus the ego relates to material that had been hidden within, and the new relationship leads to a new balance between ego and self, embracing both conscious and unconscious factors, and thus towards greater integration and growth. This can be with or without conscious insight.

The process is one of empathy and communion; and the primary relationship is between the creation and its creator, the self and the ego. The image thus becomes the mediator, and its creator becomes more of his own therapist. He thus works towards greater autonomy and self-reliance, towards the resolution of transference, towards individuation, allowing the process to unfold in its own way and in its own time. It is here that the ultimate power of art therapy lies. 'The really powerful thing is the images, and doing them.' And as Jung said, 'symbols are natural attempts to reconcile and reunite often widely separated opposites' (1967 CW 5: 259).

Thus we have seen how art therapy is used as a way of beginning to redress the imbalance between the various aspects of therapy. It can provide something of a bridge and a greater synthesis between, for example: verbal and non-verbal; unconscious and conscious; inner and outer, doing and talking; fantasy and reality, intuition and rationality – all helping towards the unity of body, mind, and spirit. In these ways it can provide a way of 'healing the split'.

If we are to believe Jung's diagnosis about the psychological ills of 'Modern Man', and his belief in the psyche's ability to heal itself – both individually and collectively – then many of the points that have emerged in this study must have a significance that goes far beyond the therapeutic setting.

© 1987 Patricia Nowell Hall

Notes

1 Robert Ornstein (1972) has made a distinction between the 'rational' functions of the left hemisphere of the brain, and the 'intuitive' functions of the right. 'Left hemisphere domination' would thus imply domination by the 'logical, thinking, analytic, masculine' ways of operating, at the expense of the 'intuitive, feeling, symbol-forming, feminine' ways of the right. Broadly speaking, in the Taoist philosophy, the left hemisphere would appear to mediate the Yang functions, while the right hemisphere is the mediator of Yin.
2 'The tail-biting Ouroboros represents the eternal circle of disintegration and reintegration. . . . It is a world-wide symbol of self-sufficiency, self-fecundation . . .' (Cirlot 1972). It was the self-sufficiency aspect John particularly pointed out.
3 Of course the kind of materials chosen is of great significance. She described the use of clay as 'more physical', 'basic and direct'. 'You can be more angry with it, or you can enclose it in your hands and be tender or caressing with it. You can manipulate it more easily than most other media.' In this way it can lend itself more easily to transformation. At the same time firing a clay image is an extra step to making it more permanent, 'holding' it for further contemplation – and thus reinforcing its message. This could be seen as another step towards autonomy.

References

Auden, W. H. (1962) *Making, Knowing, and Judging*. London: Faber, as quoted in lecture on 'Healing' given by Dr Anthony Stevens at Cumberland Lodge course 'The Arts in Therapy and Education', 1977.
Champernowne, I. (1969) Art Therapy as an Adjunct to Psychotherapy. *Inscape* I.
Champernowne, I. (1971) Art and Therapy – an Uneasy Partnership. Lecture given at the annual course of Arts in Therapy and Education, Cumberland Lodge. Published in *Inscape* 3.
Cirlot, J. E. (ed.) (1972) *Dictionary of Symbols*. London: Routledge & Kegan Paul.
Coleridge, S. T. (1802) Dejection: An Ode. In *Poems of Samuel Taylor Coleridge* (1912). London: Oxford University Press.
Coleridge, S. T. (1817) *Biographia Literaria*. London: Dent (New York: Dutton 1956).
Freud, A. (1950) Foreword to Milner, M. *On Not Being Able to Paint*. London: Heinemann.

Halliday, D. (1980) Lecture for course of Postgraduate Diploma in Art Therapy, Herts. College of Art and Design.

Hobson, R. F. (1974) Loneliness. *Journal of Analytical Psychology* 19, 1: 77.

Hobson, R. F. (1985) *Forms of Feeling*. London: Tavistock.

Jones, M. (1953) *The Therapeutic Community: A New Treatment Method in Psychiatry*. New York: Basic Books.

Jones, M. (1962) *Social Psychiatry in the Community, in Hospitals and in Prisons*. Springfield, Ill.: Charles Thomas.

Jung, C. G. (1930) *The Psychology of the Child Archetype*. Collected Works vol. 9, pt 1. London: Routledge & Kegan Paul.

Jung, C. G. (1953) *Two Essays on Analytical Psychology*. Collected Works vol. 7. London: Routledge & Kegan Paul.

Jung, C. G. (1960) *The Structure and Dynamics of the Psyche*. Collected Works vol. 8. London: Routledge & Kegan Paul.

Jung, C. G. (1961) *Modern Man in Search of a Soul*. London: Routledge & Kegan Paul.

Jung, C. G. (1962) *Commentary on The Secret of the Golden Flower* (translated by Cary Baynes). London: Collins and Routledge & Kegan Paul.

Jung, C. G. (1966) *The Practice of Psychotherapy*. Collected Works vol. 16. London: Routledge & Kegan Paul.

Jung, C. G. (1967) *Symbols of Transformation*. Collected Works vol. 5. London: Routledge & Kegan Paul.

Jung, C. G. (1970) *Mysterium Coniunctionis*. Collected Works vol. 14. London: Routledge & Kegan Paul.

Kramer, E. (1971) *Art as Therapy with Children*. New York: Schocken Books.

Milner, M. (1950) *On Not Being Able to Paint*. London: Heinemann.

Ornstein, R. E. (1972) *The Psychology of Consciousness*. San Francisco: W. H. Freeman; London: Cape (1975); Harmondsworth: Penguin (1975).

Perls, F. (1971) *Gestalt Therapy Verbatim*. New York and London: Bantam Books.

Pietrone, P. (1986) It Takes Two to Get You Better. *Guardian*, 16 August.

Rhyne, J. (1973) *Gestalt Art Experience*. Monterey, Cal.: Brooks/Cole.

Rogers, C. (1957) The Necessary and Sufficient Conditions of Therapeutic Personality Change. *Journal of Consulting Psychology*, 22: 95–103.

Schwartz, C. (1978) The Child Archetype. Lecture given at Champernowne Trust course of the Arts in Therapy and Education.

Stern, K. (1966) *The Flight From Woman*. London: George Allen & Unwin.

Winnicott, D. M. (1971) *Playing and Reality*. Harmondsworth: Penguin.

Acknowledgements

I would like to give special thanks and appreciation to all the ex-patients involved in this study – for their insight and honesty, their images and their words, and for all they have shared with me, entrusted to me, and taught me.

7 | Art therapy in adolescence: a metaphorical view of a profession in progress

Diane Waller

Adolescence: an energetic, creative, turbulent, lethargic, murderous, bewildered state of being.

Introduction

My own interest in art therapy began while I was a student of fine art in Oxford. Edward Adamson visited the Ashmolean Museum where we had our studios and gave a talk to accompany an exhibition of paintings from Netherne Hospital. I was intrigued and excited by the paintings, curious about the people who had painted them, and curious about Adamson's approach. For the first time I heard that there were people called 'art therapists', and I resolved to become one. That was in 1967. After many months of searching for information about my chosen occupation, I discovered that there was no training, no career structure, and in the words of the then secretary of the British Association of Art Therapists (BAAT) I learned that 'If you want to work as an art therapist you'll have to persuade a hospital to take you on, and you'll need to be determined and to make your own way.' Being by nature something of a maverick, being completely undecided as to what I would do with my art training (the idea of teaching did not appeal and I was not single-minded enough to be a 'full-time' artist), having discovered that studying anthropology had been helpful to me as an artist, and being ready for a challenge, art therapy seemed a good choice.

I joined BAAT, which was then only 3 years old, visited several art therapists, and fairly soon acquired a part-time art therapy post in a psychiatric hospital, working with adolescents. Although I only stayed in this post for a year before moving to the Paddington Centre for Psychotherapy and the Royal College of Art, I remember it as one of the most powerful learning experiences I have ever had. I think, however, I survived on intuition and luck and because the children were so responsive to art. As anyone knows who has worked with adolescents, it is perpetually challenging, exhausting, and sometimes infuriating, but rarely boring. I suppose it is because I feel in touch with the adolescent part of myself – a part which is sometimes positive and creative, sometimes seeking security and boundaries, and at other times rebelling against established 'norms' – that I have the idea that the profession (of which I am now firmly a part) is in a stage of its development which could be likened to adolescence. I've therefore chosen this exciting but difficult developmental stage as a model from which to view art therapy now.

I shall attempt to take the position of 'a participant observer' and freely admit to the subjective nature of my presentation. Some of my biases and influences I can declare here: these are known to me – Marx, De Beauvoir, Fromm, John Berger, the anarchist Koprotkin, the nineteenth-century Russian novelists, and more recently, Bateson, Fairbairn, Bion, and Foulkes; several generations of art therapy students; and my colleagues. Other influences of which I am not fully aware will, no doubt, be spotted by discerning readers!

Progress and pitfalls in the development of a profession

'Probably every profession has been through this phase in the process of becoming established – that is – of acquiring statutory authority to practise. The individual practitioner in addition to responsibility to his client or patient, has to accept the obligations of membership to a professional body which is accountable to society through the state. Accountability implies regulation of training and the right to practise. A boundary is drawn between legitimate and illegitimate practitioners. Regulation is the price to be paid for safeguarding an exclusive right to practise.'

(Khaleelee 1982: 1)

While assembling thoughts and material in preparation for this chapter, I came across the above passage in a report entitled 'Psychotherapists and the Process of Profession Building' produced by the Organisation for Promoting Understanding in Society (OPUS). I made an immediate connection with the current position of art therapists within and outside the National Health Service in Britain. The report was based on 'Psychotherapists and Society', a workshop 'to share experiences of the professional role' held in London in

November 1982. The workshop explored the question of whether and how psychotherapists could combine within a single and recognized profession with statutory registration. It was attended by forty-three psychotherapists affiliated to no less than sixteen different institutions.

The aim of the workshop was defined as: to contribute to the building of psychotherapy as a profession by enabling practising psychotherapists of different orientations to share their experience of working with patients and to identify areas of common ground. It asked two main questions: What are the expectations and needs of society for psychotherapeutic services? What are the limitations and failures of psychotherapy, as perceived by practitioners of the various schools in relation to these expectations and needs?

In the report of the workshop, Olya Khaleelee identified two important issues which she felt had arisen: the extent to which the professional practitioner as a person is the instrument of treatment; and the problem of providing support and replenishment for the psychotherapist. 'This mirrors the patient's wish for the psychotherapist to be the 'perfect mother' and it is similarly unattainable. Understanding and accepting such processes could help in tackling the problems of coming together as a profession' (Khaleelee 1982: ii). Such issues as were identified in this report of a psychotherapy workshop struggling to come to terms with 'professionalism' are, it seems to me, entirely relevant to art therapy now.

Art therapy, unlike psychotherapy, has managed to develop a structure within the National Health Service in Britain, and to produce a register of qualified practitioners. A definition of an art therapist exists, arrived at by extensive discussion between the representatives of the Department of Health, BAAT, and the union ASTMS (Association of Scientific, Technical and Managerial Staff) which represents the majority of art therapists. It is as follows:

'[An art therapist is] a person who is responsible for organising appropriate programmes of art activities of a therapeutic application with patients, individually or in groups, and possesses a degree in art or design or a qualification considered equivalent for entry to an accepted postgraduate training course, and also a qualification in art therapy following the completion of an accepted course at a recognised institution of further or higher education.'

(DHSS 1982)

On the basis of this definition, art therapists, along with music therapists, moved in 1981 from an *ad hoc* grade within the National Health Service to a position on the Whitley Council, under the wing of the Professional and Technical 'A' Committee.

If we compare the definition of an art therapist with those of other so-called paramedical staff, we see that the major element in the definition is the contribution made by an *art* training of normally four years' duration. This is an amazing achievement on behalf of art therapists. The fact that training in art *therapy* has existed since around 1970, over ten years before professional recognition, played a major part in getting the definition accepted. In the words of one civil servant at the Department of Health and Social Security in 1978, 'art therapists have put the cart before the horse'. He meant that training existed for something which had not yet been identified or defined, other than in *ad hoc* terms, by the DHSS itself! It would be wrong to give the impression that this was an easy achievement. The definition was desired by and approved by the membership of BAAT (which then numbered about 400 and represented the majority of art therapists in Britain). It had been fought for by the staff of the three training courses and officers and council members of BAAT, aided by ASTMS officers and sympathetic Members of Parliament. It involved years of pioneering work, carefully documented case studies, and hours of unpaid labour in the form of attending meetings, writing papers, lobbying MPs, negotiating with government departments, and so on.

Despite some quite strong differences of opinion in the BAAT Registration and Training Sub-Committee of 1976, unity was reached on appropriate 'core course' requirements for training courses in art therapy. As Hinshelwood points out in his article 'Questions of Training', such consensus has not yet been achieved as far as psychotherapy is concerned:

'Entry to most professions is automatically restricted through a recognised training resulting in a certificate of competence. One of the curiosities about the psychotherapy profession is that it lacks such a *rite de passage* . . . this is one of the major obstacles to achieving a traditional professional status for psychotherapy.'

(Hinshelwood 1985: 7–8)

In the case of art therapy, a driving force for unity seemed to be a firm belief in the value of the visual arts generally, and specifically in their potential to provide a means of expression and communication not usually available within hospital or other 'clinical' settings. A powerful identification with the role of 'artist' (and perhaps 'outsider') in the face of the medically dominated and hierarchical structure of the NHS may also have played a part.

Many of the art therapy educators and prominent practitioners of the late 1970s had been influenced by 'anti-psychiatry' movements of the 1960s; by writers such as Goffman and Szasz and Illich, by R. D. Laing, and by workers like Joe Berke, whose sensitive association with Mary Barnes at Kingsley Hall inspired many art therapists. Others had been strongly influenced by the ideas of Jung, and some had undertaken Jungian analysis.

It is probably true to say that most art therapists at that time saw art therapy as an 'alternative' treatment. Some were suspicious that colleagues might be tempted to 'sell out' and ascribe a 'medical' orientation to their work in the hope of easier recognition by the National Health Service. Others feared too 'educational' an approach, which might risk censor from the NHS. These anxieties, and the various differences of opinion which have to exist within a healthy organization, were submerged during the intense campaign to achieve professional recognition.

Recent developments within the Training and Education Committee of BAAT have put the spotlight back on some of the differences. But with a solid base to work from they can now be pursued more openly. An example of the kind of task which faced the committee recently is that of a course review, and more specifically, the review of a previously approved training in art therapy. In the Personnel Memorandum of 1982, this course had been given provisional approval by the DHSS because it was, in fact, an option within a postgraduate art education training. The hope was that the educational establishment which sponsored the option would be able to give sufficient resources to enable it to become a full-time Diploma in Art Therapy. But for reasons which were no doubt to do with the politics of higher education at the beginning of this decade, it remained an option. BAAT conducted its own review and came to the same conclusion as the DHSS, namely that the option, despite its long standing and important contribution to art therapy and the excellence of the teaching, could not continue to be an 'approved' course.

Given the professional aspirations of art therapy, it was hardly reasonable to continue to claim that part of another profession's initial training could suffice as an equivalent to a full Diploma in Art Therapy. The realization that art therapists were actually a professional body with some influence came as a shock to everyone, including those members who had fought so hard for this eventuality. Fantasies which had once revolved around the authority of the DHSS now featured the Council of BAAT, who were accused of 'destroying' an art therapy course. To some, BAAT became a bad and destructive parent, but to others it became a firm and wise parent.

Fears were expressed that the art-based, creative potential of art therapy might be sacrificed in favour of a reductive, diagnostic approach, as if it were necessary for there to be an 'either/or' solution. The positive side of this difficult period was that much hard thinking and re-examination of fundamental assumptions concerning training in art therapy is being undertaken by art therapy educators and by BAAT representatives on the current Training and Education Committee.

A further stage in the professional development of art therapy was marked around the same period, in the form of the 'Principles of Professional Practice', a document drawn up by a working party of BAAT and approved by the AGM of 1984. Members had persistently asked for such a document and were fully involved at all stages. Questionnaires were sent out, inviting members to make comments on a range of issues – such as referrals, the holding of exhibitions of patients' work, and minimum working facilities that should be provided for art therapists. But the response was just under 20 per cent.

The sub-committee charged with the task of preparing what was, in effect, a code of practice, immediately became the target for hostile projections; the committee were perceived by many members as imposing an arbitrary set of rules on art therapists – yet it was the members themselves who had pressed Council to draw up the code by passing a motion with a huge majority in favour at the previous AGM! And the code also had the aim of protecting art therapists as well as their clients.

Although the questionnaires clearly had the aim of involving the members, they were seen as an imposition and threatening, and further proof of the authoritarian nature of the Council. Similarly, an AGM had voted unanimously to establish a register of qualified art therapists, and much pressure had been put on Council to get on with the task. Again, members were fully consulted about the format of the register and how they would wish to appear on it. It was made clear that all current full members would be considered registered yet, time and time again, art therapists expressed anxiety about 'who will be on the register and who will see it?'

The process went ahead, notwithstanding the lack-lustre response from members, and the register was presented to members at the 1986 AGM. Since then there has been an enormous increase in qualified art therapists joining BAAT! Yet many members were initially reluctant even to provide their *working* addresses for the register, such was the fear that the register might be misused. There may be good reasons for reticence, but given the fact that other professional workers (physiotherapists, for example) have a register so that they may be contacted by other workers who may wish to refer a patient, or by their colleagues who may want to refer a client moving to another town, and that art therapists are keen to develop a community service, the secrecy is puzzling – especially from a group which wishes to promote itself.

It seems as if there is a hidden desire to have a hostile and malevolent force to conquer. If none is easily perceived, then one must be created. Just as the adolescent is prone to split and polarize in order to contain the conflicting feelings within, so the profession is constantly in danger of fragmentation during its struggles towards growth.

Hinshelwood's comment about psychotherapy is interesting to note: 'One of the most striking features of the profession is its fragmented state, in which rivalrous groups claim allegiance to different theoretical orientations and protect themselves by arcane terminologies that restrict the possibility of interchange' (Hinshelwood 1985: 17). Using an object relations model he postulates that the dynamics of the fragmentation arise from two main kinds of internal situations: first, that the therapist needs to maintain a supporting, 'loving' relationship with her patients, and that frustration, dislike, hatred, or fear of the therapist's own object gets directed frequently towards colleagues; and secondly, that the therapist needs to act out their own reparative demands – especially powerful if the therapist has gone into the work with the aim of repairing damaged objects, in which case reparation may seem to require omnipotent or magical skills.

Professionalism, with its advantages and problems, is well on the way for art therapy, being desired and at the same time feared by art therapists. However, the structure in which art therapists find themselves in the NHS is proving frustrating, and a reform of the Whitley grading is now being sought, along with other members of the paramedical professions who are also seeking a structure more appropriate to clinical work (actual *treatment* of patients) than the hierarchical 'head count' system. In such a system, promotion can only be achieved after Senior I by having a number of staff subordinate in one's department. For art therapists, this means that only two Head III posts exist in Britain, given that art therapy 'departments' usually contain only one or two therapists.[1]

The 'head count' system was opposed by BAAT when art therapists were seeking to join the Whitley Council, but they were obliged to accept this structure, which was part of the link to occupational therapy and the other paramedical professions. The result of this low-ceiling structure, where advancement stops for most at Senior I, is that art therapists leave the profession after four or five years' service, leaving far too small a pool of 'elders' to support its growth. Quite clearly, a structure that rewarded clinical work and gave scope for advancement to the one or two art therapists in a hospital would have been sensible. One can ask why this was not possible in 1981, and why art therapy was linked to occupational therapy, when there was good evidence to show that the link was an administrative accident and that there was no historical support for it in philosophical terms.

Bearing in mind the very different background and training that art therapists have, compared with other paramedical staff, it was surprising that they were considered on the same level in the first place. Indeed, if the recommendations of the so-called 'Consultative Document on Art, Music, Drama, etc. Therapy' issued by the DHSS in 1978 had been adopted, art therapy would have been incorporated into occupational therapy, giving no scope for separate development. It was only the massive counter to this document launched by art and music therapists, supported by ASTMS and other influential professional groups, which prevented this occurrence.

So this new group must have been perceived as having some clout.

Allowing a newly emergent group to have its own – and very desirable – career structure could have caused dissent and protestation among the other paramedical professions, the members of which are mainly women. They are poorly paid and have low status. Occupational therapists have had to endure a 'handmaiden' status in relationship to medical staff, and are often looked down on by nurses. A potentially militant group, politicized through long membership of unions (first the National Union of Teachers and then ASTMS) could be better contained within an existing, hierarchical, and stifling structure.

Art therapists were transformed from an '*ad hoc* grade' (which had meant that all new posts had to be approved by the DHSS and there were no negotiating possibilities on the Whitley Council) to a 'related grade', which meant that they still had no seat on the Whitley Council and had to rely on ASTMS to represent them. They were also not referred to by name until 1985, but only as a 'related grade', as were music therapists, too.

The failure to refer to art therapists by name had been a long-standing irritation: when art therapists gave evidence to the Clegg Commission[2] in 1979, a long and time-consuming exercise, this was never referred to in the ensuing report or follow-up documents. ASTMS produced a booklet in 1980 as a response to the failure by Clegg to take account of some groups in the NHS, entitled *The Forgotten Professions*, in which art and music therapists, speech therapists, chiropodists, and others stated their case. Under the section dealing specifically with art therapy it states:

'Art therapists are among the most badly treated occupations within the NHS. Not surprisingly therefore they require above average increases to place them on a par with their counterparts. We believe that increases of at least 50 per cent are needed. Again we believe this to be a conservative estimate, but it will go at least some way towards removing the very unjust circumstances in which art therapists have been placed.'

(ASTMS 1980: 47)

(Sadly, this suggestion was not taken up by Clegg at the time and has not yet been heeded.)

Interestingly, it had been a joint Whitley Council Staff–Management working party of 1976 that had come to the conclusion that there was enough evidence of art therapy being a discrete activity to have it brought under the Whitley Council. The working party gave consideration to the art and music therapy service in twenty hospitals, met sixteen art therapists, and came to the following conclusion:

'In broad terms art therapy was seen to perform one or both of two functions. The first was "rehabilitative" . . . the second "diagnostic": therapists performing such a function were generally anxious to disclaim any intention of interpreting patients' work themselves in psychiatric terms, but did contend that patients' art work could constitute useful diagnostic evidence for psychiatrists and could help them to monitor changes in a patient's condition. This second function seemed the most marked where art therapy itself was strongest and independent of occupational therapy. . . . On the whole the employment of considerable art skills and the general adoption of broadly common rehabilitative objectives gave the art therapists we saw a clear unity as a group.'

On training, the working party commented:

'As one would expect, most had a formal training in art to a high level, the normal justification for this in the minds of the therapists themselves being that it gave them a very wide range of skills and techniques which could be called upon in adapting to the different needs of individual patients.'

(*Ad Hoc* Grades: Possible Allocation to the PTA Whitley Council. Report on Joint Visits of Staff and Management Side Panels 1976)

The report also stated that for qualified art therapists supervision by another member of the remedial professions appeared to be 'unnecessary and would be resented'.

This report, so positive for art therapists, was totally ignored within the DHSS for two years, and its findings were not mentioned in the 1978 Consultative Document.

Many art therapists still work within occupational therapy departments and are managerially responsible to the Head or sometimes the District Therapist. The question of whether or not art therapy departments may be autonomous is a very important one for art therapists at this stage of their professional lives, and numerous letters are received by the Council of BAAT and regional group organizers from art therapists who are trying to separate themselves from what can appear as the 'parental' authority of occupational therapists. It is an issue which most art therapists currently practising have already encountered or are about to encounter. There are a few who were employed within autonomous departments from the start, or who created their own department, but they will not be immune from the struggles of their colleagues in other hospitals. The element of competition between the two groups cannot be denied.

Women and the profession

As members are mainly women, it was interesting to find a comment from Susie Orbach and Louise Eichenbaum, founders of the Women's Therapy Centre, on this issue:

'Competitive feelings serve to keep women in their place. Deeply instilled in each woman is an unconscious knowledge of the threshold that she cannot cross without arousing the anger and envy of other women. In this way women unconsciously collude to keep each other from self-fulfilment. Patriarchy is distilled in each woman's psychology. Competitive and envious feelings prevent her from trying to get what she needs in a society that has a huge stock of prohibitions.'

(Eichenbaum and Orbach 1985: 144–45)

Looking at the ways in which art therapists go about achieving a separate status within their institution, it is clear that we need to take account of psychological factors. However, it is also clear that the 'head count' system already described makes the task more difficult for both groups. Losing an art therapy post can mean a lower grade for the future Head Occupational Therapist, and a loss of establishment for their profession. In some cases a long vacant occupational therapy post has been filled by the establishment of a new art therapy post, in which case the occupational therapists understandably wish this to remain part of their department. The 'divide and rule' element is obvious, especially, it would appear, when the groups are women.

Yet there is no reason why art therapists and occupational therapists, both having clearly acknowledged their own professional identity, should not work together for good clinical practice (and indeed they often do). There seems to be, however, a tendency for occupational therapists to want to 'protect' art therapists from the administrative and managerial tasks necessary in managing one's own department, even a very small one. This can be seductive for art therapists, especially those on their own in large institutions and for whom 'autonomy' means a range of administrative responsibilities to be coped with on top of their clinical load, and an increasing public relations role in clarifying what they do to other staff. It is, therefore, not always a straightforward decision for an art therapist to make: to press for autonomous status in the full knowledge that, if single handed, time spent with patients will be severely restricted as managerial duties are undertaken. It is to be hoped that the new grading structures will take these difficulties into account.

The struggle for autonomy

One might ask, why is it that autonomy is so important for art therapists? Many reasons could be suggested, but I think that their background, personality, and training are factors. Art therapists have tended to see themselves, and to be perceived by others, as a radical and even subversive element in the NHS. The curious mixture of art and therapy gives rise to responses of suspicion, intrigue, fear, discomfort, patronizing attitudes, and on occasion, outright dismissal. No doubt such fantasies are not reserved for art therapists alone, and if we are to believe Wally Harbert, director of Avon Social Services Department, writing in *Community Care*:

> 'It is clear that there is a great deal of rivalry, jealousy and suspicion between the various helping professions. An eavesdropper on informal conversations soon learns that much of the casual discussion between fellow professionals consists of poking fun at people in other professional groups. The fantasies that professional carers have about one another are more vivid and more uniform than the fantasies that clients have about professionals.'

(Harbert 1985: 15–16)

However, being a 'new' group, art therapists certainly attract plenty of projections, and of course are prone to make them too. On the basis of discussion with many art therapists from different generations, qualified through training and 'grandparents', it appears than many of the pioneers arrived at their profession through a strong radical political consciousness as well as from motives of wishing to understand themselves better, or from having found art an essential means of expression, or from having intense curiosity about human beings in general. Many art therapists seek a democratic, non-hierarchical work setting, are convinced of the value of creativity, and are determined to pursue their goal of combining art and therapy. Some of the 'older generation' of art therapists were victims of too early specialization at school, having to choose either arts or sciences, when they would have preferred to combine them. 'Art therapy', as a straight-forward career choice, was not available to them. The pioneers tended to be individualists who found their own way of using their interests and skills, rather than taking a more clearly defined pathway into an already established profession, such as teaching or occupational therapy. But it is with both these groups that art therapists find themselves confused in the eyes of the public and even professional colleagues. Occupational therapy is often stereotyped by that same public (and at times by art therapists who should know better) as merely a way of passing time – just 'basket making': in others words, a traditionally female occupation which is craft oriented, low paid, low status, serving the (male) medical hierarchy, and content with the status quo. Occupational therapy had its roots in the post-war rehabilitation movement, and it is often forgotten that the majority of occupational therapists work in general hospitals with physically ill people, and only a minority in psychiatry. Occupational therapists are themselves struggling to lose their unfair image and to find a role more appropriate to rehabilitation and treatment in the 1980s.

There is reason to believe that art therapists may be more 'politically conscious' than occupational therapists. Although both are predominantly female professions, art therapists may have developed a more 'feminist' perspective in their work – among other reasons, as a result of their struggle with the 'male centred' culture of art college. The majority of art therapists are artists, most of whom will have spent four or five years in college, where they will have encountered a wide range of opinions, including strongly anarchist ones.[3] They must have then worked for at least a year before applying for entry to a postgraduate diploma course, where the average age of students is late twenties or early thirties.

Occupational therapists, on the other hand, normally enter training at 18. From 1987 it is anticipated that the national minimum entry level for all students will be two 'A' levels and five 'O' levels, except for mature students. A considerable part of their training takes place in general or psychiatric hospitals, where they are early exposed to the 'medical ethos' prevalent therein. The colleges of occupational therapy are often private institutions, so the students do not come into contact with the wide range of opinion and teaching styles open to students on undergraduate courses. There are, however, more courses now in polytechnics and colleges of technology within the public sector, and it will be interesting to see what effects this will have on the profession.

As well as looking at occupational therapy, it may be useful at this point to consider another 'caring' profession with which art therapists sometimes get identified, namely social work. Cracy Cannon, when referring to the training of social workers in *Countercourse* points out that:

'Most social work training takes place in polytechnics, which compared to universities are poorly financed . . . students do not have many opportunities to meet students and staff from other disciplines, contacts which in the university situation can be extremely important for a thorough appreciation of what is formally taught.'

(Cannon 1972: 247)

Although this may not be true in all cases of social work training, nor of all polytechnics, we can still look at the issues raised as meaningful ones for other 'caring' professions. Cannon points out that social work students tend to be insulated by virtue of their practical work placements which take them out of college for two or three days each week. The other days tend to be crammed. Many students are women, in their late twenties, with families, so there is little time for participation in wider college activities. This has a familiar sound for art therapy students. But we have to bear in mind that, prior to their art therapy training, art therapy students will have been exposed to the 'otherness' of an art training.

There is now a slight tendency for art therapy educators to wish to enrol non-art graduates in greater numbers (from nursing, occupational therapy, social work, etc.) ostensibly in the interests of a multi-disciplinary approach. Such a tendency is seen by the professional association to erode the art base of art therapy and to dilute its potential. It is felt that multi-disciplinary approaches can be encouraged in subsequent work rather than in initial training.

The increasing emphasis of recent years on pre-course work-experience for intending students of art therapy could mean that current students have been exposed for some years to 'caring' institutions and may have unconsciously absorbed a sociological theory which puts the onus on the individual as 'sick' and on the carer as 'well', and fails to take into account social, cultural, ethnic, and class factors. As Littlewood and Lipsedge (1983) point out in the their incisive study *Aliens and Alienists*, the fact that people from cultures other than white, middle-class may have a completely different set of social norms and expectations, and definitions of 'illness', is often overlooked even in some of our more progressive teaching hospitals.

One hopes that by insisting on 'relevant pre-course experience' the very qualities of freshness of perception, critical awareness, and creative problem-solving that could be expected from good art graduates will not be dulled.

Some possible contradictions in art therapy training

It seems possible that some of the attitudes which are common in adolescence might be stimulated in art therapists by some contradictions which are appearing in art therapy training. If we look again at social work and at Cannon's statement concerning their training, we might find some familiar issues:

> 'There is a basic contradiction in social work thinking. On the one hand emphasis on professionalism points to a rigorous training in the 'sciences' of psychiatry, psychology and sociology, and on the other to social workers as 'mature' personalities who have exceptional 'insight' into people's motivation. Maturity and insightfulness are not seen as qualities gained from taking a course, but are seen as characteristics which some people have and others don't. If the social worker has 'insight' plus training, then his judgements have a validity over, for example, political explanations, for the social worker 'knows' that the political militant is in fact 'acting out' his infantile authority problems. While the student's attention is turned to underlying motives he ignores the overt content of what is being said and done. In this way the rationality of political arguments is denied.'

(Cannon 1972: 248)

In the case of art therapy students, they are selected by college tutors (who tend to be influenced by 'radical' ideas) on the basis of their enthusiasm for, their demonstrated talent in, and their commitment to, the visual arts; and on their presentation at interview, their relevant work experience, and their engagement in some form of personal therapy. I have to speak now from my own experience of selecting students, though I do not feel it is so different from the experience of other art therapy tutors. I have noticed that the students tend to be the kind of people who wish to explore their own lives, to reassess relationships, and to find a new direction. They usually express a strong 'social' commitment, and are keen to accept the challenge offered in a fairly new profession. Unlike previous generations, art therapy students today could have had art therapy in mind as a career possibility while at school. Indeed a few hundred enquiries are received each year by BAAT from school children wishing to become art therapists. They are somewhat surprised to find that they will probably be at least 25 before they can start!

As the number of applicants far exceeds the number of places available, it is possible to be highly selective, and qualities such as playfulness (engendered through art work), a critical attitude, and a certain amount of 'bolshiness' yet sensitivity to others, appeal to interviewers. One of the problems facing the profession is how to preserve these qualities when it seems as if art therapy training contains similar contradictions to those of social work.

Indeed, when surveying the post-course employment of graduates we find there are problems of identity. For example, having acquired a post as an art therapist on the basis of their unique skills within, say, a social services day centre for people with a mental handicap, they quickly become absorbed into 'the team' and the pressure to conform to the prevailing culture leads them rather quickly to give up art therapy, or to limit their art therapy input to one group a week – a rather half-hearted attempt to assert independence. If this happened in only one or two isolated cases then one could say that it was an individual's choice, or problem. But it happens a lot and is a cause for concern among art therapists. If the resulting 'adolescent' attitudes provoked by the contradictions in their training as well as by the life stage of the profession could be used positively to *influence* other professions, rather than being subdued by them, then we should see some exciting developments in health care and attitudes towards 'mental illness' and its treatment. It is beginning to happen. But, in the words of Wally Harbert: 'Professional colonialism is a force to be reckoned with' (Harbert 1985: 15).

Much of the frustration felt by art therapists is, quite understandably, projected on to our own profession and its representatives, the Council, which is the committee of management of BAAT. This is a small elected group of voluntary workers, four officers and eight council members, who share various tasks from managing finances, chairing meetings, conducting negotiations with employers, and generally looking after the interests of members in particular and the profession as a whole. The Council is a mix of practising art therapists and art therapy educators, coming from different parts of Britain, meeting about once every six weeks in London. It is a useful target for projection of hostile and anxious feelings on behalf of members. It is often accused of 'not doing enough' about helping art therapists towards 'autonomy' from occupational therapy; it is blamed for 'allowing' the DHSS to avoid making a clear statement about management structures for art therapists; it is 'not doing enough' about creating establishments for art therapists within social services and education; it is 'too concerned' about NHS art therapists. At the same time, it is suspected of 'making decisions' and 'being authoritarian'. As might be expected, these perceptions of the Council are rarely expressed in writing but are muttered about and pondered over in the workplace or sometimes at regional group gatherings. A certain amount of 'acting out' takes place, which is destructive to the professional aspirations of art therapists. This includes: letting membership lapse but claiming privileges of membership; not joining but complaining about lack of support; failing to read literature distributed by the Council and its sub-committees which is designed to assist members; failing to familiarize themselves with issues which are important to the future of art therapy and improved treatment services for patients. As with any small and insecure group, hostility tends to be projected on to an outside force. This is safer than looking at the differences within the group, or examining deep seated prejudices or fantasies of one's own. It is more comfortable than attempting a political analysis of the situation. Yet, the history of art therapy reveals that art therapists have shaped their future, structured their profession as best they could given the odds, and caused their work to be recognized, because they were able to contain the splits and were sufficiently politicized (through early association with the NUT and then with ASTMS) to present a united front when it mattered. Now that there is a relatively safe structure, dissent can emerge.

Specific problems of 'elders' who are also engaged in training

It is necessary at this stage to look at the position of the 'elders' in art therapy. It does not appear an enviable one. Many 'elders' are 'untrained', being the pioneers who were practising before training existed or before the 1980 DHSS Personnel Memorandum which stated that art therapists, to be considered qualified, must possess a qualification in the 'therapeutic application of their art'. Some elders have expressed a feeling of being rejected by the younger 'qualified' art therapists and suspect that they are seen as having lower status. Art therapy educators tend to be a mix of pioneers and qualified, but by virtue of being responsible for training they become identified as elders and are on the receiving end of many projections. The cliché applied to academics generally of 'living an easy life in an ivory tower' gets applied to art therapy tutors too. It may be expressed in various forms, overt or covert – being 'not like us' (coal-face art therapists) but like 'them' (management) and being extremely powerful. Tutors are, in reality, better paid. But they certainly have many battles of their own to fight in their own workplace. For example, as they are engaged in training, they feel a great responsibility for the future generation of art therapists, and they will be trying to gauge what the needs of these people will be, as well as to take care of the current needs of students and their patients. They must tread a difficult path in providing a course which equates to other 'academic' postgraduate courses but which has an emphasis on experiential learning and clinical practice. They must be careful not to step outside their role as 'teachers' while, at the same time, drawing on their skills as therapists. Such a course makes enormous demands on the mental and physical resources of staff and students alike. The inadequate time – one year full-time or two years part-time – of the course makes for extra stress. No sooner is one student group settled in and beginning to gel, than it is time to prepare for the ending of the course, time for seeking jobs and experiencing severe panic at the task ahead.

In courses with continuous placements combined with academic and experiential work, there are pressures from those now often short-staffed and over-stretched institutions for the student to be a fully fledged staff member. So the student is faced with conflicting demands: in college, to participate fully and creatively in groups and workshops, to bring a questioning and critical approach to the lectures and seminars, and to experiment and play through their own art work; and in placement, to be a confident staff member, to present themselves as mature and sophisticated in the ways of the institution, and to be able to receive referrals – sometimes ones on which other, more experienced staff have given up!

Increasingly college tutors experience anxiety over the demands from the placements and do their best to support students in groups and individually, stressing the need for caution in referrals and regular support for the student while in the placement. (Again, this is not only a problem for art therapy students: a recent television documentary revealed an appalling situation in the NHS where student nurses may be left alone, in charge of a ward at night, because of lack of funds and shortage or more senior staff.)

Sometimes tutors are puzzled by the hostility they receive from the placement staff – it can be blatant and cruel on occasion, and directed towards 'the college' (that impersonal noun comes in very handy at such times!). The grass was never so green as in the colleges, apparently. Yet these tutors are constantly on the receiving end of conflicting demands from their own institutions. Only three centres offer a Diploma in Art Therapy, the officially recognized training. Two are in very small departments in large institutions, and the third in a smallish art college where it has the doubtful honour of being only one of two postgraduate areas in the college. All three are subject to the strictures of the National Advisory Body, the Council for Academic Awards or the University Grants Committee, the local authorities, and the Department of Education. All must fight for funding in the same way as courses in, say, English, fine art, or maths.

Although art therapy training seems to be following a model similar to that of most psychotherapy training, with the emphasis on relating theory to practice and including experiential work and being with patients, it takes place in the state higher education sector, and course tutors have a constant problem in trying to marry the academic with the professional in a very new area of work. The fact that the title of the course contains the word 'art' gives rise to some problems and fantasies on behalf of colleagues. Combine this with 'therapy' and fantasies run wild! There are still many myths and misconceptions about the term 'art therapy' and these are certainly prevalent in the colleges, despite strenuous public relations exercises on behalf of art therapy staff.[4]

Course leaders must make endless justifications for an appropriate, which may mean higher-than-average, staff:student ratio. A missed supervision does not equal a missed lecture: it could mean life or death when a student's client is suicidal. Or that is how it would be interpreted if a tragedy were to happen, as we have seen from press reports featuring social workers, held responsible for children being beaten or killed; even though their team was abysmally short-staffed and did their best, the supervisors are still deemed to be at fault.

To marry the needs of a range of clinical and educational placements with the needs of students and their patients, and with those of the academic framework of the college, is a masterly balancing act, needing plenty of support in terms of secretarial and administrative back-up. Unfortunately these are just the areas liable to 'cuts'. When a department has chosen to remain small, it is not seen to need much support, and justifications flow regularly from the art therapy department to central administration, and grind through committees of academics for consideration. Validating bodies (such as the Council for National Academic Awards (CNAA)) or advisory committees can be useful friends in this situation, taking the role of 'protective parent'; but it rather undermines the professional integrity of the art therapy staff who have been making the same arguments for years!

Most tutors, as a matter of principle, continue to practise as therapists and conduct research in addition to their heavy teaching/supervisory role. Wider college responsibilities need to be taken on, as much to create a sense of belonging as to promote the discipline and to be seen as 'just like others'. These same tutors must carry the counter-transference feelings of the students towards their patients – the sometimes aggressive and punitive wishes. Sometimes, and inevitably, these feelings are experienced by tutors towards the students and towards 'the college' as parent. It is often the case that 'the elders', in the form of art therapy tutors, experience adolescent feelings towards their own institution. So at times the grass can look burnt rather than green to those that graze on it.

To return to the OPUS report which I mentioned at the beginning of this chapter, in relation to counter-transference feelings, Khaleelee points out that:

'It is therefore highly likely that the therapist will also be in need at times for a perfect mother to contain these feelings. Trainees and others still in analysis have this resource; some also receive continuing support from a supervisor but these are a minority. This need is then likely to be carried into the professional body and to be vested there in 'the elders' who may actually be former therapists of younger members or at any rate belong to the 'parental' generation. They, of course, cannot meet such a need and in any case are themselves practitioners with needs of their own. So the projection gets pushed back, the therapist experiences failed dependency and unconsciously continues the search for the perfect mothering institution.'

(Khaleelee 1982: 22)

Dealing with frustration while searching for an identity

This, then, leads to splitting within the profession. In art therapy, as we have seen, the target for projection may be the professional association, BAAT, and its Council in particular, and also the regional groups which are an integral part of, and funded by, BAAT. Attendance at regional delegates meetings, once very high, dropped off to a low in 1985, then improved again in 1986 before the AGM where the register was presented. There are always issues for debate between the regional groups and the Council and it is vital to have an arena for discussion, for opinion to be shared and difficulties aired, and for joint solutions to be found where possible. With low attendance, a valuable opportunity is missed. Some regional co-ordinators, having taken on the job partly out of frustration at what they saw as the Council's lack of action, or out of concern for 'grass-roots' members (even though Council members are also members of regional groups and grass-roots members themselves) or from a genuine wish to help and offer support to the profession, find the same lack of support for their carefully planned activities. Some co-ordinators even found the majority of attenders to be non-art therapists and wrote to the Council to check if this was acceptable!

They, in turn, feel rejected and seek to project their disappointment:

perhaps the regional areas have been wrongly drawn up; there is not enough money coming from BAAT; or morale is low because of the status of art therapists which means that people are too exhausted or too poor to travel; BAAT is too concerned with NHS art therapists; and so on.

Adolescence is an exhausting process and the energy required to maintain the split is enormous. The splitting off of bad parental projections on to the Council leaves its members feeling beleaguered and attacked, and it is then only too easy for the process to begin within the Council itself. Lack of enthusiasm for taking on an officer's post (seen as a really hot seat) and fear of being perceived as an authority figure, in other words, as 'one of them', are some of the results. There is indeed much work for officers (and all Council members), all done voluntarily, but it is of a less frustrating and menial kind than in past years, and more able to be shared by a bigger group. So the increase of workload cannot be blamed for this reluctance to take on certain responsibilities. In past years, of course, art therapy was fighting to establish itself and did not contain the contradictions previously referred to in training and professional status.

One way of avoiding the contradictions is to escape them by taking on another professional training. Many art therapists who work in social services areas, where there is as yet no official establishment for them, have considered, or have actually undertaken, social-work training. Some have been pressured by their institution to do so. Other art therapists have trained as psychotherapists. They can then wear whichever hat they prefer depending on the situation. It appears though that those with the social-work training have left art therapy, whereas those with psychotherapy training have continued to actively engage in professional work, either as art therapists or art therapy educators, or both. Perhaps this is because the psychotherapy training enables art therapists to spot the contradictions and to live more easily with them; or to feel more secure with an 'older' professional hat to put on. Insufficient evidence is at hand to go further into this question but it would be a fascinating area for research.

It is obviously important that art therapists who take on another training should remain within the profession if it is to grow and not lose its vitality. Living with the painful frustrations of a growing and changing profession is not easy. Yet these feelings are mirrored in the fear of growth and change which is often expressed by our clients. It is valuable to explore these parallels in a group with other art therapists, preferably one with a social-political orientation as well as a psychodynamic one. While on the course, trainee art therapists do have a regular forum in which they can make connections. When they leave the course, they experience a profound sense of loss and anger towards the 'parent' course. There is a sense of abandonment and even betrayal, of being set adrift in a hostile sea. If not explored and worked through, such feelings can lead to rejection of the models of art therapy which had been examined, experienced, and chewed over during the course, in favour of easier options. These may be undertaken in order to placate (in fantasy) the employing institutions, or worse, because they were considered questionable practice by course tutors. The profession is so small that it can little afford art therapists diverting their skills or losing sight of them altogether.

When encountering a model which is firmly built into the culture of the institution in which they are employed, about which they have strong reservations, or when wishing to implement new methods of working, it is important that art therapists have a place to sound out opinion. They may well be isolated in their institution. Without support, they are more likely than ever to become de-skilled, or to adopt a defensive attitude towards their colleagues, leading to much unhappiness and lack of recognition for their work. Evidence of this having happened is, sadly, only too readily available in the files of the professional association.

It is not only unfortunate for the art therapist, but it also deprives the patient of a different form of 'treatment' from the predominantly verbal therapies, or from reliance on medication. Indeed, art therapy could be said to have one advantage over verbal psychotherapy, in that there is usually a concrete example of the process of therapy to show: a painting or an object that acts as a record of what has gone on between patient and therapist. It is a major, early, and often unverbalized anxiety among art therapy students that their patients will not wish to draw or make something, and that they will have nothing to show their tutors or colleagues. The art work then becomes proof that the student is an art therapist and not a pseudo-therapist. But excessive anxiety on behalf of the therapist will communicate itself to the patient, who is already probably frightened at the prospect of putting brush to paper. Sometimes the mutual anxiety is so overpowering that weeks go by without a mark being made, and the patient misses the chance to engage in a possibly liberating experience. What needs to be distinguished here is the ability of the skilled therapist to wait until the patient feels secure enough to make a mark, and the over-anxiousness of the trainee who needs the art work to prove to self and others that they have a rightful place in 'the team'. And the team frequently expect to see 'pictures', and get suspicious if they do not appear.

One recalls the days when art therapists were obliged to take paintings from their sessions to the psychiatrist, who then used them for purposes of analysis or diagnosis, or in their own relationship with the patient. Perhaps some of the anxiety which art therapists experience in this area of their work is a hangover from those days. The 'hand-maiden' role slips away but gradually.

Insecurity about one's role leads to less effective practice in the long run. But art therapists have such a short time to come to terms with their position as newcomers to a team during training, and the notion of being 'different' from others, although sought for and necessary, is also feared. More advanced courses and post-course groups are sorely needed to strengthen the identity of art therapists. But resources are scarce in higher education. Peer-group supervision is often available through the regional group network and this is invaluable, but not always enough. For art therapists, especially if their profession is going through an adolescent period, need parental figures to knock against, and ones who will survive. A very healthy sign in the profession is the growing acknowledgement by members of the need for such supervision at all stages, and creative solutions are being sought and found. Thanks to the initiative of some therapists, employers are beginning to accept supervision as a fully justified element in the job description, and are enabling art therapists to take time during their working day for this important task.

Art therapists and artists in hospitals: defining their roles

Problems in accepting 'professionalism' and all that it means are, of course, by no means confined to art therapists. But for the reasons explored in this chapter, it is a particularly acute preoccupation at present. There is a healthy aspect to the ambivalence of art therapists towards professionalism, given that some aspects of the process result in exclusion, narrow-mindedness, and territorial warfare. However, taking the positive side of the process, it is extremely unhelpful when professional aspirations are ignored and scorned by groups who one would expect to be allied. For example, the recent Committee of Inquiry into the Arts and Disabled People set up by the Carnegie UK Trust under the chairmanship of Sir Richard Attenborough, did not initially see part of their brief as being to investigate the role of arts therapists with disabled people. (Disabled in this sense included people who are mentally ill and mentally handicapped as well as those with physical disabilities.) Art therapists have been involved with all these groups, and especially with mentally ill people, for at least fifty years. Eventually, after some pressure from the arts therapy associations – that is, from art, music, drama, and dance therapists – the Committee set up a sub-committee specifically to look at the arts therapies.[5]

There is now, following the publication of the 'Attenborough' Report, some suggestion that some hospital artists (not art therapists and not trained in therapy) see themselves performing the same function as art therapists. It seems as if we are going back in time! However, at the moment, artists in hospitals have a safe position. They are not seen to be challenging the medical or clinical professions, nor are they generally competing for resources, being either voluntary workers or funded through charities or Manpower Services schemes. It goes without saying that they are usually very badly paid for doing work (such as murals) which if carried out for any of our leading banks or commercial organizations would reward them handsomely.

Artists in hospitals can be kept in their place by virtue of not having one. A hospital need make no commitment to them, but gains a useful and enthusiastic worker who might transform the environment: as the Attenborough Report says:

'Endless cream and grey painted corridors and intimidating waiting areas have been transformed with paintings, murals and humorous signposting. Patients, visitors and staff benefit from the visually relaxing environment. A playground designed for bed-bound and wheel-chair bound children is just one of the many examples where the sensitive imagination of artists has complemented the standard health service provision. The presence of the arts team has significantly improved the atmosphere of the hospitals, health centres and clinics which they serve.'

(Attenborough 1985: 32)

But, in the words of the Committee again:

'We recognise that in some instances when the arts are being used informally with people who are disturbed, guidance will be needed from professional arts therapists who are suitably qualified.'

(Attenborough 1985: 74)

Running through the report, included in a five-page chapter dealing with the arts therapies, is a plea for the arts to be taken seriously:

'The arts should never be regarded as open only to a privileged élite. The arts are for everyone. To some degree it is within everyone's capacity to reinterpret their own experience, and to share the experience of others by involvement in the world of art. Over the ages, the arts have been the field for and have prompted some of the finest achievements of the human spirit.'

(Attenborough 1985: 2)

Somehow it seems to have slipped the notice of the Committee that art therapists are also artists (the basis of our professional recognition) and that they are available for those patients who might wish to use their skills in whatever way the *patient* wishes. Art therapists do not seek out patients to 'do therapy'; nor do they presume to try to engage people who happen to have a disability in a therapeutic relationship, unless specifically asked by that person or parent or guardian.

The deep suspicion about 'therapy' which emerged time and time again throughout the Committee's deliberations has certainly puzzled art therapists who have heard themselves described on occasion as 'agents of a repressive system' and have been advised by a prominent member of the Committee that 'disabled people don't want therapy'. It seems as if art therapists have now become, as a group, a target for 'artists'' projections. I had begun to postulate that this might have something to do with the essentially 'female' nature of art therapy – just over 65 per cent of the practitioners are women, and the 'caring' professions, except medicine, are usually seen as female preserves. In her study 'Why do so many women become art therapists?' Lynn Walters (1986) makes some interesting observations about the lack of recognition given to women artists throughout art history. She suggests that women find it harder to identify themselves as artists during and after art school. On interviewing a group of male and female art therapists she also discovered that the men put more emphasis on 'doing' and the women on 'being'. The art element of art therapy was seen as more important to the men, who had a stronger identity as individual artists, using their skills as artists within the therapeutic process to communicate with the patient. The women, on the other hand, seemed to focus primarily on the relationship between themselves and the patient. Certainly it seems as if the emphasis on 'doing' which one finds in various descriptions of work carried out by hospital artists would fit into the 'masculine' mode as defined by Lynn Walters. But if, as I suspect, the majority of 'hospital artists' turn out to be women, then they will no doubt join the ranks of the low-paid sisterhood.

Overall, Lynn Walters found that there was actually very little difference in the way that male and female art therapists perceived their work, except for the slightly greater importance given to art in the transaction by men. However, she discovered the following quote from Gibb, which we can speculate on:

> 'Instrumental therapies are goal oriented, seeking effective answers to problems, whereas expressive therapies are emotional, dynamic and more concerned with self exploration. The concept of instrumental versus expressive was originally developed to define gender roles within the family but when applied to therapy there is evidence that women are more successful as expressive therapists than men.'
>
> (Gibb 1984: 26)

What is interesting, apart from the male/female question which I have just drawn attention to briefly, is that no committee of inquiry was set up to help art or music therapists to achieve a place within our hospitals, and no funding bodies came forth to enable them to be employed in the past, and they show little signs of doing so in the future. Based on the experience of the fund raisers of a major Arts Therapy Congress in 1985 in London, art therapy is not a very deserving cause in the eyes of most charities and trust funds. We wonder why this is so, when 'hospital arts' has attracted substantial funding. Is it because art therapists have fought against the 'voluntary' status so much admired, especially in women, in our British society, or that 'therapy' conjures up unpleasant possibilities – the unconscious let loose, looking at one's innermost feelings – or because of the many misperceptions of the art therapist's role previously referred to, in particular the question of 'diagnosis' where it is feared that the art work may be, as it were, used in evidence to pronounce a person 'mad'? This is the very thing that art therapists themselves have fought against. Or could one problem be that art therapists tend to work with mentally ill people, who are not usually on the receiving end of much public sympathy? Or are art therapists suspected of 'polluting' the art form, of engaging in 'unaesthetic practice'? And that, despite the pleas of the Committee, the arts are really a very élitist area into which certain groups, at certain times (children, primitives, näives, the insane, women, and now the disabled) can be admitted?

Art therapists, identified as they are with their background as 'artists' and struggling to come to terms with the issues involved in being part of a largely medical grouping, feel uneasy about the splitting off of 'arts therapists' and 'hospital artists' though they fully acknowledge that access to the arts is as important for people who happen to be in hospitals, community homes, etc. as it is for the general public. Perhaps the lack of a clear role for artists in our society is a fundamental problem which needs to be addressed by all artists, whether they be therapists or not.

It sometimes feels as if art therapists are between two powerful parent bodies: on the one hand, the so-called 'Art World' and on the other, the 'Medical World'. The tension of being in between is a dynamic and creative one, but a painful state to maintain. And the price to pay for developing professionalism is a high one. Yet there are rewards, both in providing an alternative form of expression and a chance for self-determination and change for people who are seeking this, and in public acknowledgement of the work coming forth in the form of increased job possibilities, and opportunities to write, to speak to others about art therapy, to make videos, etc.

If, as I believe, art therapy is a profession going through adolescence, then this adolescence is taking place at a time of financial stringency and rapid changes in British society, and when there are strong tendencies towards preservation of territory by existing power groups; and powerful monied patrons place bets on surer horses than art therapy. Art therapists need to realize that they no longer have to justify their existence over and over again. They have proved their worth and can now concentrate on making what they do more effective and relevant to the patients' needs. Along with music therapy, they are now watching the emergence of the professions of drama, and dance movement therapy, and witnessing their struggles.

The regular meetings of the arts therapy profession representatives, under the auspices of the Carnegie Trust following publication of the Attenborough Report, have been useful and educational. But even in this potentially supporting and positive situation for art therapists, one senses tendencies coming from 'outside' to underestimate the primary skills of these arts therapists, that is, in the practice of their individual art form, by the all-embracing term 'creative therapist'. Remembering the 1978 DHSS Consultative Document, which referred to art, music, drama, etc. therapy, and the concern expressed to BAAT officers that if art and music therapy became separate professions then the way would be open for all the 'et ceteras' to do likewise, it should make us even firmer in our resolution to maintain the art basis of our profession. We can share and combine with other interpretative and performing arts therapists according to the desires and aspirations of all of us, where we think it valuable for clients, rather than seeing ourselves at the mercy of economic expediency. To put it crudely, four for the price of one will not do!

Conclusion

The unique combination of art and therapy and the way in which art therapists have achieved professional status has made Britain a focus for imitation in this area. If some of the adolescent aspects of art therapy, that is its creative, subversive, change-seeking, and critical-of-status quo attitudes can be harnessed for the benefit of patients, whether they be in hospital or in the 'community', and the institutions in which they are treated, and art therapists themselves, and the more negative, self-destructive, conventional and 'whingeing' bits can be dealt with appropriately (or at least acknowledged) then the future of the profession looks very good indeed. But, one might say, that is a very idealistic and rather naïve attitude to take, especially given our current economic climate. I would reply, that attitude is part of what being an adolescent is all about. Long may it last!

© 1987 Diane Waller

Notes

1 The arrival of the Griffiths Report and the reorganization of the NHS towards community care will necessitate radical re-thinking not only of clinical but managerial structures. (Griffiths, R. (1983) *NHS Management Enquiry.* London: DHSS.)

2 The Clegg Commission was a Standing Commission on pay comparability appointed by the Prime Minister in March 1979 to examine terms and conditions of employment of particular groups of workers referred to it by the government in agreement with employers and the unions. It was chaired by Professor H. A. Clegg. The Report No. 4 *Professions Supplementary to Medicine* (London:

HMSO March 1980) was the one which should have featured art therapists.
3 See Madge, C. and Weinberger, B. (1973) *Art Students Observed*. London: Faber & Faber.
4 See Waller, D. and Gilroy, A. Art Therapy in Practice in D. Steinberg (ed.) (1986) *The Adolescent Unit*, Chichester: Wiley, for a fuller account of this phenomenon.
5 BAAT's submission to the Committee for Inquiry into Arts and Disabled People can be found in Waller, D. *Inscape* Summer 1984, and an update on the relationship of BAAT to the Committee in *Inscape* Spring 1985. (*Inscape* is published twice a year by the BAAT.)

References

ASTMS (1980) Art therapy. In *The Forgotten Professions*: Evidence to the Standing Committee on pay comparability on behalf of speech therapists, radiographers, technical instructors, art therapists, helpers, chiropodists. London: ASTMS.

Attenborough (1985) *Arts and Disabled People*. Report of a Committee of Inquiry under the chairmanship of Sir Richard Attenborough. London: Carnegie UK Trust.

Cannon, C. (1972) Social workers: training and professionalism. In T. Pateman (ed.) *Countercourse: A Handbook for Course Criticism*. London: Penguin.

DHSS (1982) Personnel Memorandum PM(82) 6 March.

Eichenbaum, L. and Orbach, S. (1983) *Understanding Women*. London: Penguin.

Gibbs, M. S. (1984) Woman therapists working with women. In C. M. Brody (ed.) *New Theory and Process of Feminist Therapy*. New York: Springer.

Harbert, W. (1985) Professionalism. *Community Care* October 10.

Hinshelwood, R. (1985) Questions of training. *Free Associations* 2.

Khaleelee, O. (1982) *Psychotherapy and the process of profession building*. London: OPUS.

Littlewood, R. and Lipsedge, M. (1983) *Aliens and Alienists*. Harmondsworth: Penguin.

Walters, L. (1986) Some proposals which could explain why so many women choose art therapy as a career. Unpublished Postgraduate Diploma in Art Therapy thesis, Goldsmiths' College, London.

Acknowledgements

My thanks to Dan Lumley, Andrea Gilroy, Joan Woddis, and Robin Davis who read and commented so helpfully on the drafts; to Christopher Cornford and Frederic Samson who encouraged me back in 1969; to Donna Haber of ASTMS from whom I learnt such a lot, especially in the period 1975–81.

Name index

Adamson, E. 188
Antony, S. 57, 59
Attenborough, Sir R. 208–09
Auden, W.H. 160
Avens, R. 95, 103, 105
Axline, V. 62

Barnes, M. 59
Berke, J. 191
Bettelheim, B. 113
Bick, E. 125
Bowlby, J. 40, 121
Bowyer, R. 62
Burns, R.C. 72n

Cannon, C. 199–200
Case, C. ix, 36–71, 96
Cassirer, E. 74–5, 83–91, 95, 102
Cézanne, P. 117
Champernowne, I. 158–59, 164, 183
Cirlot, J. 186n
Clegg, H.A. 195, 212n
Cohen, F. 30
Coleridge, S.T. 164, 167

Dalley, T. ix, 1–34

Darwin, C. 40
Deri, S. 22
Dubowski, J. 3–4

Ehrenzweig, A. 3, 5
Eichenbaum, L., 196–97

FitzHerbert, K. 31–2
Fordham, M. 97
Frazer, J.G. 75, 98–9, 101
Freud, A. 181
Freud, S.: art and aesthetics 6–9; dream analysis 2, 5–6, 20; grief 41–2; play 61; sublimation 119; transference 16, 79
Fuller, P. 114, 117
Furman, R. 59

Gellner, E. 76
Gibb, M.S. 210
Gilroy, A. 213n
Glendinning, V. 144
Gordon, R. 59
Gorer, G. 59
Gorham-Davies, R. 17
Greenson, R. 96–7
Griffiths, R. 212n

Index of case studies

Subject index

'active imagination' 9, 84, 167–68
adults, and art therapy 157–86; chaos
181–83; patients' views 163–71;
setting 158–59; therapist's role 159–
63; therapy 171–81
aesthetics: and art therapy 5–6; 21; and
psychoanalytic theory 6–10
aggression 118–19; *see also* sadism
'aloneness' 166; *see also* space
anxiety 16, 20–1
art: Freud and 6–8; Jung and 9, 160–
61; and play 20–5, 68–71; projection
in 111–13; as therapy 1–34, 182
art therapy 1–34; aesthetics and 5–6,
21; as 'alternative' treatment 192; art
and 3–4; art and play 20–5, 68–71;
autonomy for 197–200; and children
25–9, 36–71, 128–56; in education
29–34; group 163–67; imagery in
77–9; loss and 36–71; patients'
experiences of 157–86; play and 19–
20, 20–5, 68–71; process of 2, 5–6;
profession of 188–212; and
psychoanalytic theory 2, 6–10, 109–
26; setting for 36–9, 158–59; and
symbolism 109–26; therapist's

experiences of 128–56; training in
200–05; transference in 16–19, 74–
107; use of 1–5; *see also* therapist
Association of Scientific, Technical and
Managerial Staff (ASTMS) 190, 194–
95, 202
Attenborough Report 208–09, 212

Bataks 75, 87
Bible 74, 130
boundaries of play 63–6
British Association of Art Therapists
(BAAT) 188, 191–96, 201–02, 205–
06

Carnegie Trust 208, 212
chaos, value of 181–83
children, in art therapy 25–9; case
studies 26–9, 128–56 (*see list*); and
loss (*q.v.*) 36–71; in schools 29–34;
see also development; play
Clegg Commission 195, 212–13n
communication 21, 23–5, 85, 166–67;
see also interpretation; symbolism
counter-transference 18, 81–2, 97–8
creativity: Freud on 2–3, 7–8; and

.